The Complete Guide to SAP NetWeaver® Portal

 PRESS

SAP PRESS is a joint initiative of SAP and Galileo Press. The know-how offered by SAP specialists combined with the expertise of the Galileo Press publishing house offers the reader expert books in the field. SAP PRESS features first-hand information and expert advice, and provides useful skills for professional decision-making.

SAP PRESS offers a variety of books on technical and business related topics for the SAP user. For further information, please visit our website: www.sap-press.com.

Marty McCormick, Matt Stratford
Content Integration with SAP NetWeaver Portal
2009, 388 pp., hardcover
ISBN 978-1-59229-226-4

Marcus Banner et al.
Developer's Guide to SAP NetWeaver Portal Applications
2009, 423 pp., hardcover
ISBN 978-1-59229-225-7

Loren Heilig et al.
SAP NetWeaver: The Official Guide (2nd Edition)
2008, 495 pp., hardcover
ISBN 978-1-59229-193-9

Alfred Barzewski et al.
Java Programming with SAP NetWeaver (2nd Edition)
2009, 694 pp., hardcover
ISBN 978-1-59229-181-6

Manish Chaitanya

The Complete Guide to SAP NetWeaver® Portal

Galileo Press

Bonn • Boston

Galileo Press is named after the Italian physicist, mathematician and philosopher Galileo Galilei (1564–1642). He is known as one of the founders of modern science and an advocate of our contemporary, heliocentric worldview. His words *Eppur si muove* (And yet it moves) have become legendary. The Galileo Press logo depicts Jupiter orbited by the four Galilean moons, which were discovered by Galileo in 1610.

Editor Kelly Grace Harris
Copyeditor Julie McNamee
Cover Design Graham Geary
Photo Credit iStockphoto.com/contour99
Layout Design Vera Brauner
Production Graham Geary
Typesetting Publishers' Design and Production Services, Inc.
Printed and bound in the United States of America

ISBN 978-1-59229-403-9

© 2012 by Galileo Press Inc., Boston (MA)

1st edition 2012

Library of Congress Cataloging-in-Publication Data
Chaitanya, Manish.
The complete guide to SAP Netweaver portal /
Manish Chaitanya.—1st ed.
p. cm.
ISBN 978-1-59229-403-9—ISBN 1-59229-403-0
1. Web site development. 2. Web portals—
Computer programs. 3. SAP NetWeaver. 4. Business
enterprises—Computer networks. I. Title.
TK5105.8885.S24C48 2012
006.7—dc23
2011049146

FSC
www.fsc.org
MIX
Paper from
responsible sources
FSC® C014174

Contents at a Glance

Dear Reader,

I'm tempted to start this letter with a pun about how this book is your portal to... well, you know where I'm going with this. I'll spare you. Terrible jokes aside: Welcome to *The Complete Guide to SAP NetWeaver Portal*! This reference will serve as a day-to-day companion to your work, and I'm confident you will find a wealth of useful information within its pages.

Drawing on his years of experience with SAP, Manish Chaitanya has gone to great lengths to make sure this book provides everything you need to know in order to do your job effectively. Throughout the project, I was continually impressed by Manish's dedication to the schedule, detailed attention to editorial direction, and seemingly superhuman patience with his pesky and demanding editor (me). In the end, his efforts have resulted in a superb product that I'm proud to have been involved in.

Of course, we at SAP PRESS are always eager to hear your opinion. What do you think about *The Complete Guide to SAP NetWeaver Portal*? How could it be improved? As your comments and suggestions are the most useful tools to help us make our books the best they can be, we encourage you to visit our website at *www.sap-press. com* and share your feedback about this work.

Thank you for purchasing a book from SAP PRESS!

Kelly Grace Harris
Editor, SAP PRESS

Galileo Press
Boston, MA

kelly.harris@galileo-press.com
www.sap-press.com

Contents

Introduction

SAP NetWeaver Portal is the preferred way for web-enabling applications in an SAP landscape, providing users with a single point of access for SAP and non-SAP applications and systems. Because of the increased importance of SAP NetWeaver Portal, it is essential to not only develop, implement, and configure a portal correctly, but also to administer it regularly to ensure its smooth functioning and to be able to detect problems at an early stage.

This book covers the full lifecycle of an SAP NetWeaver Portal implementation, from the installation and blueprint phrase through to the go-live and support phase. We will walk you through the big picture of SAP NetWeaver Portal implementations: a portal's place in the landscape, the architecture of SAP NetWeaver Portal, and how the portal handles client requests. We will also take a deep dive into user interface development on various technologies—including portal components, Web Dynpro Java, and Web Dynpro ABAP—with the aim of familiarizing you with various development options and giving a primer on the technologies. Finally, we will focus on the administration of SAP NetWeaver Portal, which is as important as the implementation; it is essential to ensure that the portal is available to end users without disruption, and early detection of problems is critical to this point. We will explain the various administrative activities needed for maintaining SAP NetWeaver Portal in a safe and reliable condition; for example, user administration, security administration, transports, single sign-on, and integration with backend systems. In addition, there are activities like disaster recovery, backup and restore, monitoring, etc. that are needed while the implementation is going on as well as after the implementation has been completed. This book serves as a hands-on guide for consultants and implementation teams in handling the above activities smoothly.

Who This Book Is For

This book is aimed at developers and consultants who are currently working with SAP NetWeaver Portal, or who are new to SAP NetWeaver Portal. Because the book presents an end-to-end discussion of working with SAP NetWeaver Portal, there are necessarily some chapters that will be of more interest to administrators, and others that will be of more interest to developers.

The book starts with an overview of the various features of SAP NetWeaver Portal, and then takes a dive into the installation and initial configuration steps that make the portal ready for implementation. Subsequent chapters discuss the various steps of implementation, including blueprinting, development, and configuration. After completing the discussion on implementation, we discuss concepts in disaster recovery, high availability, and backup and restore. The last chapter then discusses monitoring the SAP NetWeaver Portal system using various tools and logging and tracing.

What This Book Covers

The chapters are organized as follows:

▶ **Chapter 1**
This chapter provides an introduction to SAP NetWeaver Portal. It starts by discussing the needs for an enterprise portal, and then explains how SAP NetWeaver Portal fulfills these needs. It also covers the most important features that SAP NetWeaver Portal provides, including Knowledge Management, Collaboration, Unification, federated portal networks, and external-facing portals.

▶ **Chapter 2**
This chapter discusses the architecture of SAP NetWeaver Portal and explains how it is dependent on the SAP Application Server (AS) Java. It discusses how the Portal Runtime works and how it responds to client requests. This chapter also discusses the server administration tools and shows how basic administration can be done using these tools.

▶ **Chapter 3**
This chapter explains the basic steps for installing SAP NetWeaver Portal and performing the initial configurations. We talk about preparing for the installation, the installation itself, and post-installation steps. Then we discuss various initial configuration steps, such as UME configuration, landscape configuration, and service configuration. We also discuss how to customize the logon screen of the portal.

▶ **Chapter 4**
This chapter discusses integrating SAP NetWeaver Portal with other SAP systems. We discuss various single sign-on scenarios between SAP NetWeaver Portal and

other SAP systems and how to configure them. We also discuss how the portal roles can be distributed to SAP backend systems and how roles from SAP backend systems can be uploaded to SAP NetWeaver Portal.

▶ **Chapter 5**

This chapter discusses blueprinting for SAP NetWeaver Portal installations. We explain how to gather information about the functional and non-functional requirements, and consider what questions should be asked by an SAP NetWeaver Portal consultant to understand these requirements. We also discuss the various UI technology options for developing user interfaces, including the advantages and disadvantages of each technology.

▶ **Chapter 6**

This chapter discusses the most common type of activity an SAP NetWeaver Portal consultant performs: portal content development. We discuss how to create roles, worksets, pages, and iViews, as well as how to assign content to users and translate content into different languages. We also discuss how portal branding is done and how themes are assigned to users. Finally, we discuss how to integrate various SAP and non-SAP content with SAP NetWeaver Portal and how to implement business packages.

▶ **Chapter 7**

This chapter discusses the various technologies for developing applications for SAP Portal. It focuses on each technology and provides development examples. We begin by discussing portal components development, and then we discuss developing applications using Web Dynpro Java and Web Dynpro ABAP technologies.

▶ **Chapter 8**

This chapter discusses implementing a federated portal network (FPN). We begin by exploring the various content sharing scenarios between portals, and discuss what kind of content sharing can happen between two SAP portals, as well as between an SAP and a non-SAP portal. We then discuss how to manage FPN and WSRP connections for sharing to take place. Finally, we discuss how content is exposed by the producer portals and how content is consumed by the consumer portals.

▶ **Chapter 9**

This chapter discusses the high availability of SAP NetWeaver Portal, as well as backup and restore strategies. We discuss what high availability means and how it works for SAP NetWeaver Portal. The aim of this chapter is to give an overview of these concepts, and not to go into the details of a specific high availability implementation.

▶ **Chapter 10**
This chapter discusses various monitoring technologies for ensuring that the portal is running properly and there are no impending failures. We discuss how SAP NetWeaver Administrator can be used for various monitoring activities. We also discuss logging and tracing and how logging can be configured to suit your needs. Finally, we discuss PCD objects and troubleshooting techniques.

All coding samples and screenshots were prepared using the initial SAP NetWeaver Portal 7.3, available at the time of the writing of this book (December 2011). With subsequent releases of SAP NetWeaver Portal, some of the screens may change.

Manish Chaitanya

SAP NetWeaver Portal is a single point of access for SAP and non-SAP applications running on various platforms.

1 SAP NetWeaver Portal Basics

In this chapter, we demonstrate and explain what a portal is and why it is needed. We'll discuss the positioning of SAP NetWeaver Portal in relation to SAP's other products and consider the important features that SAP NetWeaver Portal provides.

1.1 General Introduction to Enterprise Portals and SAP NetWeaver Portal

SAP NetWeaver Portal provides various services needed for an enterprise portal implementation. Some of the common requirements of an enterprise portal, such as single sign-on (SSO), integration, federation, personalization, and many more, are built into SAP NetWeaver Portal, as you'll see in this section. We also introduce the key terminologies related to the packaging of SAP NetWeaver, and discuss the mapping between use cases and installable software units. This will help you identify the components that are needed during the installation of SAP NetWeaver Portal.

1.1.1 Enterprise Portal Services

The Web has become the preferred gateway for making any information available to a large number of people. Within an enterprise, a centralized enterprise portal makes sense because it allows you to provide a secure and unified role-based access point to a large number of enterprise systems and processes with a consistent look and feel. The following are some of the basic services of any enterprise portal:

▶ **Single sign-on (SSO)**
SSO is a feature that allows a user to sign in once to a central system and have access to information from multiple systems without having to sign in to each

system again. Enterprise portals provide the capability to implement SSO between various systems of an enterprise.

▶ **Integration**
Enterprise portals can integrate data, functions, and content from multiple systems and still provide a single point of access and navigation for all of the systems.

▶ **Federation**
Federation is an important feature of an enterprise portal and allows for decentralization of the content creation and management. An enterprise portal can integrate content provided by other portals into a single navigation structure. Thus the content can be managed at various sources and the access can still be provided by a central enterprise portal.

▶ **Customization**
Customization of enterprise portals allows an enterprise to implement a portal to suit its unique needs. It allows an enterprise to decide what kind of content and other features it needs so that the portal can be customized to cater to those needs.

▶ **Personalization**
Personalization is more specific than customization. Whereas customization allows a portal to suit an enterprise, personalization allows the portal to suit a user. A user can select the look and feel, content, and layout of SAP NetWeaver Portal based on his tastes and based on the flexibility provided by the system administrators.

▶ **Access control**
In an enterprise, not everyone has the same level of authorizations. An SAP NetWeaver Portal allows access control to content based on the job role or function of each user. This ensures that a user is only able to perform the functions that he is eligible for.

▶ **Enterprise search**
An enterprise usually has a large pool of structured and unstructured content. *Enterprise search* is a mechanism used to search for information within an enterprise in a structured way. As you'll see in later chapters, enterprise portals provide a way to get a structured view of the unstructured content.

> **Note**
>
> This book differentiates between a web portal and an enterprise portal. A web portal, such as Yahoo!, MSN, and AOL, provides access to features such as email, stocks, news, entertainment, and so on, whereas the content and features provided in an enterprise portal are more enterprise centric.

SAP NetWeaver is the SAP platform that powers SAP business applications. Apart from the core platform, SAP NetWeaver provides optional technology components that enable customers to do the following:

▶ Extend the reach of SAP and non-SAP applications to more people and via new devices and consumption models

▶ Integrate SAP and non-SAP applications and processes into heterogeneous landscapes

▶ Extend existing SAP processes

▶ Compose new processes spanning SAP and non-SAP applications

▶ Securely manage and deliver information to people in multiple geographic locations at the same time

▶ Manage the lifecycle and infrastructure of SAP applications

1.1.2   Key Terms for Understanding SAP NetWeaver Packaging

Starting with SAP NetWeaver 7.0, SAP has started packaging SAP NetWeaver components a little differently. This section defines some of the terminology.

▶ **Usage types**
Usage types of SAP NetWeaver are software units that can be installed and configured. Some usage types, such as AS Java (Application Server Java) can be installed independently, whereas some usage types, such as EPC (Enterprise Portal Core), need the usage type AS Java to be installed. SAP systems with usage types are the main building blocks of SAP NetWeaver. They are identified by unique SAP system IDs (SAPSIDS) and are configured for a certain purpose, as indicated by usage types. Usage types have the following characteristics:

  ▶ Consist of one or several functional units

  ▶ Structuring elements for SAP software on a technical level

- ► Independent installation units that can be chosen and installed to achieve a set of functionality
- ► Determine the intended purpose of a system and the role it plays in a given use case
- ► Realized by installing and configuring a collection of software components
- ► Give a logical view of the SAP NetWeaver technology platform
- ► May depend on other usage types that should be installed in the same system
- ► Can run in the same system together with other usage types that are not a prerequisite

- ► **Standalone engines**
  Standalone engines of SAP NetWeaver are additional installable software units. They do not work as full-blown systems of SAP NetWeaver but as standalone engines that provide a specific function in combination with one or more SAP NetWeaver systems. Standalone engines are not part of a usage type. They do not run on SAP NetWeaver AS ABAP (AS ABAP) or SAP NetWeaver AS Java (AS Java).

- ► **Client**
  Clients are additional installable programs or tools. They reside either on local frontend PCs accessed by users or on backend systems where they act as client programs within an SAP NetWeaver system landscape.

- ► **Optional standalone units**
  Optional standalone units are additional software units that you can install separately. They are based on AS Java and provide specific (server) functions in combination with one or more SAP systems.

- ► **Functional units**
  An installed, configured, and activated unit of SAP NetWeaver that provides a set of functions. Functional units are bundled into usage types as the installable unit. After the installation of a usage type, you select those functional units that you want to use in your system landscape and configure them.

1.1.3 Mapping of Use Cases to Installable Software Units

SAP NetWeaver Portal falls under the use case "Integrating and Self-Servicing Content with SAP NetWeaver Portal" and needs the following usage types installed:

- AS Java

- SAP NetWeaver Product Description

- AS Java Extensions

- EP Core–Application Portal

- EP – Enterprise Portal

- Portal Add-on (for building communities with wikis and forums only)

Figure 1.1 shows the system landscape aspects for SAP NetWeaver Portal.

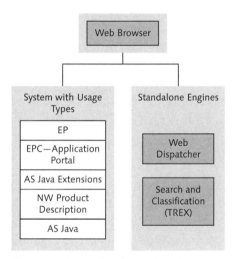

Figure 1.1 System Landscape Aspects

As shown in Figure 1.1, SAP NetWeaver Portal runs on the AS Java platform. The EPC (EP Core) usage type is required for running the basic enterprise portal functions. The EP usage type is needed for running SAP NetWeaver Portal as a full-blown corporate portal that includes Knowledge Management and Collaboration, federated portal networks, Web Page Composer, wikis, and so on. The Portal Add-on usage type is needed for building communities with wikis and forums. The NW Product Description usage type contains metadata for SAP NetWeaver (for example, about comprised software components and their interdependencies); this usage type is always included when you install a Java usage type. Finally, the AS Java Extensions usage type enables you to create development components in SAP-specific technologies on top of JEE; for example, for service composition. In addition, standalone engines such as Web Dispatcher and Text Search and Classification Engine (TREX) can be installed for additional functionality, but are not required.

1.2   Features of SAP NetWeaver Portal

SAP NetWeaver Portal offers a single point of access to SAP and non-SAP information sources, enterprise applications, information repositories, databases, and services inside and outside the organization—all integrated into a single user experience. It provides you with the tools to manage and analyze this knowledge and to share and collaborate on the basis of it. With its role-based content and personalization features, SAP NetWeaver Portal enables users—from employees and customers to partners and suppliers—to focus exclusively on data relevant to daily decision-making processes. As a unified interface to these applications, the SAP NetWeaver Portal helps each user quickly access the right resources and be as productive as possible.

This section focuses on introducing the important and more commonly used features of SAP NetWeaver Portal. We introduce the basic concepts without going into too much detail in this chapter. At the end of this section, you will have a feel for what SAP NetWeaver Portal is all about and how it fits into the overall SAP NetWeaver strategy. Subsequent chapters of this book will then focus on the specific topics and go into the details of implementing each feature.

1.2.1   Portal Platform and Framework

The portal platform runs on SAP Web Application Server's (hereafter referred to as AS Java) Java EE stack and is deployed as a Java EE application. The portal platform consists of the following:

▶ **Portal framework**
  The portal framework is a virtual environment that enables the portal as development and runtime environments. Applications that run on the portal—both out-of-the-box and custom applications, and both business and portal-related applications—are developed with various technologies such as Portal Development Kit (PDK) components, Web Dynpro, Visual Composer, Web Page Composer, Business Server Pages (BSPs), and so on.

  The portal framework provides a set of services to enable existing SAP and non-SAP business applications to be integrated into the portal, as well as to build new applications. Such services include navigation, object-based navigation, Portal Content Directory (PCD) services, and so on:

▶ **Database**
The portal stores data required by the portal at runtime in the same database used by AS Java. All of the system configurations as well as custom configurations are stored in this database. This database can also be used for storing custom application-specific data.

▶ **User persistence store**
User persistence store is the storage area containing information about users, such as directory servers. This system works with the mechanism that implements security systems for authentication and authorization, the User Management Engine (UME), which is an SAP proprietary mechanism that allows access to various content using SSO.

Figure 1.2 shows the various components of the portal platform.

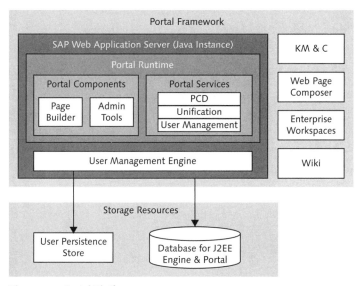

Figure 1.2 Portal Platform

1.2.2 Knowledge Management

An enterprise typically has a huge amount of structured and unstructured information. With the Knowledge Management (KM) functional unit, SAP NetWeaver provides a central, role-specific point of entry to structured and unstructured information from various data sources. This information can exist in different formats such as text documents, presentations, or HTML files. Workers in an organization can access information from different sources such as file servers, their intranet, or the Web. A generic framework integrates these data sources and provides access to the information contained in them through the portal in a structured fashion.

The KM functional unit supports you in structuring information and making it available to the correct target audience in the correct structure. You can use the different functions of KM on all content of integrated data sources, as long as the technical conditions are met. KM is a part of SAP NetWeaver Portal. The entire functional scope and configuration of the KM capabilities are available in portal iViews.

The KM functional unit is a part of the EP usage type. To use the full scope of the KM functional unit in SAP NetWeaver, you need the Text Search and Classification (TREX) standalone engine. If the landscape consists of a TREX engine, you should normally distribute TREX and SAP NetWeaver Portal on different servers for better scalability and performance.

Figure 1.3 shows various components of KM.

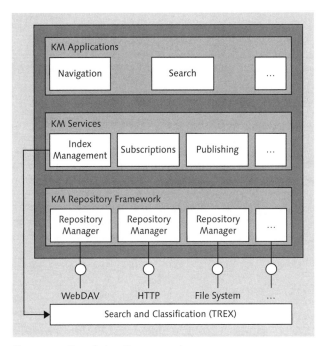

Figure 1.3 Knowledge Management

Technical Components of Knowledge Management

The KM framework includes many technical components, as described here:

▶ **Repository framework**

The repository framework is the physical storage location for documents. It provides a range of basic functions for documents and folders that are managed by KM. It enables the integration of documents into a virtual hierarchy and a namespace. The documents can be stored on different systems (Windows, Web-DAV, or HTTP). Repository managers are used to access these systems. There are internal repositories and external repositories, depending on the system. You can also connect additional external data sources by using partner-provided software and an open interface.

▶ **Repository services (KM services)**

KM provides many services for documents, such as indexing, subscription, status management, and so on. The repository services are used to connect the individual repositories with these services as needed.

▶ **Global services (KM services)**

Global services are the services provided by KM that are responsible for tasks required by all repository managers of applications. Using the index management service, for example, the SAP NetWeaver standalone TREX engine can access the content of the connected repositories through the repository framework to index, classify, and search documents.

▶ **KM applications**

KM applications can be used to access documents and administration tools. You can, for example, use form-based and time-dependent publishing if you want to publish documents. You use the XML Forms Builder for form-based publishing of documents, which allows you to create XML forms using a graphical user interface (GUI). You can then use these forms to create structured documents. You use the navigation iView template provided by KM to navigate in repositories and folders, find the documents you need, open them, and edit them with the appropriate program. In addition, you can use the search functionality to find documents matching specific criteria.

▶ **Search and Classification (TREX)**

The SAP NetWeaver standalone TREX engine enables various types of search and classification operations on the documents managed by KM.

Features of Knowledge Management

Now that we've seen the technical components of KM, let's discuss some of the important features of KM, as listed here:

▶ **Integrating repositories**
Unstructured information can be stored in various types of repositories such as file servers or third-party document management systems. You can use precon-figured repository managers to integrate various repositories and to make their content accessible to users through a central entry point in the SAP NetWeaver Portal. Open application programming interfaces (APIs) provided by SAP allow customers and partners to develop repository managers for other storage systems too. You can also store documents in one of KM's repositories that SAP pro-vides.

▶ **Navigating in folders**
By using the iViews provided by SAP, SAP NetWeaver Portal users can navigate in the folders of all integrated repositories and access the documents these repositories contain. Access to folders and documents managed by KM is con-trolled using permissions.

The user interface (UI) for navigating in folders can be configured flexibly and modified to suit various roles. You can personalize the presentation of the UI per your preferences. APIs also allow you to extend the UI by integrating your own functions into the standard system.

▶ **Search**
The search function provided by SAP can find documents in all integrated repositories connected to KM. The system displays only documents for which the current user has read permission in the results list.

Apart from the documents, you can also include the content of websites in your indexes using web crawlers. This information is then also available through the search functions in your portal. The search functionalities in SAP NetWeaver Portal are provided by the standalone TREX engine.

▶ **Taxonomies and classification**
A *taxonomy* is a hierarchical structure of categories in which you can classify the documents according to content, organization, or other criteria. Documents that are stored in different repositories can be included in the same category. Tax-onomies enable SAP NetWeaver Portal users to navigate in a uniform structure

throughout an organization even if information is stored in heterogeneous storage locations in an unstructured format.

After the initial configuration has taken place and a taxonomy has been created, the system automatically classifies new and changed documents. You can define rules for automatic classification of documents.

► **Knowledge Management services**
KM services are the functions that you can use on the content of all connected repositories as long as the technical conditions are met. Examples of these services include subscriptions, ratings, public reviews, feedback, and personal notes. You can also develop new services based on the open APIs provided by SAP.

► **Document creation and publishing**
Every portal user can create information in the portal, provided the user has the necessary permissions. Using the SAP NetWeaver Portal iViews provided by KM, you can upload documents that you created using a PC application directly to a KM folder. You can also use forms provided by KM in SAP NetWeaver Portal to create information directly in the web browser.

The publishing process of a document is supported by various functions such as the approval workflow. You can define your own rules for the workflow for publishing the documents in any KM folder. You can also assign various metadata to documents and other objects to make the knowledge available in your company more usable. For example, you can enable a rating service for the documents, which will enable users to rate any document, providing information that can be useful for all users.

1.2.3   Collaboration

With its collaboration capabilities, SAP NetWeaver Portal allows communication and collaboration between users in the portal. This allows SAP NetWeaver to bring together users regardless of time and geographic location. For example, members of a project can communicate and collaborate within their project space within the portal. Virtual rooms can be created for a project's team members for common access and organization of documents, applications, and ideas.

Like the SAP NetWeaver Portal and KM, the Collaboration component is part of SAP NetWeaver Portal. From a technical perspective, Collaboration is dependent on the system components of the SAP NetWeaver Portal and KM.

Some of the features of Collaboration are as follows:

▶ **Making services available**
You can configure how the system makes services available for collaboration in the following applications:

  ▶ Collaboration launchpad, which allows central access to contacts and services in the portal header

  ▶ Member list of rooms

  ▶ Context menu for user names

  ▶ User details iView

▶ **Virtual rooms**
Based on predefined templates provided by SAP, you can create virtual rooms for collaboration and communication within teams and project groups within an organization. A virtual room allows the members to access shared data and services independent of their location.

▶ **Groupware integration**
For collaboration in the portal, you can integrate the email and scheduling services (Microsoft Exchange) used in your company.

▶ **Asynchronous collaboration**
For asynchronous collaboration, the following functions are available:

  ▶ Online discussions

  ▶ Online management of tasks, sessions, and documents

  ▶ Online entry of feedback, ratings, and comments

  ▶ Information sharing in forums

  ▶ Information sharing in wikis

▶ **Real-time collaboration (RTC)**
For real-time collaboration (RTC), the following functions are available:

  ▶ Interactive online access to applications (application sharing)

  ▶ Interactive online exchange of information (instant messaging)

▶ **Integration of third-party services**
In addition to the services provided by SAP for RTC, you can also integrate third-party services, for example, WebEx, in the portal.

> **Note**
>
> The RTC capabilities in SAP NetWeaver are recommended for scenarios that include using instant messaging and application-sharing services by a specific group of portal users. One-to-one application sharing sessions and chat sessions can be done with up to eight users. Because RTC is resource intensive, for large portal installations, the performance and sizing impacts of RTC should be considered. For more information, see SAP Note 948298.

As shown in Figure 1.4, Collaboration features run on the KM platform of the EP usage type, so there is no other technical component requirement apart from that the KM components are running.

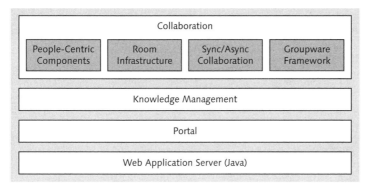

Figure 1.4 Collaboration

1.2.4 Unification

The unification capabilities of SAP NetWeaver Portal maximize the usefulness of portal navigation. Drag and relate navigation and the ability to manipulate relations between business objects increase the relevance of the retrieved data to the business context and requirements of the user. This is possible due to the ability of the unification services to resolve relations between business objects from a company's backend applications.

A simple example of the use of unification drag and relate is dragging a particular material onto an iView representing a list of customers. A result set returns a listing of all of your customers who purchase that particular material.

However, to show the added value of unification-relation resolving, suppose the content developer deletes the direct foreign-key relationship between customers and materials and edits the relation (thereby creating a manual relation), forcing it through additional steps by adding a condition from a list of regions. A salesperson performing the drag and relate operation now would still receive a list of customers who buy that particular material, but only for the region for which that salesperson is responsible.

In this section, we will first look at the capabilities provided by unification, such as drag and relate and integration capabilities. We will also look at the prerequisites for unification and the process flow for the unification scenarios.

Capabilities

The unification feature in SAP NetWeaver Portal provides the following capabilities:

▶ **Drag and relate**
Drag and relate capabilities of SAP NetWeaver Portal maximize the usefulness of portal navigation between SAP systems, including SAP ERP and SAP NetWeaver BW systems. The drag and relate functionality is not supported by versions later than SAP NetWeaver BW 3.1.

▶ **Integration**
Selecting an iView in the portal navigation panel returns the content of that iView and displays it in the content area of the portal. However, dragging a link from a displayed iView onto a drag and relate-enabled iView in the navigation panel enables the return of information based on the relationship between the business objects of the two iViews. This ability to filter content by different, but related, business objects increases the relevance of the retrieved data for the user. To enable a drag target, the DRAG&RELATE property of the iView must be set to TRUE in the property editor.

During runtime, drag and relate allows the portal user to navigate specifically to the information required by the user's roles in the organization. However, it is the content creator and/or administrator who uses and is more closely aware of drag and relate features.

Drag and relate is supported between objects of the same type, either SAP ERP transactions or BW reports and only on foreign-key relations; therefore, a foreign-key relation must exist between the business objects of the drag source and target iViews. Use drag and relate between iViews based on SAP ERP transactions and iViews based on BW reports.

The following must be true for drag and relate to work between iViews based on SAP ERP transactions and iViews based on BW reports:

▶ The business objects must be of the same type, for example:

    ▶ Controlling area (BUS0004) in SAP ERP and controlling area (T0CO_AREA) in SAP NetWeaver BW.

    ▶ Cost center (BUS0012) in SAP ERP and cost center (T0COCENTER) in SAP NetWeaver BW.

▶ A manual relation must be created using the Relationship Editor between the two objects on their primary keys.

Prerequisites

Both SAP ERP and SAP NetWeaver BW require preparation in the application at the backend for working with portal drag and relate technology. The current plug-in, which must be imported into SAP R/3 systems (for version 4.7 and earlier) to work with SAP NetWeaver Portal, is found at *service.sap.com/support*. Once there, choose SOFTWARE DISTRIBUTION CENTER • DOWNLOAD • SAP INSTALLATIONS AND UPGRADES • SAP NETWEAVER • SAP ENTERPRISE PORTAL ® ENTERPRISE PORTAL PLUG-IN • WP-PI.

Select the plug-in WP-PI 600_<YOUR_BASIS_RELEASE>. Find out your Basis release in SAP ERP by choosing SYSTEM • STATUS, and check the release of component SAP_BASIS.

In the portal, systems must be created to represent the backend applications.

Process Flow

After the prerequisites have been fulfilled, it is possible to create iViews from the portal over SAP systems in two ways:

▶ By migrating roles from the SAP system using the role upload utility of SAP NetWeaver Portal

▶ By creating individual iViews using the iView wizard framework and entering required information manually

1.2.5 Federated Portal

Organizations can implement a federated portal network using the SAP NetWeaver platform to share content between SAP and non-SAP portals.

A *federated portal network* allows organizations with a distributed landscape of portal installations, both SAP and non-SAP, to provide a single point of access to portal information, services, and applications distributed on multiple portals throughout the entire organizational network. This implementation allows existing content and configurations to be utilized by consuming content on various portals by a single portal, thereby reducing administration efforts.

Providing a single point of access vastly improves user productivity, thereby increasing the return on investment (ROI) of each portal implementation, and reducing the total cost of ownership (TCO) by way of minimizing administrative efforts.

A federated portal network is not intended to improve global performance issues between remote sites. However, some federated portal landscape configurations, combined with certain content types, may yield better performance rates compared to landscapes that have not implemented a federated portal network.

> **Implementing a Federated Portal Network**
>
> We will discuss the details of implementing a federated portal network in Chapter 8.

Each portal in a portal federation can be a producer, consumer, or both, depending on whether it exposes its content for other portals or consumes the remote content exposed by other portals, as described here:

- **Producer**
  A portal installation that provides other portals (consumers) with remote access to its content.

- **Consumer**
  A portal installation that accesses the remote content provided by another portal (a producer).

Each portal can support both local and remote users.

SAP NetWeaver Portal is WSRP (Web Services for Remote Portlets) compliant, which means you can implement a federated portal network between SAP NetWeaver Portal and other WSRP-compliant portals. It provides the following two capabilities:

▶ Other WSRP-compliant portlets on non-SAP portals can be incorporated into the SAP NetWeaver Portal federation.

▶ SAP NetWeaver Portal can expose its WSRP-compliant content for consumption by external portals.

Figure 1.5 shows a federated portal network comprising two producer portals and one consumer portal, sharing content with one another. Users log on to the portal in their location but gain seamless access to backend applications residing in other locations on the network. The remote role assignment and remote delta link modes are used to share content between SAP NetWeaver portals only, while WSRP application sharing is typically used for SAP NetWeaver and non-SAP portal content sharing.

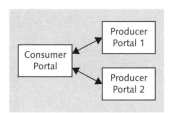

Figure 1.5   Federated Portal Network

1.2.6   External-Facing Portal

With this scenario variant, organizations can use SAP NetWeaver Portal to expose applications, services, and information over the Internet to customers, partners, and employees.

> **Note**
>
> SAP NetWeaver Portal can be implemented as an intranet portal as well as an external-facing portal.

When the portal is available over the Internet, SAP NetWeaver Portal is expected to behave like other websites. Specifically, it should perform well even in low-bandwidth situations, provide a website-like experience, and provide the business functionality. SAP NetWeaver Portal provides various tools and configuration points for implementing an external-facing portal.

By implementing an external-facing portal, companies can boost their portal project ROI by using the same platform for the company's Internet and intranet implementations. Implementing an external-facing portal is a scenario variant that exposes your portal over the Internet, so you should consider the following points:

▶ External-facing portals usually allow access to anonymous users, so you will need to create and configure content for such users.

▶ External-facing portals usually also allow self-registration for users. You will need to configure self-registration as well as create and configure content that you want to expose to the self-registered users.

▶ Security aspects need to be taken very seriously because now your portal is accessible to the general public and probably some malicious users on the Internet. You will need to make sure that the company's internal network is still safe and not accessible to unauthorized users.

In addition to registered users, an external-facing portal can be accessed by the following types of users:

▶ **Anonymous users**
Users who can view the portal content without providing a user name and password. These users are automatically assigned to a particular user (the default anonymous user in SAP NetWeaver Portal is "Guest").

▶ **Self-registered users**
Users who enter as anonymous users and then register with the portal. During registration, users set a user name and password. In subsequent visits to the portal, users log in with this user name and password. These users are automatically assigned to a particular group (the default group for registered users in SAP NetWeaver Portal is "Everyone").

Because SAP NetWeaver Portal will be made available on the Internet, it is available to everyone.

1.2.7 Enterprise Workspaces

The *enterprise workspaces* add-on was introduced with SAP NetWeaver 7.3. It provides a flexible, intuitive environment on top of SAP NetWeaver Portal, which allows business users to integrate, organize, and use various content such as applications, reports, dashboards, web content, and documents from SAP or non-SAP systems. This environment provides two types of workspaces:

▶ **Personal workspaces**
Users can organize content for their personal use.

▶ **Shared workspaces**
Users can share the content with a group by placing the content in a shared workspace.

Enterprise workspaces provide the following key capabilities:

▶ Creation and integration of custom or existing portal content

▶ Rich out-of-the-box content provided by SAP

▶ Flexible and customizable environment for users

▶ Intuitive end-user authoring tools

▶ Administration, maintenance, and content-management tools

▶ Public API for developing custom content and accessing workspace functionality

As shown in Figure 1.6, various roles come into the picture while working with enterprise workspaces.

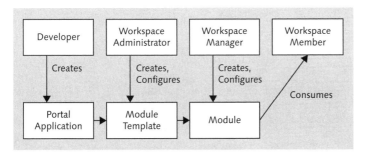

Figure 1.6 Enterprise Workspaces Workflow

Table 1.1 gives an overview of the various roles and their activities.

Name	Description
Portal Administrator	Manages, monitors, and administers the portal from within the portal administration environment. Responsible for assigning workspace roles to users and for performing various configuration tasks.
Workspace System Administrator	Responsible for configuring, customizing, managing, and monitoring the workspaces and related services.
Workspace Content Administrator	Creates and configures content to be used in workspaces.
Workspace Owner	By default, the user that created a workspace. A workspace can have only one owner who performs the following activities: ▶ Reassigns ownership of a workspace to another manager ▶ Closes a workspace ▶ Receives automatic email notifications regarding various events in the workspace lifecycle ▶ Performs all activities of a manager
Workspace Manager	Performs the following activities: ▶ Adds and removes workspace members ▶ Reassigns member roles in a workspace ▶ Views, approves, or rejects membership requests ▶ Adds and organizes pages and modules in the workspace ▶ Uploads and edits documents in a document list ▶ Adds and removes links to a link list ▶ Edits text in a text pad A workspace can have multiple managers.
Workspace Member	Views content in a shared workspace; collaborates with other members on shared applications, such as documents.
Custom Content Developer	Develops custom content for use in enterprise workspaces.

Table 1.1 Enterprise Workspaces Roles

The workspace content in enterprise workspaces is made up of modules and module templates. A *module* is a content item, such as an iView or page, which runs in a workspace page. In addition to the functionality of an iView or page, a module can also respond to workspace events. You create a module from a module template.

A *module template* is a template from which actual modules can be created in workspaces. In addition to the set of out-of-the-box module templates provided by enterprise workspaces, you can create custom module templates from existing iViews, pages, or custom portal applications.

As was shown in Figure 1.6, there are different stages in the content creation workflow. Each stage of this workflow involves different roles working on different objects. The workflow stages progress as follows:

1. Developers create custom portal applications, using the enterprise workspaces API, and deploy them to the portal. This step is optional because SAP provides a lot of out-of-the-box content.

2. Workspace administrators create module templates based on existing iViews, pages, or custom portal applications. The custom module templates then become available for use in workspaces.

3. Workspace managers or owners add out-of-the-box or custom modules to the workspace pages. Workspace managers or owners configure the module runtime settings, if applicable.

4. Workspace members navigate to the pages and work with the modules.

1.2.8   Web Page Composer

Web Page Composer is a tool provided by SAP to help business users create portal pages. Using this tool, business users can generate web content for business applications without help from the development team. Web Page Composer is based on standard SAP NetWeaver Portal capabilities, and business users can integrate content from SAP and non-SAP system to create web page content. Web Page Composer also provides tools to enhance the created pages with other content such as news, articles, and so on.

Web Page Composer has evolved to become the portal's content management system for easily creating and managing portal pages, both for integrating applications and reports, as well as unstructured content such as documents, news, and web articles. For example, imagine you are responsible for your company's intranet in your department, and you have to maintain all of the pages with the latest information such as images, news, and a document list. A colleague has asked you to update some news about a new campaign and to upload new info brochures and a how-to guide. Also, you want to provide some links to the latest sales reports with statistics and analysis about the turnover of the previous quarter.

You can also create interactive pages ad hoc; for example, without the need to involve developers. You can easily place and connect applications such as "Customer List" and "Map" on a page. Upon selection of a customer, the portal passes the address details to the other application and shows the location in the map. All this can be done easily in the portal without involving the IT department using the new Web Page Composer capabilities.

Web Page Composer offers the following services:

▶ Professional editors and business users are empowered to easily create and manage pages in SAP NetWeaver Portal.

▶ End users can actively contribute and share news and knowledge using intuitive and easy-to-use tools and templates, thus boosting their productivity and freeing up administration resources.

▶ Administrators can focus on their core tasks and innovations instead of managing content-related activities.

▶ Because Web Page Composer is fully based on the proven and scalable SAP NetWeaver platform, this ensures a reliable operation from a performance and availability point of view. In addition, Web Page Composer leverages all the open standards and frameworks for integrating any kind of information, service, or application—SAP and non-SAP.

▶ Various governance tools such as permissions, approval workflow, link checks, and so on ensure that the quality of the content is very high and only authorized people can apply changes.

▶ The additional costs for operating the solution are very small because Web Page Composer runs fully integrated with your existing portal infrastructure.

Figure 1.7 shows various activities and roles involved in working with Web Page Composer.

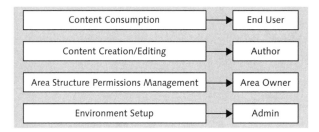

Figure 1.7 Web Page Composer Workflow

1.2.9 Wikis

A *wiki* is a website that allows users to create web pages collaboratively; multiple web pages created by users can then be interlinked. A wiki can be used for various purposes, such as group learning or project communication. A wiki usually encourages all users to create and edit content within the website by providing tools for editing web pages. With the introduction of the SAP NetWeaver 7.3 platform, SAP has integrated wiki capabilities into SAP NetWeaver Portal. Corporate wikis are now used for second-generation KM, which allows employees in an organization to easily share expertise, without training efforts.

A corporate wiki can serve a wide range of requirements and is ideally suited for various purposes such as setting up a corporate encyclopedia or quality assurance processes, managing product expertise, or project documentation. It integrates seamlessly with SAP NetWeaver Portal to provide a convenient tool for employees, distinct groups of specialists, and—by extension—the corporation as a whole. SAP provides a business package that can be deployed on SAP NetWeaver Portal for accessing wiki features.

The wiki feature provided by SAP offers all technical features for a smooth integration, including role-based entitlements, professional searches via TREX, multilanguage support, and much more. Various ways in which the wiki package can be used are listed here:

▶ **As a knowledge database/ad hoc expertise**
Wikis can be used as a knowledge database within an enterprise. Users can collaborate and create content related to the corporate processes, project related knowledge database, and so on.

▶ **Project and product documentation**
Wikis can be used to create documentation of projects and for managing knowledge about pilot projects in an enterprise. The documentation can evolve continuously and be kept updated because all users can contribute to this knowledge.

▶ **Strategic marketing/competitor information**
A corporation can use a wiki for keeping market research information up to date. They can keep information about their competitors as a knowledge database and link it to other sources of information already existing within the enterprise.

▶ **Quality management/complaint management**
A wiki can be used to track complaint incidents, known quality issues, and corresponding remedial initiatives.

The features of wikis include the following:

▶ Uniform user administration via SAP NetWeaver Portal's UME (LDAP)

▶ Integration with the role-based navigation concept of SAP NetWeaver Portal (with reading and writing rights)

▶ Integration of the SAP NetWeaver Portal/TREX search, including search results according to user rights

▶ SSO using SAP logon tickets, which requires no additional logins or passwords

▶ Integration into the navigational structure of SAP NetWeaver Portal by the Portal Content Directory (PCD)

▶ Integration into the Portal Content Studio using convenient iView wizards

▶ Supply of parallel and independent wiki instances in a single installation

▶ Multilanguage support simply by switching the SAP NetWeaver Portal language

▶ Adapting the visual appearance by using SAP NetWeaver Portal themes (project individual customizing)

1.3   Summary

SAP NetWeaver Portal offers a rich set of features and capabilities to fulfill the needs of an enterprise. With strong capabilities in portal content creation, Knowledge Management and Collaboration, portal federation networks, and so on, SAP NetWeaver Portal 7.3 is ready to take on the most complex challenges of a corporate's intranet/Internet needs. This chapter focused on introducing the various concepts and capabilities of SAP NetWeaver Portal; the next chapter will focus on more details, steps for implementing and configuring SAP NetWeaver Portal for an enterprise, and steps to effectively manage the operations on a day-to-day basis.

To implement SAP NetWeaver Portal, you first need to understand the SAP NetWeaver Portal platform and how it runs and responds to user requests. Various administration options are available so that you can use the right tools to manage the portal.

2   Architecture

The previous chapter provided an introduction to SAP NetWeaver Portal and an overview of its features and positioning. In this chapter, we will look at the portal platform, its architecture, and various components that form part of SAP NetWeaver Portal. The SAP NetWeaver Portal is a Java Enterprise Edition (EE) application that runs on the SAP Web Application Server Java stack and provides an environment for the portal components to run. SAP NetWeaver Portal is comprised of the following parts:

▶ **Portal Runtime (PRT)**
Portal Runtime is the container that runs the portal applications and generates the HTML response that is sent back to the client.

▶ **Portal Content Directory (PCD)**
Portal Content Directory is the repository for portal content objects, such as iViews, pages, roles, worksets, and systems. Information about all of the PCD objects is stored in the Application Server (AS) database.

▶ **Application Server Java (AS Java)**
AS Java is the platform on which SAP NetWeaver Portal runs.

This chapter discusses all of these components and their architecture in detail so that you can develop an understanding of the SAP NetWeaver Portal platform and how it works. We start by discussing the SAP NetWeaver Portal architecture in terms of the various components that make up the platform. Then we move to discussing various administration tools that the platform provides along with the usage scenarios of each tool. We will then discuss the SAP NetWeaver Portal Runtime in terms of how client requests to SAP NetWeaver Portal are handled by the portal at runtime.

2.1 AS Java Architecture

This section focuses on the architecture, administration, and configuration of SAP AS Java, on which SAP NetWeaver Portal runs. It introduces you to the general architecture of a Java application server.

2.1.1 Cluster Architecture

AS Java is based on cluster architecture. An AS Java server cluster consists of many parts: one or more Java instances, a central instance, and a database. Figure 2.1 shows various parts of the cluster.

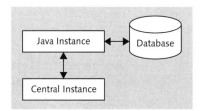

Figure 2.1 Java Cluster

Figure 2.1 shows the general architecture of an AS Java cluster, which can typically contain more than one Java instance. The main criterion driving the number of Java instances in a cluster is the scalability requirement; when the demands from the system are high, more instances are added. Individual Java instances can be deployed on the same box or on different boxes, and each Java instance can also have multiple server nodes.

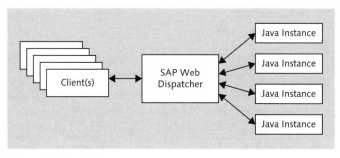

Figure 2.2 Load Balancer

When there are multiple Java instances in a cluster, a load balancer is needed to balance the incoming requests. SAP Web Dispatcher, for example, can be used to balance the load of web requests between multiple Java instances. Figure 2.2 depicts such an architecture.

2.1.2 Java Instance

The Java instance is the actual runtime environment that AS Java provides for running the applications. The Java instance consists of an Internet Communication Manager (ICM) and one or more server processes, which are also known as server nodes. The ICM handles the requests from clients and sends these requests to the individual work processes; after processing, it returns the response to the clients, as shown in Figure 2.3.

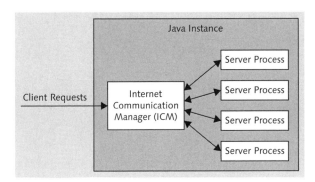

Figure 2.3   Java Instance

Each server process runs a Java Virtual Machine (JVM) and is multithreaded, meaning that each server process can handle multiple requests simultaneously.

2.1.3 Central Instance

The *central instance* is an important part of an AS Java cluster. Every AS Java cluster has one central services instance. This instance is responsible for exchanging lock administration messages between the instances, and load balancing within the cluster. Central services run on one physical machine and have a separate instance number.

The SAP central instance is comprised of the message server and enqueue server, both of which are described next.

Message Server

The message server maintains a list of all server processes in the AS Java cluster and provides information about their availability to the ICM. It also represents the infrastructure for data exchange between the participating server processes.

The message server is responsible for the following tasks in the AS Java cluster:

▶ Notification of events that arise in the cluster (e.g., when a server process is started or stopped)

▶ Communication between different server processes

▶ Forwarding of messages and requests to all participants

▶ Preparation of login information for the SAP Web Dispatcher

▶ Exchange of cache information in the cluster

The message server is addressed through the cluster manager of one of the server processes in the Java cluster, as shown in Figure 2.4.

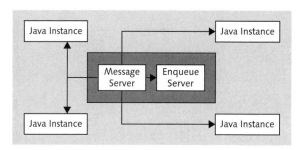

Figure 2.4   Central Instance

Enqueue Server

The enqueue server manages logical locks. It runs on the central services instance of the Java cluster, manages the lock table in the main memory, receives requests for setting or releasing locks, and maps the logical locks to the database. The enqueue server has two important tasks:

▶ Perform internal synchronization within the AS Java cluster

▶ Process applications' requests to lock and unlock objects, as well as manage the lock table with the existing locks

The enqueue server can be configured for high availability by setting it up with the replication server and a platform-independent, high-availability solution. Every cluster also has a database that stores system and application data. Although there is one central database, it is also possible to have several application databases.

2.2 Server Administration Tools

SAP NetWeaver provides a wide range of tools to effectively manage and maintain the server. In this section, we'll discuss some of the most important tools for portal server administration.

2.2.1 Management Console

The Management Console (MC) is the centralized system management tool for SAP systems. You can perform the following tasks using the MC:

▶ Start and stop SAP instances.

▶ Display SAP log and trace files.

▶ Display the various processes running within the cluster.

▶ Monitor the system alerts.

▶ Monitor AS Java (e.g., process table, threads, garbage collection [GC] history, heap memory, etc.).

▶ Monitor the ICM for threads, connection list, and other data.

▶ View log files.

▶ Monitor the central instance logs.

▶ Monitor messages from the message server and the enqueue locks from the enqueue server.

The MC is available in three modes, as discussed next.

Web-Based SAP Management Console

The web-based MC is an applet-based management console that runs inside a web browser. You can use it to administer an SAP system remotely, but for MC to work on your machine, you need the Java plug-in installed on your browser. After meeting this requirement, you can access MC by going to *http://<host>:<port>*, where

<host> is the machine where SAP AS Java is installed, and *<port>* is the admin port for starting MC. By default, the port number is *5<instance_number>13*. For example, if the instance number is 01, then the port number will be 50113. When this URL is invoked, the applet-based console is launched, as shown in Figure 2.5.

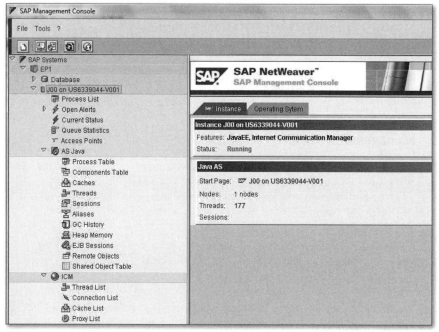

Figure 2.5 Web-Based SAP Management Console

The console lists all of the instances installed and all of the nodes within each instance. From here, you can select a node and start, stop, or restart the service. The advantage of using the web-based MC is that the console is applet-based, and administration can be done from any remote computer as long as the following requirements are fulfilled:

▸ Java Runtime Environment (JRE) 1.42 or higher is installed.

▸ The web browser supports Java, and the Java plug-in in the browser is installed and activated.

You can activate or deactivate the Java plug-in in the browser by going to TOOLS • INTERNET OPTIONS • PROGRAMS. Figure 2.6 shows the setting for Internet Explorer 7.0.

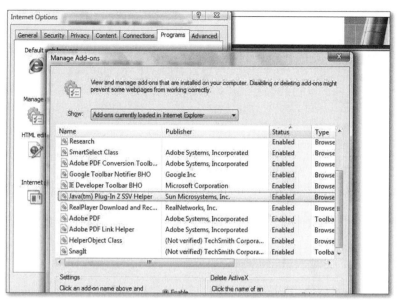

Figure 2.6 Internet Explorer Java Plug-In

Eclipse-Based Management Console in SAP NetWeaver Developer Studio

Go to Window • Open Perspective • Other • SAP Management Console to bring up the instances installed on the host you have connected to.

Standalone Microsoft Management Console

SAP provides a plug-in that allows you to monitor and administer the SAP system from the SAP Microsoft Management Console (MMC), which is only available for Microsoft Windows platforms. You can also perform all of the management activities previously mentioned using the standalone MMC. Figure 2.7 shows the MMC running on a Windows machine. As you will notice, the information provided in MMC is similar to that in the web-based MC.

The MMC lists the SAP instances running on the host machine but cannot be used to manage SAP systems running on a remote machine. You can start the MMC in one of the following ways:

▶ From the Windows Start menu, you can choose Start • Programs • SAP Management Console.

- From the SAP MMC, a configuration can be saved by going to FILE • SAVE AS. This saves the configuration as an .msc file. These configurations can be opened later by the FILE • OPEN option.

- From the command line, the following command can be executed:

```
>mmc.exe <config_file>
```

where <CONFIG_FILE> is the configuration file for the configuration that needs to be loaded. A configuration file can be saved by going to FILE • SAVE AS.

- You can specify the name of the instance to be loaded this way:

```
>mmc.exe <config_file> -SAP_R/3_MANAGERHOST <Instance_Name>
```

- From the configuration file, you can double-click a previously saved configuration.

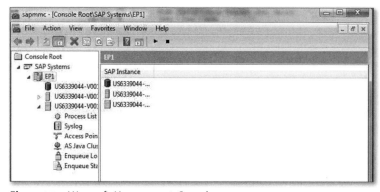

Figure 2.7 Microsoft Management Console

2.2.2 SAP NetWeaver Administrator

SAP NetWeaver Administrator is the web-based tool for administration, configuration, and monitoring AS Java. The following are the main features of SAP NetWeaver Administrator:

- A central tool for tasks such as starting and stopping instances, configuring application server and services, viewing logs and traces, and running performance analysis

- A web-based tool that allows administration activities to be done from any system using a web browser interface

▶ Accessible when the server is running and can be started by going to the following URL in a web browser: *http://<host>:<port>/nwa*

In this URL, the host is the host machine where the server is installed, and the port is the HTTP port number of the application server. The default HTTP port for an application server is *5<instance_number>00*. For example, if the instance number is 10, the HTTP port will be 51000.

Figure 2.8 shows the landing page of SAP NetWeaver Administrator.

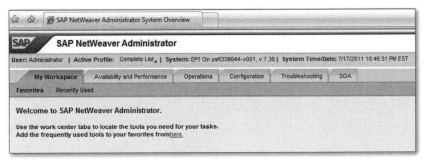

Figure 2.8 SAP NetWeaver Administrator

SAP NetWeaver Administrator functions are divided into work centers, which group similar types of functionality. Work centers are further divided into worksets, which group similar tools. The following work centers are available with SAP NetWeaver Administrator (as shown on the corresponding tabs in Figure 2.8):

▶ AVAILABILITY AND PERFORMANCE
The availability and performance work center enables you to monitor various system availability and performance parameters. It has the following tools:

  ▶ **AS Java overview**: This allows you to monitor the AS Java system on a cluster level, both online and offline. Using this application, you can detect and resolve different system problems by navigating directly to the relevant tool of SAP NetWeaver Administrator. You can also access this application by going to the following URL: *http://<host>:<port>/nwa/asjo*.

  ▶ **AS Java statistics**: This allows you to measure and analyze the performance of the activities of a Java system. This tool can provide important performance metrics such as response time, CPU time, memory consumption, etc.

  ▶ **BPM system overview**: This allows you to monitor the availability of the BPM subsystems and adapters. Using this tool, you can start a Java application as part of a troubleshooting action, check the work of the BPM functionalities, and more.

▶ **Connection monitor**: This allows you to view all JCo connections between the Java server and an ABAP system, as well as view details by selecting an entry. You can access the connection manager directly by going to the following URL: *http://<host>:<port>/nwa/connection-mon.*

▶ **Distributed transactions**: This allows you to monitor how JTA transactions are handled by the AS Java transaction service, and how incomplete transactions are recovered after a resource crash.

▶ **Guided procedures**: This allows you to view the current status of the Guided Procedures components. This tool is only available in your AS Java if you have installed the capabilities required for implementing the Creating Composite Applications scenario. You can access this tool directly by going to the following URL: *http://<host>:<port>/nwa/gp.*

▶ **Java system reports**: Java system reports allow you to monitor the AS Java system and Java applications running on the system. You can track the performances of all AS Java instances, detect and analyze the causes of various problems in AS Java, and perform tuning for productive use with AS Java. You can access this tool directly by going to the following URL: *http://<host>:<port>/nwa/java-sys-reports.*

▶ **JCo monitoring**: This allows you to monitor all the JCO connections in the system; for example, you can organize the metadata cache and change the settings for JCo traces. You can access the JCO monitoring tool directly by going to the following URL: *http://<host>:<port>/nwa/connection-mon.*

▶ **Locks**: The locks tool in this work center allows you to create and release locks. Locks in SAP are identified by their name and argument, and SAP NetWeaver Administrator sets the lock owner automatically. You can access this tool directly by going to the following URL: *http://<host>:<port/nwa/locks.*

▶ **Log viewer**: This tool allows you to view all log and trace messages that are generated in the SAP system. These log messages assist you in monitoring and troubleshooting problems. (We discuss this in more detail in Chapter 10.) You can access this tool directly by going to the following URL: *http://<host>:<port>/nwa/logs.*

▶ OPERATIONS

The operations work center allows you to maintain the operational parameters of the system and consists of the following worksets:

- ▶ Systems
- ▶ Users and access
- ▶ Data and databases
- ▶ Jobs
- ▶ Process and tasks

▶ CONFIGURATION

The configuration work center is where most of the configurations are done. Starting with SAP NetWeaver 7.1, the Visual Administrator tool—used for run-time configurations of the system—has been retired. Now the configurations are done from the configuration work center for SAP NetWeaver Administration. The configuration work center provides the following worksets:

- ▶ Security
- ▶ Infrastructure
- ▶ Scenarios
- ▶ Processes and tasks
- ▶ Connectivity

▶ TROUBLESHOOTING

The troubleshooting work center gives access to the various tools needed for troubleshooting the Java engine or applications running on the Java engine. The tools are grouped under the following worksets:

- ▶ Java
- ▶ Database
- ▶ Logs and traces
- ▶ Processes and tasks
- ▶ Advanced troubleshooting

▶ SOA

The SOA work center provides various tools for service-oriented architecture (SOA) configuration and monitoring. The various tools in this work center are grouped under the following worksets:

▶ Technical configuration

▶ Application and scenario communication

▶ Logs and traces

▶ Monitoring

2.2.3 Offline Configuration Tool

The Offline Configuration Tool, commonly known as the Config Tool, allows configuration of AS Java in offline mode. As a result, the server does not need to be running for the Config Tool to work. The Config Tool connects directly to the database, which is where all completed configuration changes are stored. For these changes to take effect, you must restart the server because the server reads all of the properties from the database during startup.

The Config Tool can run in two modes, as discussed in the following subsections.

GUI Config Tool

The UI-based GUI Config Tool can be opened by executing the batch file *configtool.bat* (in a Windows environment) at the location *<install_directory>/<system_id>/<instance_id>/ j2ee/configtool*.

In a UNIX environment, the file is named *configtool.sh*. This opens up the Config Tool UI and connects to the AS Java database, as shown in Figure 2.9.

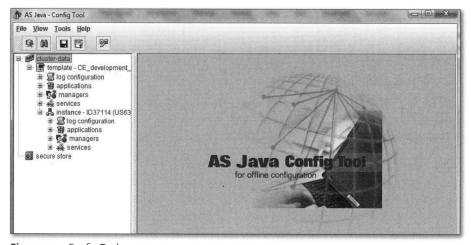

Figure 2.9 Config Tool

The following tasks can be accomplished using the GUI Config Tool:

▶ **Connect to a database**
Connect to the default database and any other databases. You can effectively connect to multiple remote systems from one machine using the Config Tool.

▶ **Configure virtual machine (VM) parameters**
Configure various VM parameters such as initial heap size, maximum heap size, and so on.

▶ **Configure services**
Configure all of the services running in AS Java, such as deploy service, classloader service, HTTP service, and so on.

▶ **Configure managers**
Configure various managers running in AS Java; for example, LogManager, SessionManager, ThreadManager, and so on.

▶ **Configure applications**
Deploy all of the SAP standard and custom applications.

▶ **Configure the cluster, instances, and nodes**
This allows you to configure the whole cluster, as well as individual instances and nodes.

▶ **Add and remove server nodes**
Add additional server nodes to the same instance. Each server instance can have multiple server nodes. When the server gets installed, by default it is installed with one server node. Adding more server nodes enables the server instance to handle higher loads and aids in load balancing the client requests.

▶ **Log configuration**
Configure logging (discussed in more detail in Chapter 10).

▶ **Export configurations**
Export configurations as an XML file and later restore the system configurations by importing the XML file.

Console Config Tool

The Console Config Tool provides a command-line interface for configuring the server parameters in offline mode. As with the GUI Config Tool, all changes made using the Console Config Tool take effect only after the server has been restarted. The Console Config Tool can be invoked by double-clicking the batch file *console-config.bat* in *<install_directory>/<system_id>/<instance_id>/j2ee/configtool*.

This opens the Console Config Tool in the command line, as shown in Figure 2.10.

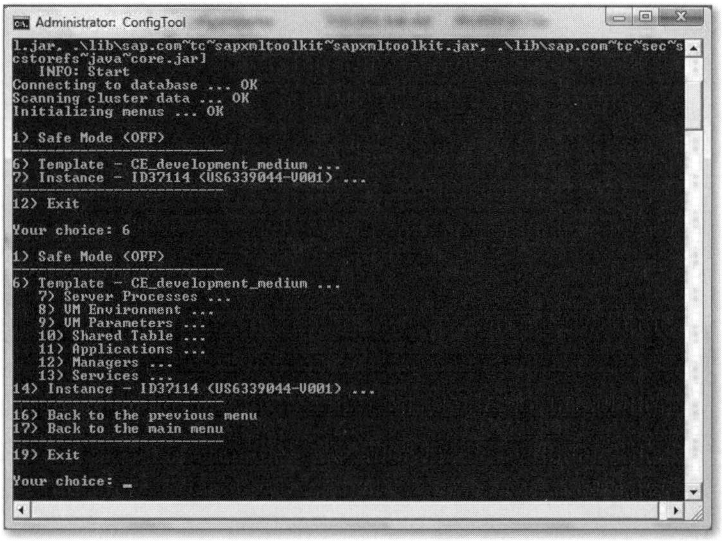

Figure 2.10 Console Config Tool

The following tasks can be performed using the Console Config Tool:

▶ Configure template and instance properties

▶ Configure VM parameters

▶ Configure shared tables

▶ Configure applications

▶ Configure managers

▶ Configure services

2.2.4 Telnet

You can also use a telnet client to administer the SAP NetWeaver application server using command-line shell commands. *Telnet* is a network protocol that can be used to connect to remote machines using a terminal connection. A telnet client allows you to connect to the application server using the telnet protocol. Telnet requires the application server to be up and running for it to work. In addition, remote administration using telnet is not possible because SAP only allows connection to the local host with telnet.

To start the telnet console, type the following command in the command line:

```
>telnet localhost <telnet_port>
```

In this case, `telnet` is the telnet client, and `telnet_port` is the telnet port of the application server. By default, the Java AS telnet port is calculated as 50000 + (100 × instance number) + 8. For example, if the instance number is 01, the telnet port will be 50108.

You can connect to the application server using the telnet protocol by invoking the telnet command. Figure 2.11 shows the telnet-based console.

Figure 2.11 Telnet-Based Console

After the telnet console comes up, enter the user name and password. By authenticating, you are logged in to one of the server processes. You can jump to another server by using the JUMP command. The command LSC gives a list of all server processes in the instance.

To view a list of all available commands, execute the MAN command. This list is shown in Figure 2.12.

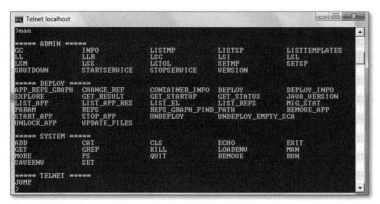

Figure 2.12 Telnet Commands

As shown in Figure 2.12, the commands are grouped together by the functionality they provide. To view the message syntax and message documentation of a command, execute the following:

```
>MAN <command_name>
```

Here, `<command_name>` is the name of the command for which you want to see the documentation.

2.3   Portal Runtime

Portal Runtime (PRT) is the runtime environment that enables SAP NetWeaver Portal to handle the client requests to the Portal Runtime Container. Because the Portal Runtime Container runs on top of AS Java, the requests are first handled by the AS Java and then forwarded to the Portal Runtime Container. In this section, we will first explore the Portal Runtime Container and then see how the client requests are handled by AS Java and the Portal Runtime Container.

2.3.1   Portal Runtime Container

As discussed earlier, the Portal Runtime Container is the platform that runs portal applications. It provides an environment on top of AS Java for running portal-based applications. The PRT is a Java-based framework and is delivered as part of the EP-BASIS-API package, which has the following parts:

▶ tc~epbc~prtc~basis
A Java EE library containing the Java Naming and Directory Interface (JNDI), registry, and concurrency application programming interfaces (APIs).

▶ tc~epbc~prtc~api
A Java EE library containing the PRT APIs.

▶ tc~epbc~prtc~core
A Java EE service containing the PRT APIs implementation as a web container extension.

2.3.2 Request Handling by the Server

The client requests for the portal normally start from a client browser. The request is processed in the server, which returns a response to the client. This processing of requests takes place in two places for SAP NetWeaver Portal. First the request is handled by the AS Java and then processed by the PRT. In this section, we will discuss these processing steps.

As we have discussed earlier, the SAP NetWeaver Portal container is deployed in the AS Java as a Java EE application. This Java EE application defines the following two servlets:

▶ **Gateway**
Handles requests for the portal home page.

▶ **PRT dispatcher**
Handles the requests for specific portal components.

SAP NetWeaver Portal is accessed via *http://<host>:<port>/irj*, where *<host>* is the host server where the portal is running, and *<port>* is the HTTP portal of SAP NetWeaver Portal.

The following steps are executed in the SAP NetWeaver Portal Java EE application when a client makes an HTTP request to the portal:

1. When the request reaches the Java EE engine, it identifies that the request is for the Java EE application irj, which is the portal application. Every Java EE application has a *web.xml* file in the *root/WEB-INF* directory; this *web.xml* file contains the servlet definitions and servlet mapping that decides which servlet of the application should be invoked based on the request URL pattern. The gateway and PRT dispatcher servlets are defined in the *web.xml* file for the irj application.

The Java EE engine reads the *web.xml* file and selects a servlet based on the URL and the servlet mapping defined in the XML file, which, in this case, is the gateway servlet.

2. The gateway servlet again reads the parameters defined in the *web.xml* file. It then redirects the request to the portal launcher PRT application if the application requires authentication, or it redirects to the application that enables anonymous requests if an anonymous login is required.

3. The Java EE engine receives the redirection request and again reads the *web.xml* file to process it. This time, it redirects the requests to the PRT dispatcher servlet based on the URL.

4. Every portal component has an XML *portalapp.xml* file that defines the configuration of the portal component. The PRT reads the *portalapp.xml* to see if the AuthScheme property is set to anonymous. If authentication is needed, then the runtime checks if the user is already authenticated by checking for a valid cookie or a valid user name and password. If the runtime doesn't find one, then it redirects the request to the user management login page. After the user logs on successfully, a cookie is created on behalf of the user to identify the session for subsequent requests, and the request processing continues.

The portal launcher component calls the desktop service of the portal to render the appropriate portal desktop for the user. Figure 2.13 shows these steps.

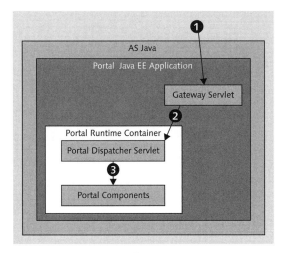

Figure 2.13 Request Handling in AS Java

2.3.3 Request Handling by Portal Runtime

By now, you know that the PRT is actually a Java EE application named `irj` that is deployed in the AS Java. The `irj` application has a servlet named `prt`, which handles all of the requests coming to the PRT. To handle a request, SAP NetWeaver Portal builds a portal object model (POM), which is a tree of all the components involved in generating the HTML response.

SAP NetWeaver Portal creates nodes for each component in the POM. PRT creates a root node called the portal node; all other components involved will be created as child nodes. SAP NetWeaver Portal always creates a page builder node to display an HTML page as a response.

Figure 2.14 represents a POM tree for a component running inside PRT. The POM can become pretty complex for requests that involve multiple components.

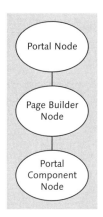

Figure 2.14 Portal Object Model

The following is the sequence of method calls during POM and content creation:

1. `doOnNodeReady()`
   Called on a component when the node representing the component is added to the POM tree. Called once for each component.

2. `doOnPOMReady()`
   Called on each node when no more nodes are to be added to the POM tree. The PRT traverses the tree from top to bottom, calling the method for each component.

If a node is created in a `doOnPOMReady()` method, the new node's `doOnNo-deReady()` method is called and then the `doOnPOMReady()method` finishes execution. Next, the `doOnPOMReady()` method of the new node is called.

3. Request event handlers
   This category of methods is called if there are request events for special nodes. These events are specific to your application and the events in your code.

4. `doBeforeContent()`
   Called just before content creation. The PRT traverses the tree from bottom to top, calling the method for each component.

5. `doContent()`
   Called to retrieve content from the top-most component in the POM tree. `doContent()` is called only in default mode. An alternative method is called for other modes. For example, if you are in `help` mode, then the method `doHelp()` is called. The mode can either be set by sending a parameter `prtmode` in the request URL or can be set manually during POM creation by calling the method `setNodeMode()` of the `INode` interface.

6. `doAfterContent()`
   Called on each node when that component's `doContent()` (or alternative method) is finished.

2.3.4 Starting and Stopping SAP NetWeaver Portal

As we have seen, SAP NetWeaver Portal runs on top of AS Java, so starting and stopping the latter automatically stops and starts SAP NetWeaver Portal.

The start and stop of AS Java can be done in various ways:

▶ Using the Management Console (MC)

▶ Using the Microsoft Management Console (MMC)

▶ Using a command line (UNIX only)

We discuss each of these options in the following subsections.

Management Console

To start the SAP NetWeaver AS Java using the MC, follow these steps:

1. Start the MC.

2. In the console, navigate to the system that you want to start.

3. Select the system. Right click, and choose START from the context menu.

4. Enter the operating system "<SID>adm" administrator credentials.

    MC then starts the SAP instance.

Figure 2.15 shows starting the SAP system from the MC.

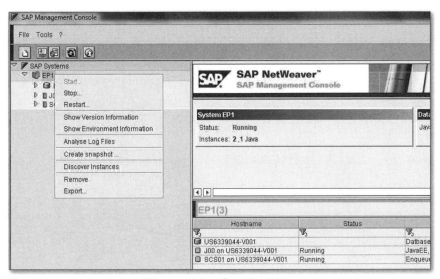

Figure 2.15 Starting SAP NetWeaver AS Java from the MC

To stop an SAP instance using the MC, follow the same steps just given, except choose STOP from the context menu.

Microsoft Management Console

To start the SAP NetWeaver AS Java using the MMC, follow these steps:

1. Start the MMC.

2. In the console, navigate to the system that you want to start.

3. Select the system. Right-click, and choose START from the context menu.

4. Enter the operating system "<SID>adm" administrator credentials. The MMC then starts the SAP instance.

To stop the SAP instance, follow similar steps as those previously mentioned, but choose STOP from the context menu instead.

Remember that this works only on Windows platforms and that you have to run the MMC on the host where the SAP instance has been installed.

Command Line (UNIX)

In UNIX environments, you can use `startsap` and `stopsap` commands to start and stop SAP instances. To execute these commands, log on as the `<sapsid>adm` user to the host where the SAP system is installed.

To start all instances running on the host, execute the following command:

```
>startsap -t all
```

If you want to start the instances separately, execute the following command:

```
>startsap -t j2ee <instance_name> [-v <virtual host name> ]
```

For example:

```
>startsap  -t j2ee JC00 -v virtual_host_1
```

Similarly, to stop an instance, execute the following command:

```
>stopsap -t j2ee <instance_name> [-v <virtual host name> ]
```

Table 2.1 gives a list of names for the `<instance_name>` parameter where `<nn>` is the instance number.

Parameter Name	Description
SCS<nn>	Java central services instance (SAP Central Services [SCS] instance)
J<nn>	Java central instance
TRX<nn>	TREX instance
ERS<nn>	Enqueue replication server instance (ERS instance)
SMDA<nn>	Diagnostics agent instance
W<nn>	Web services instance
G<nn>	Gateway instance

Table 2.1 Instance Name Parameters

To *start* the SAP instances separately using the command line, follow this sequence:

1. Database instance

2. SCS instance

3. Java central instance

To *stop* the SAP instances separately using the command line, follow this sequence:

1. Java central instance

2. SCS instance

3. Database instance

2.4   Network Architecture

SAP NetWeaver Portal implementations are most often used to expose a corporation's data and information in enterprise systems over the Web. In the majority of cases, SAP NetWeaver Portal is also exposed over the Internet. This brings a host of challenges that need to be anticipated. Because it's not uncommon to see corporate networks get hacked by malicious users, usually the most important aspect to consider is security. The network architecture of the SAP NetWeaver Portal landscape plays a large part in determining the security of the corporate portal.

There are various terms that you need to understand here:

► **Firewall**
A firewall is a device or set of devices that protect a network from unauthorized access. Corporations normally have a firewall between their networks and the Internet to prevent direct access to their networks by outside users.

► **Demilitarized zone (DMZ)**
DMZ is a subnetwork within a network that has limited access to the rest of the network. In a network, there are services that need to be exposed to external users (e.g., email, websites, etc.). However, exposing these servers to the Internet also means risking unauthorized access by malicious users. To minimize this risk, servers are kept in a separate subnetwork so that even if these hosts are compromised, other business systems inside the network are safe.

▶ **Proxy server**
A proxy server is a gateway that makes sure that the requests are not going directly to the application servers. They are instead redirected by the intermediate servers, thus adding an extra layer of security.

Figure 2.16 shows a simple network architecture of a typical portal implementation where the portal is exposed to the outside world.

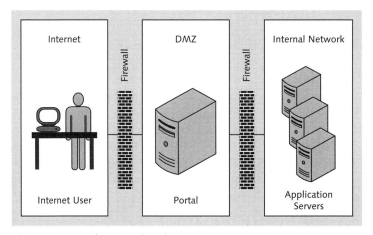

Figure 2.16 Simple Network Architecture

In the figure, the SAP NetWeaver Portal—which will be accessed by users outside the network—has been placed in a DMZ. There, the portal server has very limited access to the internal network, which is a high security zone. The firewall between the external world and the DMZ ensures that access to the DMZ is limited. Another firewall lies between the DMZ and the internal network, which makes any external access to the internal network very difficult. All of the servers that contain sensitive data are part of the high security internal network.

More complex network architecture is shown in Figure 2.17. In this architecture, another layer of DMZ has been added; the outer DMZ contains proxy servers. Two common proxy servers are SAP Web Dispatcher and Apache Web Server.

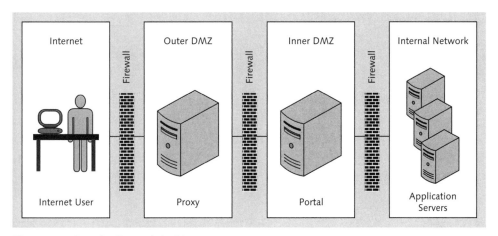

Figure 2.17 Complex Network Architecture

2.5 Summary

The objective of this chapter was to familiarize you with the SAP NetWeaver Portal architecture and describe how it runs inside AS Java. We emphasized that the Portal Runtime (PRT) is a Java EE application deployed on the AS Java platform and that this application provides the environment for deploying and running portal components. We also discussed various administration and configuration tools and their usage. Finally, we explained how a typical client request reaches AS Java and how it gets handled by AS Java and PRT before a response is returned to the client. The aim of this chapter was to build a foundation for your understanding of how things work in SAP NetWeaver Portal.

In the next chapter, we will look at the installation and initial configuration steps for SAP NetWeaver Portal.

This chapter explains the installation and initial configuration steps needed for an SAP NetWeaver Portal implementation.

3   Installation and Configuration

In the previous chapter, we explored SAP NetWeaver Portal architecture, and discussed how it runs on top of SAP NetWeaver Java AS. This chapter takes you through the high-level installation process of SAP NetWeaver Java AS and SAP NetWeaver Portal.

For the scope of this book, we will discuss the installation of SAP NetWeaver 7.3 on Windows Server 2008 R2 and the SAP MaxDB database. The entire installation process has been divided into preparation, installation, and post-installation steps. After the installation and post-installation sections, we will discuss some of the initial configuration needed for any SAP NetWeaver Portal implementation, including transport layer security configuration and user management configuration. We'll also see how the system landscape is created in the portal, discuss Universal Worklist configuration, and then explain the new transport and change recording feature that was introduced with SAP NetWeaver Portal 7.3.

3.1   Preparation for Portal Installation

This section discusses the preparation steps that you must perform for the standard installation option. Each step is discussed in the following subsections.

3.1.1   Disabling the Windows Server 2008 Firewall

The Windows firewall is turned on by default on Windows Server 2008 R2 and is configured to allow only a small set of Windows-specific inbound IP connections. By default, outbound connections are not limited to rules and are therefore not restricted by the firewall. The default firewall settings are valid for the out-of-the-box installation of Windows Server 2008 R2. These settings apply to local policies. For domain policies that override local policies, other rules might apply.

To avoid any problems with nonconfigured TCP/IP ports that are used by the SAP system, disable the firewall on all Windows hosts before you install the SAP system with SAPinst. SAP recommends that you either secure network access to the SAP application servers with a real physical firewall or use a router access control list (ACL). Follow these steps on the Windows Server 2008 R2 for this configuration:

1. Click START • ADMINISTRATIVE TOOLS • WINDOWS FIREWALL WITH ADVANCED SECURITY.

2. Right-click WINDOWS FIREWALL WITH ADVANCED SECURITY, and click PROPERTIES.

3. Choose the relevant profile (in most cases, DOMAIN PROFILE), and set the FIREWALL STATE to OFF.

3.1.2 Performing Basic Windows Preparation Steps

Perform some basic Windows preparation steps such as the following:

1. **Check the Windows file system.**
   Make sure that you are using the Windows NTFS on the machine where you are installing the server by doing the following:

   ▶ Choose START • ALL PROGRAMS • ADMINISTRATIVE TOOLS • COMPUTER MANAGEMENT • DISK MANAGEMENT. Right-click the relevant disk.

   ▶ Choose PROPERTIES • GENERAL. The system displays the type of file system in use.

   ▶ Check that the file system is Windows NTFS.

2. **Check the Windows domain structure.**
   If you are doing a domain installation, check that all SAP system hosts are members of a single Windows domain. You don't need to do this if you are doing a local installation and not a domain installation.

3. **Ensure Windows Server 2008 performance.**
   Windows Server 2008 R2 provides three plans (Balanced, High Performance, and Power Saver) for power options. Make sure that HIGH PERFORMANCE is selected as the default power option by following these steps:

▸ Choose START • CONTROL PANEL • POWER OPTIONS.

▸ In the SELECT A POWER PLAN window, select HIGH PERFORMANCE.

3.1.3 Required User Authorization for Running SAPinst

Although SAPinst automatically grants the rights required to the user account used for the installation, you have to check whether this account has the required authorization to perform the installation. The authorization required depends on whether you intend to perform a domain or local installation. If necessary, ask the system administrator to grant the account the necessary authorization before you begin. The installation will abort if you attempt the installation with an account that does not have the required authorization.

3.1.4 Preparing the SAP System Transport Host

The transport host has a directory structure that is used by the SAP transport system to store transport data and metadata. When you install an SAP system, SAPinst creates the transport directory on the global host in *\usr\sap\trans* by default.

If you do not intend to use the directory structure of the system you are going to install but want to use either another new transport directory on a different host or an existing transport directory in your system landscape, you need to prepare that transport host as follows:

▸ If the directory structure already exists, you must set up its security to allow the new system to write to it.

▸ If the directory does not yet exist, you must create the core directory structure and a share to export it for other computers as well as set the security on it. Complete the following steps:

   ▸ Create the directory *\usr\sap\trans* on the host to be used as the transport host.

   ▸ Share the *usr\sap* directory on the transport host as SAPMNT, and set the permission for EVERYONE to FULL CONTROL for this share. This enables SAPinst to address the transport directory in the standard way as *\\SAPTRANSHOST\SAPMNT\trans*.

▸ If the transport directory already exists, grant EVERYONE the permission FULL CONTROL for the transport directory.

3.1.5   Preparing the Installation Media

The physical installation media is normally obtained as part of the installation package but can also be downloaded from the SAP Service Marketplace at *http://service.sap.com/swdc* by going to Download • Installations and Upgrades • Installations and Upgrades • Entry by Application Group • <SAP Solution> • <SAP Product> • <SAP Release> • Installation and Upgrade • <Operating System> • <Database>.

If you download the installation media, note that the media might be split into several files. In this case, you have to reassemble the required files after the download. To extract the downloaded SAR files, use the latest SAPCAR version (the compression utility), which you can find on the SAP Service Marketplace at *http://service.sap.com/swdc*. Follow these steps:

1. Create a download directory on the host where you want to run SAPinst.

2. Identify all download objects that belong to one installation medium according to one or both of the following:

   ▶ **Material number:** All download objects that are part of an installation medium have the same material number and an individual sequence number: *<material_number>_<sequence_number>*. For example, 55245262_1 and 55245262_2.

   ▶ **Title:** All objects that are part of an installation medium have the same title, such as *<solution><media_name><OS>* or *<database>*RDBMS*<OS>* for database media.

3. Download the objects to the download directory.

4. Extract the individual download objects using SAPCAR, starting with the lowest sequence number (e.g., 51031387_1, then 51031387_2, etc.).

5. When SAPCAR asks if you want to replace existing files, for example, *labelidx.asc*, always accept with Yes.

3.2   SAP NetWeaver Portal Installation Steps

After you have completed the preparation steps, you are ready to begin installing the software. This section describes how to run the installation tool SAPinst. SAPinst includes a GUI client and a GUI server, which both use Java. In the following section, the GUI client and GUI server are called "SAPinst GUI." This procedure describes an installation where SAPinst and SAPinst GUI are running on the same host.

SAPinst creates the installation directory *sapinst_instdir*, where it keeps its log files, which is located directly in the *%ProgramFiles%* directory. If SAPinst is not able to create *sapinst_instdir* there, it will try to create *sapinst_instdir* in the directory defined by the environment variable TEMP. SAPinst creates a subdirectory for each installation option called *<sapinst_instdir>\<installation_option_directory>*, which is located in *%ProgramFiles%*.

SAPinst extracts itself to a temporary directory (TEMP, TMP, TMPDIR, or System-Root). These executables are deleted after SAPinst has stopped running. Directories called *sapinst_exe.xxxxxx.xxxx* sometimes remain in the temporary directory. You can safely delete them after the installation has completed.

The temporary directory also contains the log file *dev_selfex.out* from the extraction process, which might be useful if an error occurs. If SAPinst cannot find a temporary directory, the installation terminates with the error FCO-00058.

During the installation, the default ports 21200, 21212, and 4239 are used for communication between SAPinst, GUI server, SAPinst GUI, and HTTP server, as follows:

▶ SAPinst uses port 21200 to communicate with the GUI server.

▶ The GUI server uses port 21212 to communicate with the GUI client.

▶ Port 4239 belongs to the HTTP server, which is part of the GUI server.

If these ports are already in use, SAPinst automatically searches for free port numbers. If the search fails, you see an error message, and SAPinst exits. If this happens — or if you want SAPinst to use specific ports — open a command prompt, and change to the required directory as follows:

```
cd /d <drive>:\DATA_UNITS\IM_WINDOWS_<platform>
```

Execute *sapinst.exe* with the following commands:

▶ `SAPINST_DIALOG_PORT=<port_number_sapinst_to_gui_server>`

▶ `GUISERVER_DIALOG_PORT=<port_number_gui_server_to_gui_client>`

▶ `GUISERVER_HTTP_PORT=<port_number_http_server>`

To see a list of all available SAPinst properties, go to the directory (*%TEMP%\sapinst_exe.xxxxxx.xxxx*) after you have started SAPinst, and enter the following command:

```
sapinst.exe -p
```

Next, we provide additional information about the prerequisites for installation and the actual installation steps.

3.2.1   Prerequisites for Installation

The following are prerequisites for installing SAP NetWeaver Portal:

▶ Make sure you have at least 300MB of free space in the installation directory for each installation option. In addition, you need 60-200MB of free space for the SAPinst executables.

▶ Check that your installation host meets the requirements for the installation options that you want to install. If you are installing a second or subsequent SAP system in an existing database, make sure that the database is up and running before starting the installation.

3.2.2   Steps for Installation

After you have verified that all the prerequisites have been met, follow these steps for installation:

1. Log on to the installation host using an account with the required user authorization to run SAPinst.

2. Make the installation media available on the installation host.

3. Start SAPinst from the installation media by double-clicking *sapinst.exe* from the directory *<drive>:\DATA_UNITS\<product>_IM_WINDOWS_<your platform>_<your DB>*. SAPinst GUI starts automatically by displaying the WELCOME screen.

4. In the WELCOME screen, choose the required options, and click NEXT.

5. If SAPinst prompts you to log off from your system, log off and log on again. SAPinst restarts automatically.

6. Follow the instructions in the SAPinst screens, and enter the required parameters. To find more information on each parameter during the input phase of the

installation, position the cursor on the required parameter and press $\boxed{\text{F1}}$. After you have entered all requested input parameters, SAPinst displays the Parameter Summary screen. This screen shows both the parameters that you entered and those that SAPinst set by default. If required, you can revise the parameters before starting the installation.

7. To begin the installation, choose START. SAPinst starts and displays the progress of the installation. When the installation has finished, SAPinst shows the message "Execution of *<Option_Name>* has completed."

During the last restart of AS Java performed by SAPinst, the portal starts the processing and uploading of the new portal archives. It takes approximately 15 to 90 minutes before the deployment is completed and the portal is launched. Do not stop SAPinst or AS Java during this phase.

If you copied the installation media to your hard disk, you can delete these files when the installation has successfully completed.

3.3   Post-Installation Steps

After you have successfully installed a standard SAP NetWeaver 7.3 system, follow the post-installation steps outlined in this section.

3.3.1   Updating Database Statistics

You have to update database statistics if you have installed software units or usage types based on AS Java. Make sure that the database is up and running before continuing, and then follow these steps:

1. Log on as user `<sapsid>adm` to the host where the database instance is running.

2. Open a command prompt, and execute the following command:

```
dbmcli -d <DBSID> -u control,<pwd> sql_updatestat "SAP<SAPSID>DB.*"
```

For example:

```
dbmcli -d QE1 -u control,ctrlpwd sql_updatestat "SAPQE1DB.*
```

3.3.2 Logging On to the Application Server

Check that you can log on to the application server after the installation. The application server should be running before you continue with the following steps:

1. Start a web browser, and open the following URL: *http://<host >:5<Instance_Number>00*. You must always enter a two-digit number for *<Instance_Number>*. For example, do not enter "1" but instead enter "01".

2. Log on by clicking the icon of any of the provided applications, for example, the SAP NetWeaver Administrator.

3.3.3 Logging On to SAP NetWeaver Portal

After you have verified the application server, verify that SAP NetWeaver Portal has been installed successfully and that you can log on.

To log on to the portal you just installed, make sure that the server is up and running, and then follow these steps:

1. Start a web browser, and open this URL: *http://<host >:5<Instance_Number>00/ irj*. This should bring you to the SAP NetWeaver Portal login page.

2. Log on with the administrator ID that was created during installation and the password that you provided as an installation parameter.

3.3.4 Installing the SAP License

When you install the SAP NetWeaver platform, a temporary license is automatically created; you must install a permanent license soon after installing the application server. The license key is bound to the hardware key of the host where the message server is running. To install the license, first you need to get a license from SAP by going to *http://service.sap.com/licensekey*.

After you have the license key, log in to the SAP NetWeaver Administrator at *http://<HOST>:<PORT>/nwa* and navigate to CONFIGURATION • INFRASTRUCTURE • LICENSES. The screen will show the current licenses installed with the validity dates as shown in Figure 3.1.

To install a new license, click the INSTALL FROM FILE button. In the popup that appears, choose the file, and click ADD. This should add the license to the system.

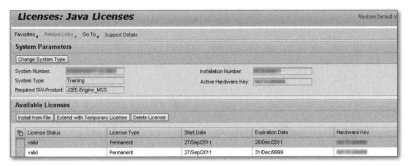

Figure 3.1 SAP Licenses

3.3.5 Secure Sockets Layer Protocol for Database Server Communication

The SAP MaxDB database server supports the Secure Sockets Layer (SSL) protocol. You can use this protocol for communication between the database server and its client (here, the AS). SSL guarantees encrypted data transfer between the SAP MaxDB database server and its client applications. In addition, the server authenticates itself to the client.

There is a performance cost for SSL because the data has to be encrypted, which requires time and processing power. To use SSL, you need to do the following:

1. Install the SAP Cryptographic Library on the client host and on the server host machines.
2. Generate the Personal Security Environment (PSE) on the server (SSL Server PSE) and on the client (SSL Client PSE).

3.3.6 Ensuring User Security

You need to ensure the security of the users that SAPinst created during the installation. Table 3.1 at the end of this section lists the following users:

▶ Operating system users
▶ SAP MaxDB system users

During the installation, SAPinst by default assigns the master password to all users created during the installation, unless you specified other passwords.

In all cases, the user ID and password are encoded only when transported across the network. Therefore, we recommend using encryption at the network layer, by using either the SSL protocol for HTTP connections, or Secure Network Communications (SNC) for the SAP protocols dialog and remote function call (RFC). Make sure that you perform this procedure before the newly installed SAP system goes into production.

For the users discussed in the following subsections, take the precautions described in the relevant SAP security guide, which you can find on SAP Service Marketplace at *http://service.sap.com/securityguide*.

After the installation, operating system users for SAP system, database, and host agent are available as listed in Table 3.1.

User Type	User	Comment
Operating system users	<sapsid>adm	SAP system administrator
	<dasid>adm	Administrator for the diagnostics agent
	sapadm	User for central monitoring services
	sqd<dbsid>	SAP MaxDB database administrator
	SAPService<SAPSID>	User to run the SAP system
SAP MaxDB database users	SAP<SAPSID>DB	SAP MaxDB database owner
	CONTROL	SAP MaxDB database manager operator
	SUPERDBA	SAP MaxDB database system administrator

Table 3.1 Users Created During Installation

If you have chosen the option Use Java Database, the User Management Engine users are stored in the database (Java UME), and you can manage users and groups with the UME web admin tool and the SAP NetWeaver Administrator only.

If you have chosen the option USE ABAP, the UME users are stored in an external ABAP system (ABAP UME), and you can manage the users and user security policies in the ABAP stack.

3.4 Transport Layer Security Configuration

After the SAP NetWeaver Portal has been installed and post-installation steps have been completed, the next step is often to configure transport layer security. Because SAP NetWeaver Portal is usually accessed by a large number of people, and many times the data transfer between the users and SAP NetWeaver Portal can be confidential, the security of the data while being transferred becomes very important.

Because SAP NetWeaver Portal normally connects to the SAP backend, securing the connection between SAP NetWeaver Portal and the SAP backend helps safeguard the exchange of confidential data. Figure 3.2 shows a typical scenario of a user connecting to SAP NetWeaver Portal using a web browser and SAP NetWeaver Portal connecting to SAP backends.

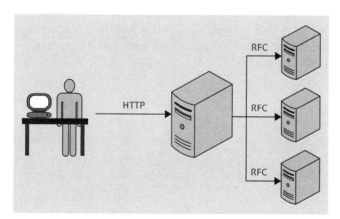

Figure 3.2 Transport Layer Security

As shown in Figure 3.2, the connection between the user's web browser and SAP NetWeaver Portal is an HTTP connection. In SAP NetWeaver Portal, the HTTP layer is secured by using the SSL method.

The connection between SAP NetWeaver Portal and the SAP backend is usually an RFC connection that is secured using the SNC method. In this section, we will look at the configurations needed for SSL and SNC.

3.4.1 Configuration of SSL for SAP NetWeaver Portal

Because SAP NetWeaver Portal runs on AS Java, the SSL configuration is done at the AS Java level. Follow the steps discussed in the following subsections to configure SSL on AS Java.

Step 1: Installation of SAP Cryptographic Library for SSL

Download and extract the SAP Cryptographic Library that can be used for this purpose from the SAP Service Marketplace. Three files are important: a DLL file (for Windows), a license ticket file (*.lst* file), and a configuration tool (*sapgenpse.exe*). The DLL file and the configuration tool should be copied to the *C:\usr\sap\EP1\SYS\exe* folder, and the ticker should be copied to the *C:\usr\sap\EP1\J00\sec* folder.

The installation can also be done by using the SAP NetWeaver Administrator. Log on by going to *http://<host>:<port>/nwa*. After you are inside SAP NetWeaver Administrator, go to CONFIGURATION.SECURITY.SSL. In the section SAP JAVA INSTANCES, select the SSL library and the ticket file, and save. After saving, the SSL status should be green. The screen will look like Figure 3.3.

Figure 3.3 SAP Crypto Library Installation with SAP NetWeaver Administrator

Step 2: SSL Configuration

After the SAP Cryptographic Library has been installed, open the SAP NetWeaver Administrator by going to *http://<host>:<port>/nwa* and following these steps:

1. In SAP NetWeaver Administrator, go to CONFIGURATION • SECURITY • SSL.

2. In the SAP JAVA INSTANCES section, choose the appropriate Java instance.

3. In the SSL ACCESS POINTS section, click ADD. The screen should look like Figure 3.4.

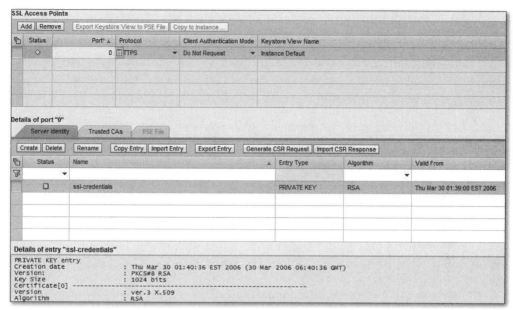

Figure 3.4 SSL Configuration with SAP NetWeaver Administrator

4. Enter the port number for HTTPS, CLIENT AUTHENTICATION MODE, and KEYSTORE VIEW NAME, and then save. The new SSL access point should be set up as shown in Figure 3.5.

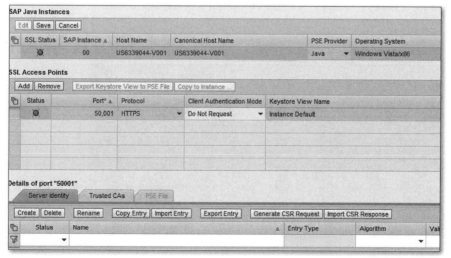

Figure 3.5 SSL Access Point

3.4.2 Configuration of SNC for Securing AS Java to AS ABAP Connections

The RFC connections from AS Java to AS ABAP can be secured by making used of SNCs. This section assumes that the SAP Cryptographic Library is installed per steps mentioned in Section 3.4.1.

Next, we discuss the steps required for the SNC configuration.

Step 1: Creating a Personal Security Environment (PSE)

To create the SNC PSE, use the command sapgenpse.exe as shown here:

```
>sapgenpse get_pse -p <PSE_Name> -x <PIN> <Distinguished_Name>
```

For example:

```
>sapgenpse get_pse -p MY_PSE.pse -x mypin CN=SAPNW, O=Company, C=US
```

This command will create the file *MY_PSE.pse* with PIN mypin. The distinguished name when using this PSE is CN=SAPNW, O=Company, C=US.

You will find sapgenpse in the file path *<drive>:\usr\sap\<Instance_Name>\SYS\exe*.

The file path where the PSE file is saved is defined by the environment variable SECUDIR. If the environment variable SECUDIR is not defined, then it is saved in the user's home directory. You can execute the sapgenpse.exe command to know where your PSE file will be saved as shown in Figure 3.6.

Figure 3.6 PSE File Location

Step 2: Creating Credentials for AS Java

After creating the PSE file, you need to create the credentials for the AS Java for it to be able to access the PSE. You need to execute the following command to create the credentials:

```
> sapgenpse seclogin -p <PSE_Name> -x <PIN> -O [<NT_Domain>\]<user_ID>
```

This creates the credential files for the user specified. The user ID should be the use under which the AS Java runs, which is, `<sid>adm` for UNIX and `SAPService<SID>` for Windows. For example:

```
>sapgenpse seclogin -p MY_PSE.pse -x mypin -O SAPService<SID>
```

Step 3: Maintaining an Access Control List (ACL) on AS ABAP

We saw all of the configurations needed in AS Java. In AS ABAP, you need to maintain an ACL to make sure it is communicating with the correct component. To maintain the ACL, perform the following actions:

1. In AS ABAP, go to Transaction SM30.

2. Enter "VSNCSYSACL" as the TABLE/VIEW, and click MAINTAIN.

3. Enter "E" in the TYPE OF ENTRY, and click OK.

4. Here you can create new entries for the system ID and SNC name. For the SNC name, enter the distinguished name you created earlier with the prefix "p:". Also check the ENTRY FOR RFC ACTIVATED checkbox (Figure 3.7).

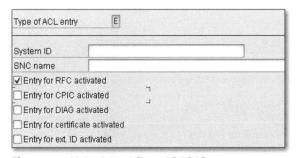

Figure 3.7 Maintaining ACL on AS ABAP

3.5 User Management Configuration

User management of SAP NetWeaver is provided by the user management functionality of AS Java. AS Java's user management configuration console can be accessed by going to *http://<host>:<port>/useradmin*.

After you log on, the user administration screen will look like Figure 3.8.

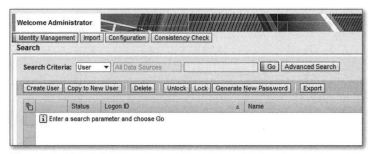

Figure 3.8 User Administration in AS Java

On this screen, click CONFIGURATION. Alternatively, you can also access it from the USER ADMINISTRATION tab from SAP NetWeaver Portal. For this, log on to the SAP NetWeaver Portal from *http://<host>:<port>/irj*, and go to the SYSTEM ADMINISTRATION • SYSTEM CONFIGURATION • UME CONFIGURATION as shown in Figure 3.9.

Figure 3.9 User Administration in Portal

You can also access the user management console from the SAP NetWeaver Administrator by going to *http://<host>:<port>/nwa/identity*. After logging on successfully, you will reach the IDENTITY MANAGEMENT screen, as shown in Figure 3.10.

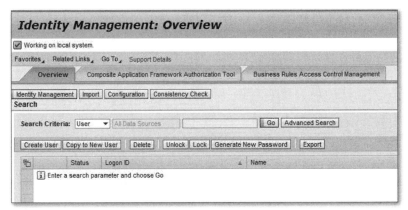

Figure 3.10 User Admin in SAP NetWeaver Administrator

On this screen, click CONFIGURATION to go to the UME configuration page. The UME configuration page looks like Figure 3.11.

Figure 3.11 User Management Configuration

The UME, which is part of SAP AS Java, provides the user management services to AS Java and SAP NetWeaver Portal, as discussed in the following section.

3.5.1 The User Management Engine (UME)

The UME is the centralized management service that provides the user management functionalities for AS Java and all applications running on AS Java (e.g., SAP NetWeaver Portal). The UME can connect to a wide variety of data sources, and, by default, the UME connects to AS Java's database. The UME most commonly uses a corporate Lightweight Directory Access Protocol (LDAP) or SAP backend as the user store, as shown in Figure 3.12.

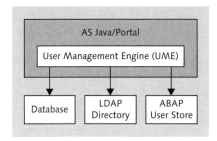

Figure 3.12   The UME

The UME can connect to more than one source at the same time and provides the following functionalities:

▶ **User administration**
This feature provides the functionalities for creating, editing, and deleting users, groups, roles, and so on. It also supports import and export of users, roles, and groups.

▶ **Security settings**
Settings such as password policy, password expiry policy, and others.

▶ **Self-service scenarios**
If enabled, it allows users to register themselves and edit their data.

Next, we'll see how the UME is configured for SAP NetWeaver Portal.

3.5.2   Configuration in SAP NetWeaver Portal

There are many steps in the configuration of the UME. This section outlines the basic and most commonly used UME configurations needed for SAP NetWeaver Portal.

Data Sources

The most important UME configuration involves data sources. It defines which user store will be used for SAP NetWeaver Portal and is the repository where the information about users, groups, and roles is stored. The availability and connectivity of a configured data source is a must for the AS Java to start.

The UME can connect to the following types of data sources:

▶ **Database of AS Java**

The AS Java database can be used as the UME when the UME is used only by applications running on the same portal, and third-party systems don't need access to the UME. The configuration file for this scenario is *dataSourceConfiguration_database_only.xml*.

▶ **LDAP directory**

This is the most commonly used data source for SAP NetWeaver Portal installations. Many corporations already own an LDAP directory for storing the information about users, and it make sense to use the same user store as the data source for the UME. This way, the portal uses the same users and attributes as all of the other systems in the corporate network. LDAP data source configuration files for SAP-supported LDAP directories are delivered with SAP AS Java.

There are two options for using the LDAP directory as the user store:

▶ **Option 1: Read/write service**

In this option, you can create and change the users, groups, and so on in the LDAP directory using SAP NetWeaver Portal's UME. When you create or change a user in the user administration of SAP NetWeaver Portal or in the identity management from SAP NetWeaver Administrator, the changes are reflected in the LDAP directory. The following data source configuration files are available for this scenario:

```
dataSourceConfiguration_<LDAP_directory_vendor>_not_readonly_
db.xml
```

```
dataSourceConfiguration_<LDAP_directory_vendor>_deep_not_readonly_
db.xml
```

▶ **Option 2: Read-only service**

This option does not allow you to create or change the users and groups from the LDAP directory. Any users or groups that you create in SAP NetWeaver Portal's user administration are stored in the local database of AS Java. The users and groups from the LDAP are available in SAP NetWeaver Portal for display only. The following configuration files are available for read-only service:

```
dataSourceConfiguration_<LDAP_directory_vendor>_readonly_db.xml
```

```
dataSourceConfiguration_<LDAP_directory_vendor>_deep_readonly_
db.xml
```

▶ **SAP ABAP user store**
The UME can use the ABAP AS as its user store. Selecting the data source can be done either during or after the installation. After installation, the data source can be changed, but after you have selected a data source other than the AS Java database, you cannot change the data source again. After selecting the data source, the next step is to edit the UME properties to configure it according to your needs.

Configuring UME Properties

There are many properties in the UME that need to be set for any implementation (e.g., LDAP directory connection details, password policy, password expiry, notification email, self-registration, etc.). SAP NetWeaver provides various tools for editing the UME properties:

▶ Expert mode in the user management configuration page

▶ SAP NetWeaver Administrator

▶ Config Tool

The first two tools are online tools, meaning that the server must be running to configure the UME. The last one, Config Tool, is an offline tool, which means that the SAP NetWeaver Portal server or AS Java does not need to be running. However, changes done using the Config Tool take effect only after the server cluster has been restarted. Now we will discuss how the UME properties can be changed by using each mechanism:

▶ **Expert mode in user management configuration page**
Using the export mode of user management configuration, you can make the UME changes that apply at the global level of the instance. To enter the export mode, first open the user management configuration, and then click OPEN EXPERT MODE button. The screen shown in Figure 3.13 lets you do basic UME properties editing.

▶ **SAP NetWeaver Administrator**
You can access the expert mode in the user management configuration from SAP NetWeaver Administrator, too. Go to the user management configuration using SAP NetWeaver Administrator as previously explained, and then click the OPEN EXPERT MODE button. This opens the UME properties editor as shown in Figure 3.13.

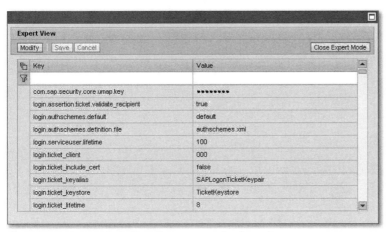

Figure 3.13 Expert Mode User Management Configuration

▸ **Config Tool**

To edit the UME properties using the Config Tool, follow these steps:

▸ Start the Config Tool, and then click SWITCH TO CONFIGURATION EDITOR MODE.

▸ On the configuration page, go to CLUSTER_CONFIG • SYSTEM • CUSTOM_ GLOBAL • SFG • SERVICES • COM.SAP.SECURITY.CORE.UME.SERVICE • PROPERTYSHEET PROPERTIES.

▸ Change to edit mode, and double-click PROPERTYSHEET PROPERTIES.

▸ Select the property that you want to change, and double-click to open the property in a new pop-up window.

▸ Enter the new value in the CUSTOM-VALUE field, and click OK.

▸ Save and restart the server.

3.6   System Landscape

The portal system landscape refers to the landscape of SAP and non-SAP systems to which the SAP NetWeaver Portal connects. SAP NetWeaver Portal can connect to many types of SAP and non-SAP systems, and SAP provides templates for creating such systems. In this section, we will explore how to create and edit various systems in the system landscape of SAP NetWeaver Portal, test system connections, and create aliases for the systems.

3.6.1 System Landscape Overview

The System Landscape Overview tab gives an overview of all the systems created in the portal. You can reach the SYSTEM LANDSCAPE OVERVIEW tab by logging on to SAP NetWeaver Portal and then going to SYSTEM ADMINISTRATION • SYSTEM LANDSCAPE. Figure 3.14 shows the SYSTEM LANDSCAPE OVERVIEW tab.

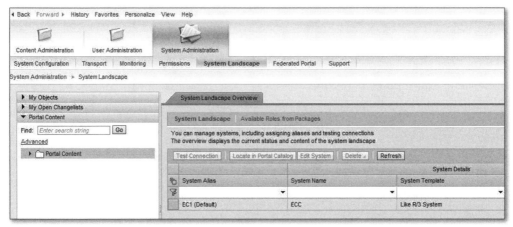

Figure 3.14 System Landscape Overview

This screen lists all of the systems that have been created in SAP NetWeaver Portal. From this screen, you can edit or delete a system, and test a connection to ensure that the portal is able to connect to the defined system with the mentioned properties.

3.6.2 Creating Systems

To create a system, first go to SYSTEM ADMINISTRATION • SYSTEM LANDSCAPE, and then complete the following steps:

1. Go to the folder in which you want to create the system object. Right-click, and choose NEW • SYSTEM.

2. The system presents all of the predefined templates for creating the system (see Figure 3.15). Select a template, and click NEXT.

3. On the next screen, enter the system name, ID, and description, and click NEXT.

4. On the next screen, define an alias, and click NEXT. You can define multiple aliases here if you want.

5. On the next screen, provide the connection and login details for the system that you want the portal to connect to, and then click NEXT.

6. The system tries to connect to the chosen system. Click FINISH to close the system creation wizard.

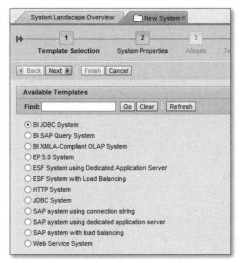

Figure 3.15 Creating a System

3.6.3 System Aliases

A system alias is a logical name for a system. A system can be assigned multiple logical names, which are used in the applications. Although there can be any number of aliases assigned to a system, at least one alias must exist for every system. Each alias assigned to any system must be unique in the system, meaning that no two systems can share a common alias. One important point to note about aliases is that they are not transported when the system object is transported, so when you transport your system to a new environment, you need to create system aliases in the new system manually.

Figure 3.16 shows the user interface (UI) for maintaining system aliases.

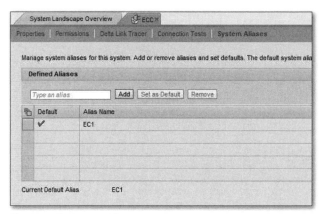

Figure 3.16 System Aliases

To open the SYSTEM ALIAS MAINTENANCE screen, go to SYSTEM ADMINISTRATION • SYSTEM LANDSCAPE. Then navigate to the system, and choose OPEN • SYSTEM ALIASES from the context menu, as shown in Figure 3.17.

Figure 3.17 Opening System Aliases Maintenance

3.7 Universal Worklist (UWL) Configuration

The Universal Worklist (UWL) is a component provided by SAP NetWeaver Portal that gives users centralized access to their work and the relevant information in the portal. The UWL can collect tasks and notifications from multiple provider systems—such as SAP Business Workflow, Collaboration Task, Alert Framework, and Knowledge Management—and present all the items in a single unified view. In most SAP NetWeaver Portal implementations, you will be integrating the UWL with SAP Business Workflow to get the task items from the SAP backend.

In this section, we consider a scenario where you are integrating the UWL with the SAP backend, and discuss the necessary steps involved.

3.7.1 Basic Configuration of the UWL

Before you perform basic UWL configuration, you must make sure that the following prerequisites are fulfilled:

▸ Each UWL user should have a backend user ID set up.

▸ The users must have authorization for function group SWK1 and Transaction SWK1.

▸ You should have a portal system configured for the backend system to which you want to connect (we discussed creating a system in Section 3.6). Also make sure an alias has been configured for the system. (Figure 3.18 shows a system that has been configured with aliases.)

▸ Single sign-on or user mapping should be set up for users.

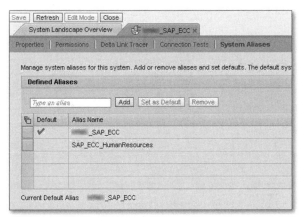

Figure 3.18 System Configured with Alias

If these prerequisites are met, you can go ahead with the UWL configuration. In SAP NetWeaver Portal, navigate to SYSTEM ADMINISTRATION • SYSTEM CONFIGURATION • UNIVERSAL WORKLIST & WORKFLOW • UNIVERSAL WORKLIST – ADMINISTRATION. Figure 3.19 shows the UWL configuration page.

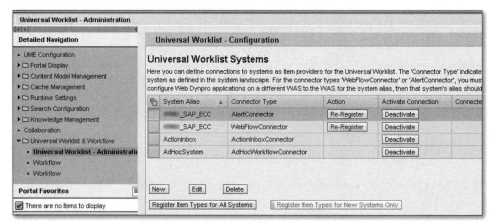

Figure 3.19 UWL Configuration Page

Here you can create, edit, and delete systems from which you want to get work items. If you want to configure a new system, click on the NEW button; this will bring up the input form for creating the system (Figure 3.20).

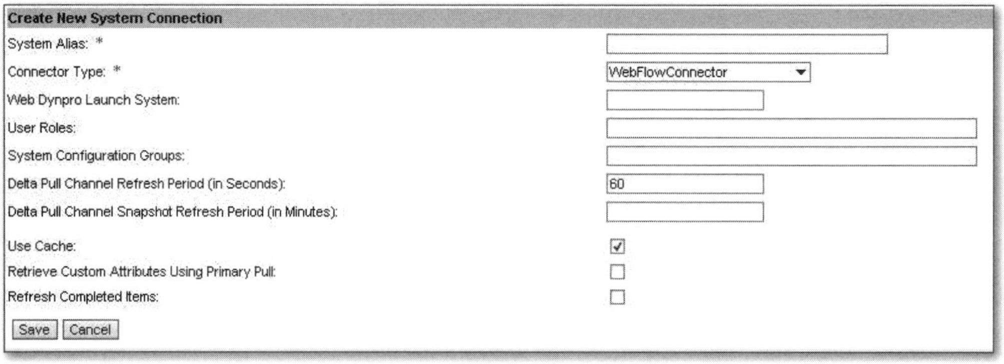

Figure 3.20 Creating a New System for the UWL

This is where you can specify the system alias of the backend system to which you want to connect. One of the most important parameters here is the CONNECTOR TYPE parameter; Figure 3.21 shows the drop down values for the CONNECTOR TYPE field. (WebFlowConnector is the connector type that refers to the connector for SAP Business Workflow.)

Figure 3.21 Connector Types

After creating the configuration, you must register the backend system item types with the UWL. To do this, click on the REGISTER ITEM TYPES FOR ALL SYSTEMS button. This will register the item types and give a success message after successful registration.

Now click on CLICK TO MANAGE ITEM TYPES AND VIEW DEFINITIONS. This is where you will find all the configurations for the item types stored in XML files. Figure 3.22 shows the XML files that store the UWL configurations for the item types in SAP NetWeaver Portal.

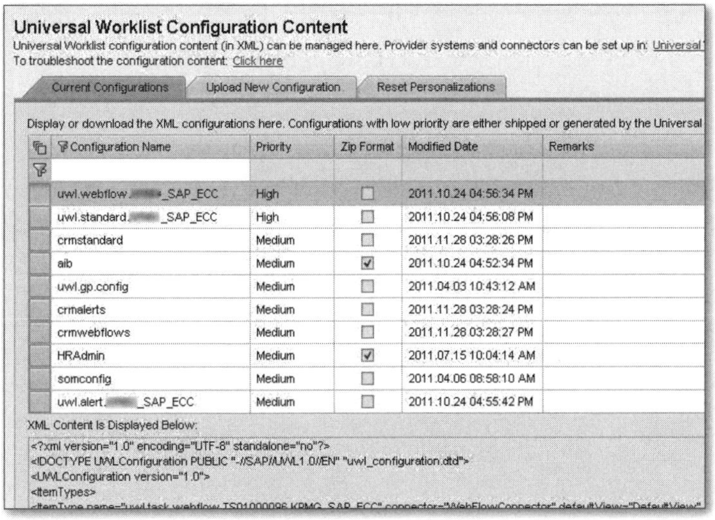

Figure 3.22 UWL XML Configurations

The configuration that gets generated when you register the item types is in the default name format *uwl.webflow.<System_Alias>*. When you select an XML configuration, the XML source is shown below. Here you can upload new configurations as well as download and delete existing configurations.

To upload a new configuration, go to the UPLOAD NEW CONFIGURATION tab. Specify a configuration name for the new configuration, choose an XML file to upload, and click on the UPLOAD button. This uploads the new configuration. Figure 3.23 shows the screenshot for uploading new UWL configurations.

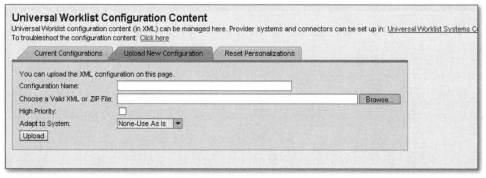

Figure 3.23 Uploading New Configurations

As you can see, the ADAPT TO SYSTEM field has a dropdown that lists all the system aliases available for the UWL; in addition, it also offers a NONE-USE AS IS option. If you select a system from the dropdown, the configuration will only be valid for that particular system. However, if you select NONE-USE AS IS, then this configuration will be valid for all the systems.

You have now completed the basic UWL configuration. Next, you need to clear the UWL cache, so that the UWL loads all the content based on the new configurations. To do this, go back to the UWL configuration main page and click on CACHE ADMINISTRATION PAGE as shown in Figure 3.24.

In the CACHE ADMINISTRATION page, click on the CLEAR CACHE button (Figure 3.25).

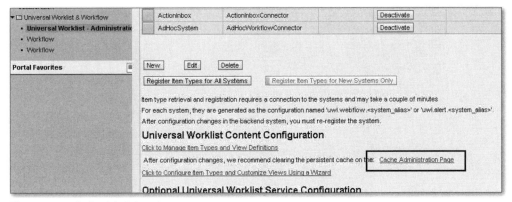

Figure 3.24 Cache Administration

Figure 3.25 Clearing the UWL Cache

Now when you preview the UWL iView, you will be able to see the work items from the SAP backend in the user interface shown in Figure 3.26.

Figure 3.26 UWL User Interface

The UWL iView can be found in the portal catalog by going to the path *portal_content/ com.sap.pct/every_user/general/iViews/com.sap.netweaver.bc.uwl.iviews/com.sap.netweaver. bc.uwl.uwl_iview*, which is shown as the selected iView in Figure 3.27.

Figure 3.27 UWL iView

3.7.2 Customizing UWL Views

SAP provides the standard UWL with default configurations. By configuring the XML file, you can change many properties of the UWL, such as the order of columns, which columns are included, etc.

The definition of each view or tab of the UWL can be found in the standard UWL XML configuration. By default, the *uwl.standard* configuration with low priority contains the default configuration of each view. To change the view, you will first need to download the standard configuration file from SAP NetWeaver Portal. Select the *uwl.standard* configuration and click on the DOWNLOAD CONFIGURATION button from the UWL CONFIGURATION CONTENT page. This is shown in Figure 3.28.

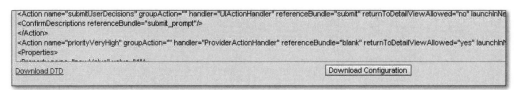

Figure 3.28 Downloading a Configuration

Download and save the XML file to your local PC. If you want to change the properties of the default view, create a new XML file, name it based on your preference, and create the structure in the XML file as shown in Listing 3.1:

```
<?xml version="1.0" encoding="UTF-8" standalone="no"?>
<!DOCTYPE UWLConfiguration PUBLIC "-//SAP//UWL1.0//EN"
"uwl_configuration.dtd">
<UWLConfiguration version="1.0">

</UWLConfiguration>
```

Listing 3.1 New XML Configuration

Now, in the *uwl.standard.xml* file that you downloaded, look for the view configuration for view name DefaultView, as shown in Figure 3.29.

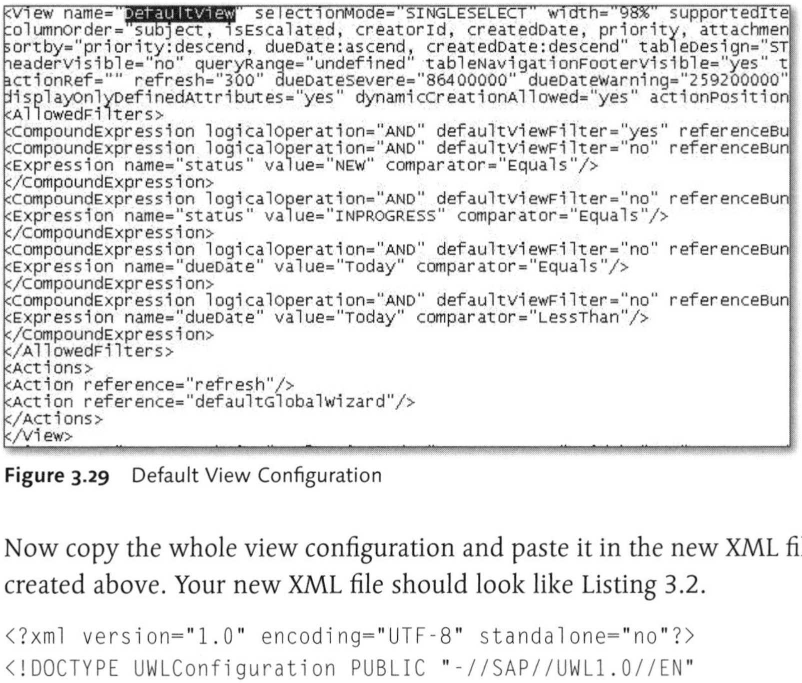

Figure 3.29 Default View Configuration

Now copy the whole view configuration and paste it in the new XML file that you created above. Your new XML file should look like Listing 3.2.

```
<?xml version="1.0" encoding="UTF-8" standalone="no"?>
<!DOCTYPE UWLConfiguration PUBLIC "-//SAP//UWL1.0//EN"
"uwl_configuration.dtd">
<UWLConfiguration version="1.0">
<Views>
<View name="DefaultView" selectionMode="SINGLESELECT"
width="98%" supportedItemTypes="uwl.task" columnOrder="subject,
isEscalated, creatorId, createdDate, priority, attachmentCount,
dueDate, status" sortby="priority:descend, dueDate:ascend,
createdDate:descend" tableDesign="STANDARD" visibleRowCount="10"
headerVisible="no" queryRange="undefined" tableNavigationFoot
erVisible="yes" tableNavigationType="CUSTOMNAV" actionRef=""
```

```
refresh="300" dueDateSevere="86400000" dueDateWarning="259200000"
emphasizedItems="new" displayOnlyDefinedAttributes="yes"
dynamicCreationAllowed="yes" actionPosition="bottom"
referenceBundle="tasks">
<AllowedFilters>
<CompoundExpression logicalOperation="AND" defaultViewFilter="yes"
referenceBundle="filter_display_all"/>
<CompoundExpression logicalOperation="AND" defaultViewFilter="no"
referenceBundle="filter_new">
<Expression name="status" value="NEW" comparator="Equals"/>
</CompoundExpression>
<CompoundExpression logicalOperation="AND" defaultViewFilter="no"
referenceBundle="filter_inprogress">
<Expression name="status" value="INPROGRESS" comparator="Equals"/>
</CompoundExpression>
<CompoundExpression logicalOperation="AND" defaultViewFilter="no"
referenceBundle="filter_duetoday">
<Expression name="dueDate" value="Today" comparator="Equals"/>
</CompoundExpression>
<CompoundExpression logicalOperation="AND" defaultViewFilter="no"
referenceBundle="filter_overdue">
<Expression name="dueDate" value="Today" comparator="LessThan"/>
</CompoundExpression>
</AllowedFilters>
<Actions>
<Action reference="refresh"/>
<Action reference="defaultGlobalWizard"/>
</Actions>
</View>
</Views>
</UWLConfiguration>
```

Listing 3.2 New UWL Configuration File

In the XML in Listing 3.2, you can change the properties of the view as you wish; these properties are shown in bold. Once your changes are done, your XML is ready to be uploaded. You can upload this new XML file as described in Section 3.7.1. When you upload, choose the HIGH priority option so that the configuration takes precedence over the standard configuration provided by SAP. After uploading the XML, refresh your UWL; you should see the new changes reflected.

3.7.3 Item Launch Configuration

When you launch a work item from the UWL to perform a transaction, the action can be performed using a variety of UI technologies: SAP GUI, BSP, or Web Dynpro, depending on what configuration has been used. The configuration for launching an item can be performed in two ways: by registering the SAP backend item types with the UWL, or by editing the XML file. We discuss these options next.

Registering the SAP Backend Item Types with the UWL

In the SAP backend, launch configuration for task types is done in Transaction SWFVISU, the task visualization transaction. Figure 3.30 shows a screenshot of the task visualization transaction.

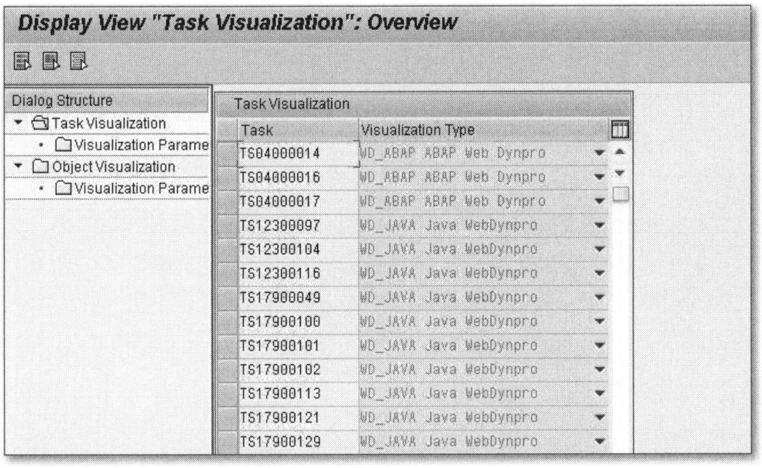

Figure 3.30 SAP Backend Task Visualization

You will see that each task has been assigned a task visualization type. Figure 3.31 shows that the TASK VISUALIZATION menu has many options. You can choose WEB DYNPRO JAVA, WEB DYNPRO ABAP, BSP, PORTAL PAGE, PORTAL iVIEW, etc. for launching the item.

Figure 3.32 shows the parameters that can be configured for the item launch, using Web Dynpro ABAP as the visualization type. For the item launch to work properly, you need to specify the Web Dynpro ABAP application name and namespace. You can also specify any dynamic parameter that you want to pass to the application via the DYNPARAM parameter.

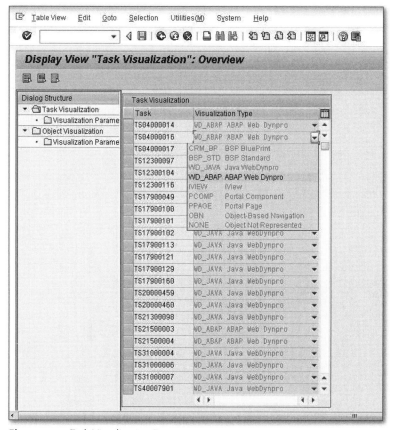

Figure 3.31 Task Visualization Types

Figure 3.32 Task Visualization Parameters

After you have performed your configurations in Transaction SWFVISU, you need to re-register your UWL connector so that the new configurations are included in the XML configuration file. To re-register the items, go to the UWL configuration page. As shown in Figure 3.33, click on the RE-REGISTER button for the connector system from where you want to get the new item launch configurations.

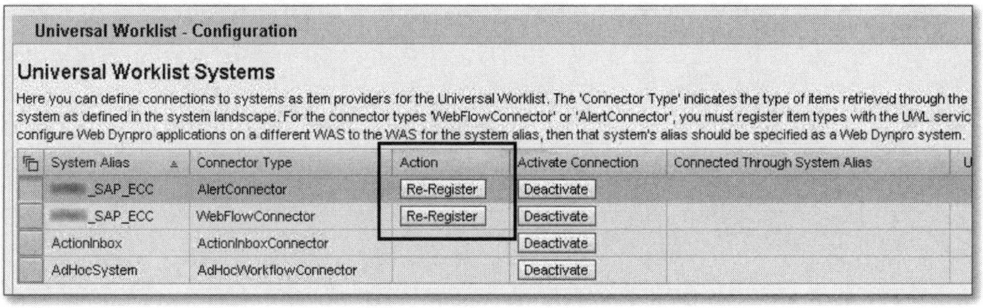

Figure 3.33 Re-Registering Item Types

After the re-registration is successful, clear the UWL cache. The new item launch configuration will now take effect for all users.

Editing the XML File

Another way to do item launch configuration is to change the UWL XML configuration file directly and upload the new configuration to the portal. We will see an example of such configuration here. Let us assume that for a particular task type, we have created an application and have created a portal iView that should be launched when the item is launched in the UWL.

To begin, create an XML file with the structure shown in Listing 3.3.

```
<!DOCTYPE UWLConfiguration PUBLIC "-//SAP//UWL1.0//EN"
"uwl_configuration.dtd">
<UWLConfiguration version="1.0">
<ItemTypes>

</ItemTypes>
</UWLConfiguration>
```

Listing 3.3 XML Structure for Item Launch Configuration

Now add a new item type with a unique name within the `<ItemTypes>` tag, referring to the backend task ID (Listing 3.4).

```
<ItemType name="uwl.task.webflow.TS91100919"
connector="WebFlowConnector"
```

```
defaultView="webflowView" defaultAction="launchIView">
</ItemType>
```
Listing 3.4 Adding the Item Type

After creating the item type with a unique name, you must map this item type to a task type in the SAP backend. We do this with the tag `ItemTypeCriteria`. As shown in Listing 3.5, the backend task ID is specified as an external type.

```
<ItemTypeCriteria
externalType="TS91100919" connector="WebFlowConnector"/>
```
Listing 3.5 Item Type Criteria

Now you need to add the actual launch action to the item type. This code is provided in Listing 3.6.

```
<Actions>
<Action name="launchIView" handler="IViewLauncher">
<Properties>
<Property name="iview" value=
"pcd://portal_content/com.sap.pct/every_user/general/iViews/myiView"/>
</Properties>
<Descriptions default="Launch iView">
<ShortDescriptions>
<Description Language="en" Description="Launch iView"/>
</ShortDescriptions>
</Descriptions>
</Action>
</Actions>
```
Listing 3.6 Launch Action Configuration

As you can see in Listing 3.6, the handler has been defined as `IViewLauncher`, since we want to launch an iView. The iView property has been set to the PCD path of the actual iView and an action name has been given. Please note that this action name matches the `defaultAction` property defined for the `<ItemType>`.

The configuration is now finished, and Listing 3.7 shows the complete XML file.

```
<?xml version="1.0" encoding="UTF-8" standalone="no"?>
<!DOCTYPE UWLConfiguration PUBLIC "-//SAP//UWL1.0//EN"
"uwl_configuration.dtd">
<UWLConfiguration version="1.0">
```

```
<ItemTypes>
<ItemType name="uwl.task.webflow.TS91100919"
connector="WebFlowConnector"
defaultView="webflowView" defaultAction="launchIView">

<ItemTypeCriteria
externalType="TS91100919" connector="WebFlowConnector"/>

<Actions>
<Action name="launchIView" handler="IViewLauncher">
<Properties>
<Property name="iview" value=
"pcd://portal_content/com.sap.pct/every_user/general/iViews/myiView"/>
</Properties>
<Descriptions default="Launch iView">
<ShortDescriptions>
<Description Language="en" Description="Launch iView"/>
</ShortDescriptions>
</Descriptions>
</Action>
</Actions>

</ItemType>
</ItemTypes>
</UWLConfiguration>
```

Listing 3.7 Item Launch Configuration XML

This file can now be uploaded by following the steps in Section 3.7.1. After clearing the cache, when you test again, you will be able to launch the iView for the configured task type.

Custom UWL iViews

The SAP-delivered UWL iView is built using the Web Dynpro Java technology and gives limited options to make drastic changes. For example, if you want to integrate the UWL with a flashy website, the UWL component will look out of place. As a result, there may be times when you want to create a custom UWL application that can more closely adhere to your look and feel requirements. Although a more detailed discussion of this topic is beyond the scope of this book, SAP provides a UWL Java API that you can use to build your own UWL UI. To find the Java docs for the UWL API, visit SDN: *http://help. sap.com/javadocs/NW73/SPS03/CE/uwl/com.sap.uwl/index.html*.

> There is also a weblog that explains the process for creating a custom UWL. You can find the weblog at this URL: *http://www.sdn.sap.com/irj/scn/weblogs?blog=/pub/wlg/5450.*

It is important to note here that the UWL gives the ability to connect to multiple providers in order to get work items from different systems at the same time; all you need to do is configure a connector for each system. Apart from the standard connectors provided by SAP, you can also develop your own connectors using the Java API provided by SAP. As discussed above, you may also want to create your own custom UWL on the ABAP stack using BSP or Web Dynpro ABAP technologies. The limitation with this approach is that you will not be able to take advantage of the UWL Java API that SAP provides.

3.8   Transports and Change Recording

In any implementation of SAP NetWeaver Portal, you will perform your developments in the development environment, and then move the content to the quality and production systems. This process is called *transport.* Transports in SAP NetWeaver Portal are generally done using the export/import process, which we discuss in this section.

Before release 7.3, SAP NetWeaver Portal did not have any mechanism to keep track of changes that were made to portal content, which meant that you would need to remember the objects you changed and add them to the transport package. However, in the newest release, SAP NetWeaver Portal has a new change recording feature. We also discus this topic in this section.

3.8.1   Transports

To transport portal content, follow these steps:

1. Go to System Administration • Transport • Transport • Export.

2. In Portal Content, right-click the folder where you want to create the transport package, and choose New • Transport package.

3. In the next screen, provide the name and ID for the transport package; click Next, and then click Finish on the next screen.

4. Now that the transport package has been created, you are presented with the options to choose from. Click CONTENT to add content to the transport package, as shown in Figure 3.34.

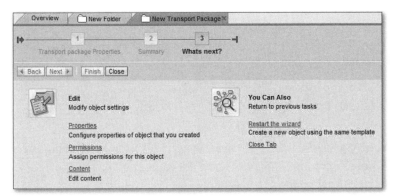

Figure 3.34 Creating a Transport Package

5. Select the objects that you want to add to the transport package. Right-click, and choose ADD TO TRANSPORT PACKAGE • OBJECT. You can also select a folder and choose ADD TO TRANSPORT PACKAGE • OBJECTS to add all objects inside a folder. This adds the objects to the transport package, as shown in Figure 3.35.

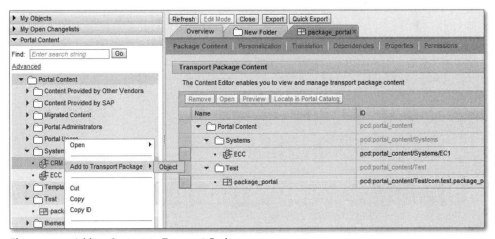

Figure 3.35 Adding Content to Transport Package

6. After the content has been added, click EXPORT to export the transport package.

7. The next screen shows the content of the transport package. From here, you can exclude objects or include objects that were earlier excluded. After finalizing the content, click NEXT.

8. Name the export file. The name should end with .epa (enterprise portal archive). Click NEXT.

9. The next screen shows the transport details and transport package details. Click EXPORT to start the export.

10. After the export completes and the exported transport package file is saved on the server, you can download the EPA file by clicking the DOWNLOAD FILE link.

11. After the export file has been downloaded, you can take this file and import it into another portal environment to transport the content of the transport package into another portal system.

To import a transport package, follow these steps:

1. Go to SYSTEM ADMINISTRATION • TRANSPORT • TRANSPORT PACKAGES • IMPORT.

2. You can import a transport package by uploading the EPA file either from the client desktop or from the server. Choose between the CLIENT and SERVER radio button options, select the EPA file to upload as shown in Figure 3.36, and click UPLOAD.

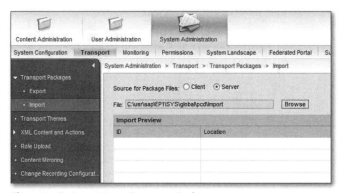

Figure 3.36 Importing a Transport Package

3. This shows the objects in the transport package. Click IMPORT to start the import.

You will receive a message when the import has successfully finished.

3.8.2 Change Recording

The new concept of *change recording* has been introduced and implemented beginning with SAP NetWeaver 7.3. Until now, the ability to record the changes done to portal content in SAP NetWeaver Portal was an important but absent functionality. As a result, the transport of portal content was not very smooth. With change recording, users can maintain, release, and transport a list of all their changes. Change lists are transported by using the Change and Transport System for Java (CTS+). Change recording needs to be activated and configured in SAP NetWeaver Portal for it to work. Follow these steps to activate and configure change recording in SAP NetWeaver Portal using SAP NetWeaver Administrator:

1. Log on to the SAP NetWeaver Administrator by going to *http://<host>:<port>/ nwa*.

2. Go to Java System properties • Overview, and click Advanced System Properties.

3. In the details section, go to the Services tab, and select the PCD Generic Layer service.

4. Selecting the service brings all of the parameters for that service into the Extended Details pane.

5. Select the property `Pcd.ChangeRecording.isChangeRecordingActive`, and click Modify. This brings a pop-up for entering a custom value for that property (see Figure 3.37).

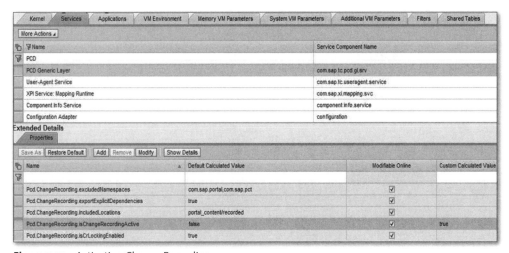

Figure 3.37 Activating Change Recording

6. Enter the new value as "true", click SET, and then click SAVE.

The change recording has now been activated. Several other properties of the PCD GENERIC LAYER are related to change recording and are worth mentioning:

▶ `Pcd.ChangeRecording.defaultUserId` is the default owner of the change lists.

▶ `Pcd.ChangeRecording.isCrLockingEnabled` defines whether the object being changed by one user should be locked for editing by other users.

▶ `Pcd.ChangeRecording.isDefaultUserEnabled` works so that all of the change lists are created with the default user ID as the owner.

After activating the change recording in SAP NetWeaver Administrator, configure it in the portal.

7. Go to SYSTEM ADMINISTRATION • TRANSPORT • CHANGE RECORDING CONFIGURA-TION, where you can manage the object locations that should be included in the change lists and locations that should be excluded from recording in the change lists (see Figure 3.38). Here you can add the locations that you want to be included in the change lists.

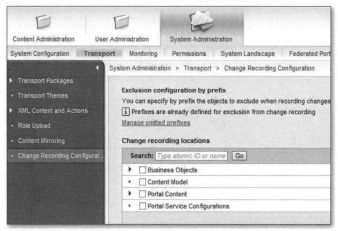

Figure 3.38 Change Recording Configuration

8. Click MANAGE OMITTED PREFIXES to add the prefixes that you want to exclude from the change list recording. After you have done this, the change recording is configured.

After the change recording has been activated and the locations configured, the objects are included in your change lists whenever you create, delete, or make changes in the included locations. You can see the change lists in the MY OPEN CHANGELISTS section next to MY OBJECTS and PORTAL CONTENT, as shown in Figure 3.39.

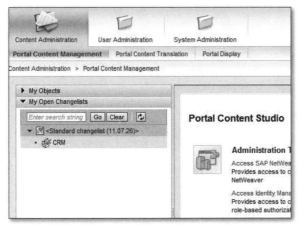

Figure 3.39 Change List

You can also right-click the change list and select OPEN IN CHANGE ORGANIZER to open the change organizer tool. The Change Organizer tool lists all of the change lists for the logged-in user; when you select a change list, it lists all of the objects included in the change list.

3.9 Summary

This chapter covered the basics of SAP NetWeaver Portal and the portal architecture. You have also seen how SAP NetWeaver Portal fits into the SAP NetWeaver platform. This chapter began with a discussion of SAP NetWeaver Portal implementation by outlining the preparation, installation, and post-installation steps. It also addressed the various configurations needed with respect to SSL configuration and the UME configuration, and the importance of system landscape because SAP NetWeaver Portal acts as a frontend for various backend SAP systems in most of the implementations. Finally we discussed the transport mechanism followed in portal projects and the new change recording feature that was introduced in SAP NetWeaver Portal 7.3.

In the next chapter, we will learn about integrating various SAP and non-SAP applications with SAP NetWeaver Portal. We will also see how single sign-on (SSO) is handled in such integration scenarios.

SAP NetWeaver Portal can be integrated in a landscape of SAP and non-SAP systems in various ways with single sign-on. Single sign-on is an important requirement of SAP NetWeaver Portal implementations.

4 Integration with SAP Backend Systems and Single Sign-On

As discussed in earlier chapters, the main aim of SAP NetWeaver Portal is to integrate various SAP and non-SAP systems and applications and provide a role-based single point of access. One crucial challenge that you have to deal with during integration is the authentication and single sign-on (SSO) of a user across systems. When someone logs on to the portal and attempts to access an application that runs on some other system, he expects to be taken to that application seamlessly, without having to enter the user ID and password for that system again; this idea is known as *single sign-on*. Because SSO is an important challenge in any SAP NetWeaver Portal implementation, this chapter discusses some of the SSO scenarios that can be implemented with SAP NetWeaver Portal.

In addition to SSO, you may also want to distribute user roles between SAP NetWeaver Portal and SAP backend systems. For example, if you have maintained user roles in SAP ABAP backend systems, you may want to upload those roles in SAP NetWeaver Portal instead of creating separate users or groups. Similarly you might have roles defined on SAP NetWeaver Portal, which you want to propagate to the ABAP backend systems. We will discuss these scenarios in the coming sections.

4.1 Single Sign-On (SSO)

SSO is an important feature of SAP NetWeaver Portal that allows a user to sign in once to SAP NetWeaver Portal and then access various other systems and applications without having to enter the credentials again. It eases the pain of users who have to access multiple systems on a regular basis.

SAP NetWeaver Portal has two mechanisms available for allowing SSO to external systems:

▶ **Logon ticket**
SSO based on a ticketing mechanism is where the source system issues a ticket, and the target system accepts and evaluates the ticket. If the ticket is valid, it lets the user in without asking for the user name and password.

▶ **User mapping**
In this SSO mechanism, the external system's user name and password for the user are maintained in SAP NetWeaver Portal. When the user is accessing the external system, the user name and password are sent to the system along with the request. If the user name and password are correct, the system lets the user in.

In any SAP NetWeaver Portal implementation in which you have to integrate external systems with the portal, the type of SSO mechanism that will be used is an important decision to make. There are important criteria that you need to consider when making this decision. The following are the possible SSO mechanisms:

▶ **SSO with logon tickets but without user mapping**
This is the most preferred and easily managed type of SSO. To take advantage of this scenario, your backend system must be able to accept logon tickets, and user IDs of the users should be the same in the portal as well as the backend systems.

To enable this type of SSO, you need to configure SAP NetWeaver Portal to issue logon tickets and configure the backend to accept logon tickets.

▶ **SSO with logon tickets with user mapping**
SSO with logon tickets with user mapping can be done when the SSO without user mapping is not possible. To implement this scenario, the backend system must be able to accept logon tickets, and the user's ID must be the same in all of the ABAP backend systems but different in SAP NetWeaver Portal. In this scenario, a reference backend system is defined and the users are mapped in the portal with reference to this reference system.

To enable this type of SSO, you need to configure SAP NetWeaver Portal to issue logon tickets, configure the portal for user mapping with logon tickets, configure the backend to accept logon tickets, and map users to the backend IDs.

▶ **SSO with user mapping**

SSO with user mapping needs to be considered when a logon ticket SSO mechanism is not possible. To enable this type of SSO, you need only configure the user mapping on SAP NetWeaver Portal. The following are the cases when you need this scenario:

▶ The backend system is not able to accept SSO.

▶ The user IDs of the users in the ABAP backend systems are different, and the users don't have the same ID on SAP NetWeaver Portal.

As should be clear from the preceding list, various configurations are needed to enable different SSO scenarios between SAP NetWeaver Portal and other SAP systems. In this section, we discuss the major configuration steps involved in these scenarios. Specifically, we will explain how to configure SAP NetWeaver Portal to act as a logon ticket-issuing system as well as a logon ticket-accepting system; how an SAP backend system can be configured to accept the logon tickets issued by SAP NetWeaver Portal (which will be the case in most of the implementations); and, finally, how to configure SSO using user mapping.

4.1.1 Configuring SAP NetWeaver Portal to Issue Logon Tickets

Logon tickets are credential tickets issued to a user or client by SAP NetWeaver Portal after a user authenticates with SAP NetWeaver Portal. SAP NetWeaver Portal stores the logon ticket as a cookie on the user's browser. The cookie name is MYSAPSSO2, and the value of this cookie is sent by the browser for each request. Based on the validity of this cookie, the user is authenticated to various other systems that accept logon tickets from SAP NetWeaver Portal.

Logon tickets contain the user ID, but they do not contain the password. It contains the following information:

▶ User ID

▶ Authentication scheme

▶ Validity date

▶ Issuing system

▶ Digital signature

In the system landscape, SAP NetWeaver Portal can be either a ticket-issuing system or a ticket-accepting system. Usually, the system that is first accessed by the user should be the ticket-issuing system, so that the user doesn't need to enter the logon credentials a second time. If SAP NetWeaver Portal works as the system that is accessed by the users first and is responsible for generating the logon ticket, the flow is as follows:

1. After successful authentication of a user in SAP NetWeaver Portal, the portal assigns a cookie to the user that is set to the user's browser. The cookie is valid until the user either logs off or closes the browser.

2. When the user tries to access any other system within the same session, the cookie is sent to the system by the user's browser.

3. The system retrieves the user's cookies from the request and gets the SSO cookie (MYSAPSSO2). If the system finds the cookie valid, it lets the user in without asking for a password.

Figure 4.1 shows a workflow of requests when a user accesses SAP NetWeaver Portal and then accesses an external system that is part of the SSO landscape.

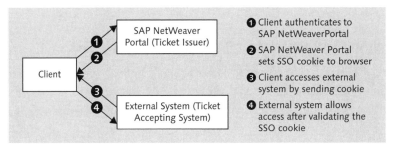

Figure 4.1 SSO Workflow

In Figure 4.1, SAP NetWeaver Portal acts as the ticket-issuing system, and the external system acts as the ticket-accepting system. (SAP NetWeaver Portal can also act as a ticket-accepting system when the SSO ticket has been issued by another system.) By default, SAP NetWeaver Portal is configured to issue logon tickets. If SAP NetWeaver Portal is not issuing logon tickets, the following steps are needed to configure it to issue logon tickets:

1. Log in to SAP NetWeaver Administrator by going to *http://<HOST>:<PORT>/ nwa*.

2. Navigate to CONFIGURATION • AUTHENTICATION AND SINGLE SIGN-ON, and then go to the COMPONENTS section in the AUTHENTICATION tab (Figure 4.2).

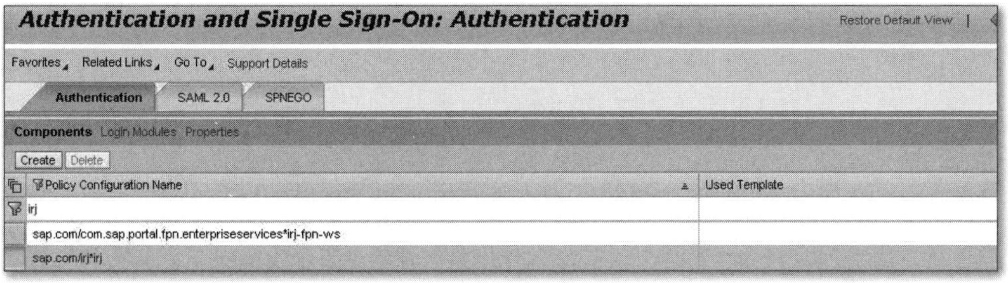

Figure 4.2 Policy Configuration

3. To search for your application in the list of policy configurations, filter for "irj" and select SAP.COM/IRJ*IRJ (Figure 4.2).

4. Your authentication scheme in the portal should be configured as shown in Listing 4.1.

```
<authscheme name="uidpwdlogon">
    <authentication-template>
        ticket
    </authentication-template>
    <priority>20</priority>
    <frontendtype>2</frontendtype>
                <frontendtarget>com.sap.portal.runtime.logon.
certlogon</frontendtarget>
    </authscheme>
```

Listing 4.1 Authentication Scheme

5. In the preceding XML example, the `ticket` authentication template is being used. In the AUTHENTICATION STACK tab, click the USED TEMPLATE dropdown, and select TICKET (Figure 4.3), as this template has been defined in the *authschemes. xml* file for SAP NetWeaver Portal.

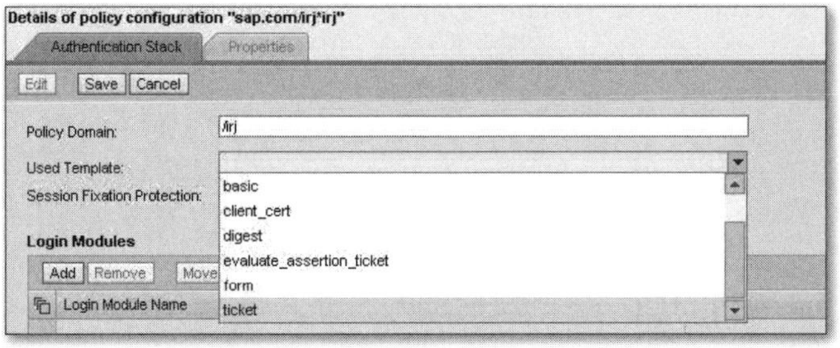

Figure 4.3 Authentication Template

6. The login module stack will appear as configured. Figure 4.4 shows that the login module has been configured to allow the user access if a logon ticket already exists. If the login module does not exist, then the user needs to authenticate, and then a logon ticket is created.

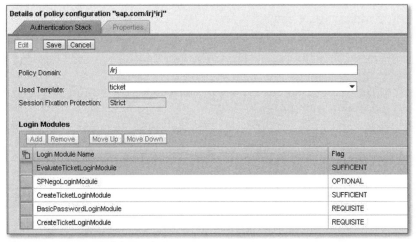

Figure 4.4 Login Module Stack

The login module configured in Figure 4.4 works like this:

▸ The EVALUATETICKETLOGINMODULE first evaluates if a logon ticket exists. If it exists, the user is allowed without being asked for a user ID and password.

▸ If a valid login ticket does not exist, the user is authenticated using SPNEGOLOG-INMODULE.

▸ If the authentication is successful, the user is allowed access, and the CREATETICK-ETLOGINMODULE creates a logon ticket for the user.

▸ If the user is not yet authenticated, a BASICPASSWORDLOGINMODULE authentication is done. If the authentication is successful, the user is allowed access, and the CREATETICKETLOGINMODULE creates a logon ticket for the user.

If you want your system to not accept logon tickets, then you will need to remove the EVALUATETICKETLOGINMODULE from the top and include BASICPASSWORDLOG-INMODULE so that an authentication is done. The flag for BASICPASSWORDLOGIN-MODULE should be set to REQUISITE, and the CREATETICKETLOGINMODULE should be set to SUFFICIENT so that BASICPASSWORDLOGINMODULE is mandatory, and the user is allowed access after a login ticket is created.

The properties of the logon ticket can be configured by editing the User Management Engine (UME) properties. To go to the UME properties for logon tickets from SAP NetWeaver Administrator, go to the user management configuration, open the export mode, and filter for "logon.ticket". This shows all of the properties related to the logon ticket configuration (Figure 4.5).

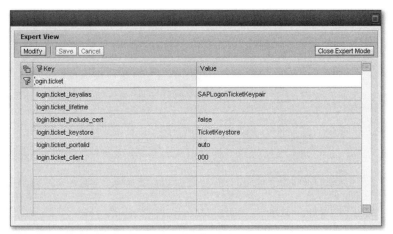

Figure 4.5 Logon Ticket Properties Configuration

After you have made your changes, you should restart the portal server for your changes to take effect.

4.1.2   Configuring SAP NetWeaver Portal to Accept Logon Tickets

We have seen how to configure Sap NetWeaver Portal to issue logon tickets. In this section, we will see how to configure SAP NetWeaver Portal to accept logon tickets. Note that SAP NetWeaver Portal uses the functionalities provided by the underlying SAP AS Java for the logon tickets.

As we have seen earlier, AS Java uses the `EvaluateTicketLoginModule` module to evaluate and accept the logon ticket. When AS Java receives a logon ticket, it evaluates the ticket for authenticity and validity and allows the user in only if found valid.

The logon ticket contains a digital signature that must be verified by the portal that is receiving the logon ticket. The digital signature is encrypted by the logon ticket-creating system using its private cryptographic key. To decrypt the digital signature, the receiving system must have the public cryptographic certificate of the ticket-using system in its keystore. That means a trust must have been established between the two systems before one system starts accepting the logon ticket from the other system.

The trust configurations can be done from SAP NetWeaver Administrator by going to CONFIGURATION • SECURITY • TRUSTED SYSTEMS • SINGLE SIGN-ON WITH LOGON TICKETS (Figure 4.6).

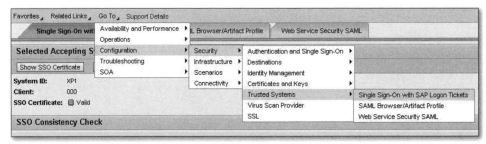

Figure 4.6 Trust Configuration

Figure 4.7 shows a list of trusted systems in the system. To create a new trusted system, click ADD TRUSTED SYSTEM.

Figure 4.7 Trusted Systems

When you click the button to add a trusted system, you get two options:

▶ By Querying Trusted System

▶ By Uploading Certificate Manually

We discuss these options in more detail next.

Adding a Trusted System By Querying the Trusted System

If you select By Querying Trusted System, you can connect to the system from here, and the system can be added as a trusted system. In the popup for trusted system selection, you need to choose the landscape type. In Figure 4.8, the landscape type selected is All Technical Systems. The list of systems provided here comes from the System Landscape Directory (SLD) to which this AS Java connects.

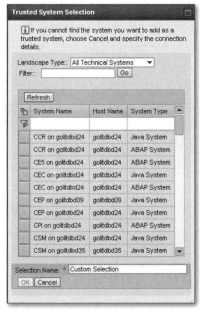

Figure 4.8 Trusted System Selection

Select the appropriate system, and click OK. You will now need to provide the connection details so that AS Java is able to connect to the server. You will need to enter details such as system type, system number, client number, host name, user name, and password (Figure 4.9).

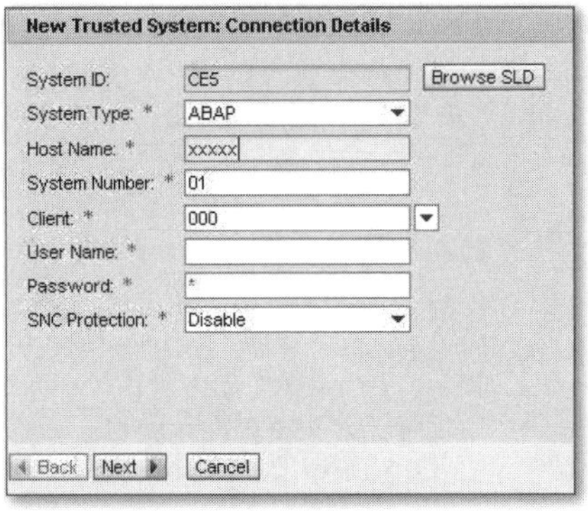

Figure 4.9 Connection Details

After AS Java connects to the server with the details provided and logs on using the user name and password you provided, it shows a confirmation screen that the trusted system is about to be added (Figure 4.10). It gives a lot of information about the logon ticket issuer's certificate, including certificate validity dates, algorithm type, and so on. When you click FINISH, the system gets added as a trusted system.

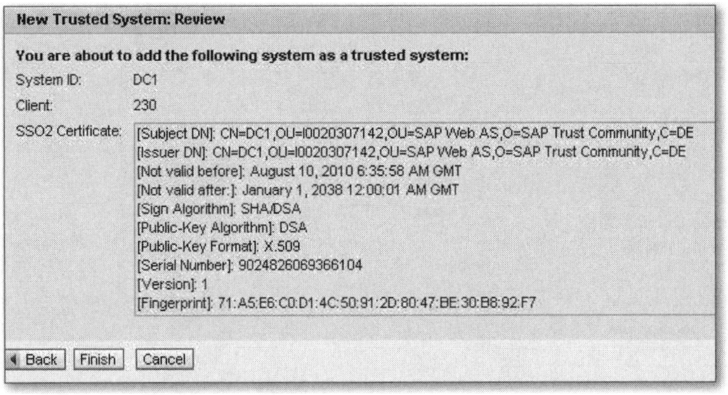

Figure 4.10 Trusted System being added

Adding a Trusted System By Uploading the Certificate Manually

To upload a certificate of a system, you should have already downloaded the certificate from the system that is going to be added as a trusted system. Click the ADD TRUSTED SYSTEM button, and select BY UPLOADING CERTIFICATE MANUALLY. You will need to provide the system ID, client, and the certificate file from the file system (Figure 4.11). If you are adding a Java system as the trusted system, the client will normally be 000.

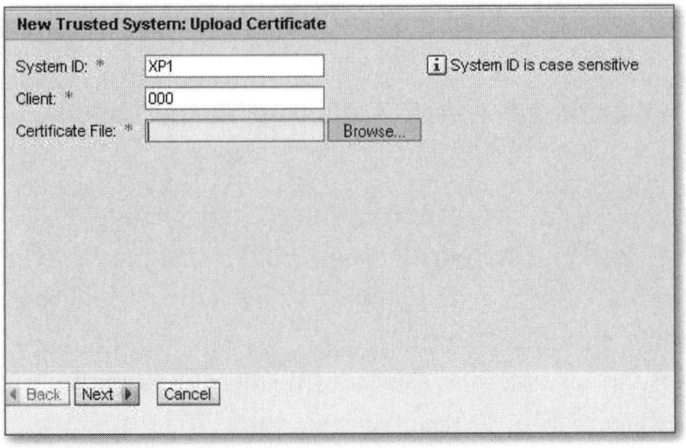

Figure 4.11 Adding a Trusted System by Uploading a Certificate

After you have provided the system details and the certificate file, the file gets uploaded and shows the details of the certificate as before (Figure 4.12). After you click FINISH on this screen, the system gets added as a trusted system.

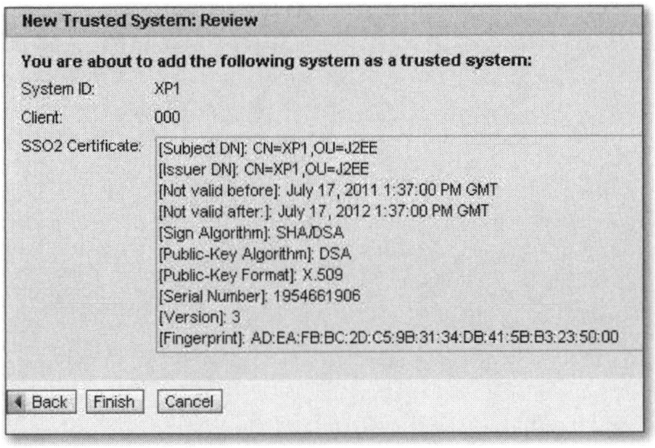

Figure 4.12 Adding a Trusted System by Uploading Certificate

After the trust has been established between the ticket-issuing system and SAP NetWeaver Portal, you need to configure SAP NetWeaver Portal to evaluate and accept the logon ticket provided by the ticket-issuing system. Section 4.1.1 explained how to configure the login modules. To make sure that SAP NetWeaver Portal accepts the logon tickets, the `EvaluateTicketLoginModule` should be added to the login module stack at the top, so that the logon ticket is first evaluated before asking for authentication. Also the flag should be set to SUFFICIENT so that if the logon ticket is valid, an authentication should not be done.

4.1.3 Configuring the SAP Backend System to Accept Portal Logon Tickets

As we have discussed earlier, SAP NetWeaver Portal often acts as the frontend system for many SAP and non-SAP backend systems. This means that SAP NetWeaver Portal acts as the single point of access for many applications running on various other SAP and non-SAP systems. In most cases, SAP ABAP systems form a major part of these external systems, so let's look at the steps needed to configure an ABAP system to accept logon tickets from SAP NetWeaver Portal.

One thing to keep in mind is that for SSO to work across systems without user mapping, the user IDs of the users need to be the same in all of the systems; otherwise, the SSO will not work.

To configure the SAP ABAP system to accept SAP NetWeaver Portal's logon ticket, follow these steps:

1. In the ABAP system, go to Transaction SM30, and maintain Table TWPSSO2ACL.

2. In this table, add a new entry for the portal server. Various details as shown in Figure 4.13 are needed.

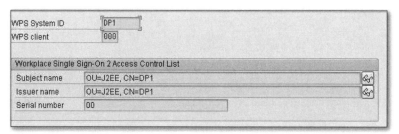

Figure 4.13 Adding the Portal in the ABAP System's Access Control List

After adding the portal details, the list of systems added to the access control list (ACL) are listed as shown in Figure 4.14.

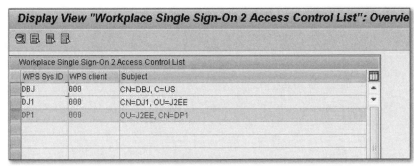

Figure 4.14 ABAP System's Access Control List

3. In the ABAP system, go to Transaction STRUST. The screen shown in Figure 4.15 appears.

Figure 4.15 STRUST Transaction

4. In the CERTIFICATE section toward the bottom, click the IMPORT CERTIFICATE button (Figure 4.16).

Figure 4.16 Import Certificate

5. You will receive a popup from which you can select the certificate file that you got from the ticket-issuing SAP NetWeaver Portal. After you select the certificate file and click OK, the details of the certificate are shown (Figure 4.17).

Figure 4.17 Certificate Details

6. Click ADD TO CERTIFICATE LIST to add this certificate to the ABAP system. Save your settings and exit.

4.1.4 Configuring SSO with User Mapping

In scenarios when the portal user ID of the user is not the same as the backend user ID, a user mapping is required. In this scenario, the backend systems are configured to accept the SSO logon ticket from SAP NetWeaver Portal, and the user IDs are the same in all of the backend systems. One of the systems in this case acts as the reference system for SAP NetWeaver Portal. Follow these steps to configure the user mapping in this scenario:

1. Make sure that you have created a system in the portal's system landscape for the reference backend system for which the user mapping will be created.

2. Open the USER MANAGEMENT property category.

3. Set the LOGON METHOD property to SAPLOGONTICKET and the USER MAPPING
   TYPE to ADMIN,USER (Figure 4.18).

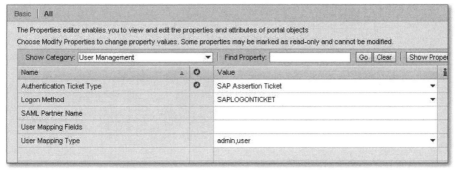

Figure 4.18 System Properties

4. Go to the user management configuration by navigating to SYSTEM ADMINISTRA-
   TION • SYSTEM CONFIGURATION • UME CONFIGURATION • USER MAPPING.

5. In the REFERENCE SYSTEM field, choose the alias of the reference system, and save
   the changes (Figure 4.19).

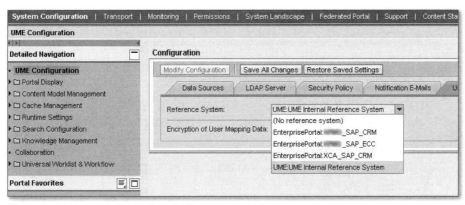

Figure 4.19 User Mapping Reference System

6. To define the user mapping for a user, go to USER ADMINISTRATION. Search for
   and select the user for whom you want to define the user mapping.

7. Go to the tab USER MAPPING FOR SYSTEM ACCESS and click MODIFY. For the
   SYSTEM field, select the system that you had chosen as the reference system
   (Figure 4.20).

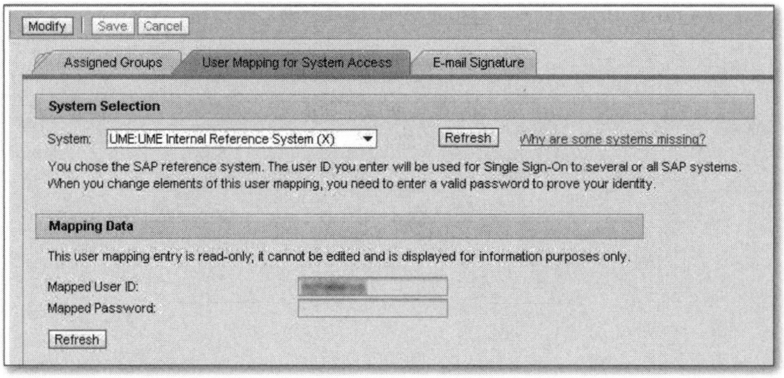

Figure 4.20 User Mapping

8. In the MAPPING DATA section, you will need to define the MAPPING USER ID and MAPPING PASSWORD from the reference system for the user.

9. After making the changes, save the entry. The user has now been mapped with the reference for SSO.

4.2 Uploading Roles from ABAP-Based SAP Systems

With SAP NetWeaver 7.3, SAP has introduced a new feature that allows you to create a portal role based on a role available in the backend. Using the New Role from Backend wizard, you can browse the available roles in a backend and then select a role to upload it along with its contents to SAP NetWeaver Portal. To use the wizard, you should already have created a portal system object for the backend system that you want to upload the roles from. Follow these steps to upload a role from the backend:

1. Log in to SAP NetWeaver Portal, go to CONTENT ADMINISTRATION, and navigate to the folder where you want to create the portal role.

2. Right-click the folder, and select NEW • ROLE • ROLE FROM BACK END (Figure 4.21).

3. In the next screen, select the role from the backend that you want to upload to SAP NetWeaver Portal. First, however, select a system alias for the SEARCH IN dropdown. This dropdown lists all of the system aliases that have been created in the portal for backend systems. After selecting a system alias, enter a search term in the SEARCH field, and click GO. The system shows two sections below

the search criteria—AVAILABLE ROLES and SELECTED ROLES—as shown in Figure 4.22. Figure 4.23 shows the roles available in the backend; the roles that the search results show in the portal corresponds to the same search results in the backend.

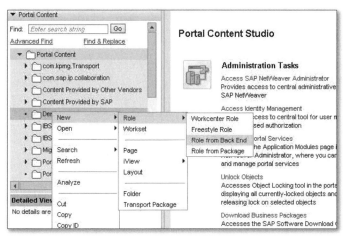

Figure 4.21 Creating a Role from the Backend

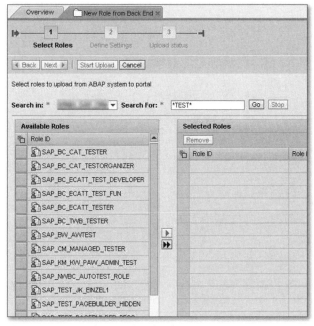

Figure 4.22 Searching Backend Role

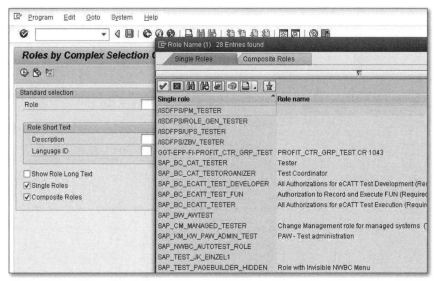

Figure 4.23 Roles in the Backend

4. You now need to select a role from the search result and add it to the selected roles. To do this, select a role, and click the ADD icon (the single-arrow icon). The selected role should now be transferred to the SELECTED ROLES section (Figure 4.24). Click NEXT.

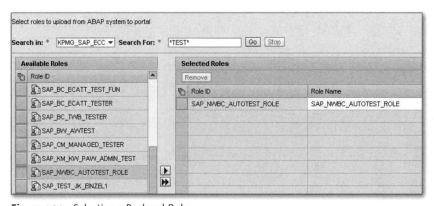

Figure 4.24 Selecting a Backend Role

5. In the next screen, choose the ID prefix and master language. After entering the required values, click START UPLOAD to·start the role upload process (Figure 4.25).

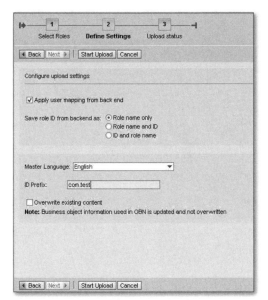

Figure 4.25   Settings for Role Upload

6. The role upload process starts to upload the selected role and all of its associated objects. There is a progress indicator on the screen that shows what percentage has been completed at any point in time (Figure 4.26). After the completion of the role upload process, you will see the status as completed and a list of all objects that have been uploaded.

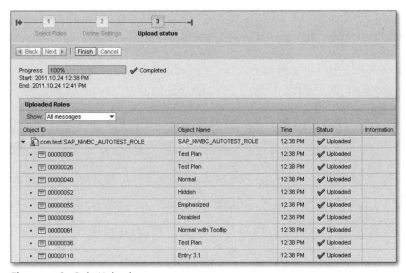

Figure 4.26   Role Upload

7. As shown in Figure 4.27, you can now open the role in the CONTENT ADMINIS-TRATION tab to see the structure of the role created.

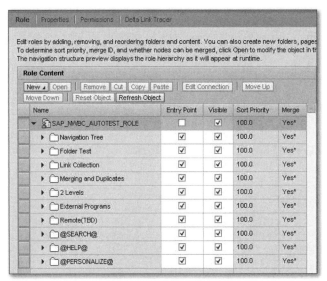

Figure 4.27   Role Uploaded from the Backend

In this section, we saw how the roles from an SAP backend can be uploaded into SAP NetWeaver Portal. In the next section, we will see how SAP NetWeaver Portal roles can be distributed to the SAP backend.

4.3   Role Distribution to ABAP-Based SAP Systems

SAP NetWeaver Portal allows you to transfer the portal roles to the backend SAP systems connected to SAP NetWeaver Portal. You will usually transfer portal roles to one backend system that acts as the central store for maintaining authorization roles for the users. Because SAP NetWeaver Portal roles are not linked with any authorization roles from an SAP backend, backend authorization roles must be mapped to the portal roles in the backend. This can be done by going to Transaction W3PR in the SAP backend system.

To distribute the roles from SAP NetWeaver Portal to the SAP backend, follow these steps:

1. Make sure that a logical system has been created in the backend in Table WP3RO-LESSYS. Go to Transaction SM30 in the backend, and create an entry for the logical system for the backend system. Make sure the checkbox for ROLE MNT. ACTIVE is checked (Figure 4.28).

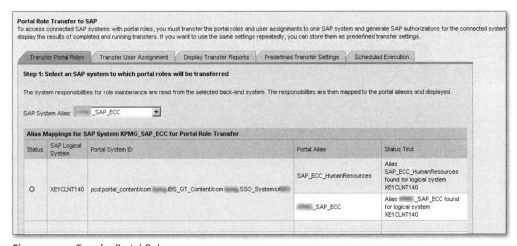

Figure 4.28 Table WP3ROLESYS in the Backend

2. In SAP NetWeaver Portal, navigate to SYSTEM ADMINISTRATION • PERMISSIONS • SAP AUTHORIZATIONS. From the SAP AUTHORIZATIONS screen, select the tab for TRANSFER PORTAL ROLES, and from the dropdown for SAP SYSTEM ALIAS, select the system alias of the system to which you want to transfer the role. Click NEXT (Figure 4.29).

Figure 4.29 Transfer Portal Role

3. In the next screen, you search for the role and select the role that needs to be transferred. Only roles that contain iViews that access the backend are transferred to the backend; for example, Business Server Pages (BSP) iViews or Web Dynpro ABAP iViews. The system alias property of an iView is checked, and the role is

transferred to the backend only if the system alias is the same as the selected system alias. Figure 4.30 shows the selection of a portal role for transfer.

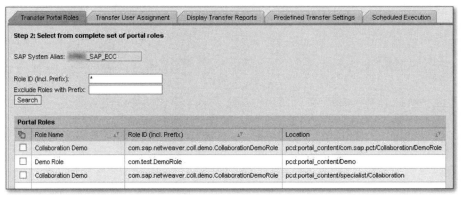

Figure 4.30 Role Selection for Transfer

4. In the next screen (Figure 4.31), check the settings that you have entered. If everything is fine, click the START TRANSFER button to start the transfer.

Figure 4.31 Start Transfer

After the transfer starts, you will see a progress bar that tells you about the progress of the transfer process. After the transfer is complete, the progress bar shows the completed status, and you will see a log of all the steps completed in the transfer process (Figure 4.32).

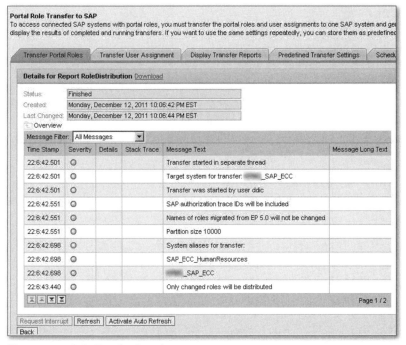

Figure 4.32 Role Transfer Complete

5. After the transfer has been completed, you can go to Transaction W3PR in the backend to see that the portal role has been transferred, as shown in Figure 4.33.

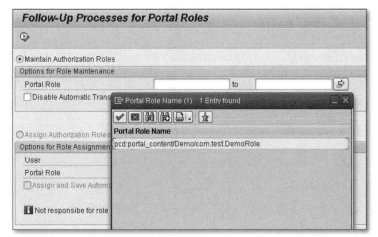

Figure 4.33 Transferred Role in Backend

4.4 Summary

This aim of this chapter was to help you become familiar with the concepts of integrating SAP NetWeaver Portal with other systems, focusing specifically on SSO. We discussed the steps needed to configure SAP NetWeaver Portal for issuing as well as accepting logon tickets. We also discussed how to configure an SAP backend to accept logon tickets issued by SAP NetWeaver Portal. Toward the end of this chapter, we discussed how roles and user data are transferred between SAP NetWeaver Portal and SAP ABAP backends.

In the next chapter, we will look in detail at how you should start your implementation and how important it is to be prepared for the blueprinting process.

Blueprinting is an important step in implementation planning that defines how you should move forward with a project.

5   Implementation Planning

Previous chapters of this book have focused on the SAP NetWeaver Portal platform and how to install and configure the portal system. At the end of all of these steps, we will have a simple portal with basic configurations. The usual next step is to implement the portal per the customer needs. This is when the consulting team needs to start customizing SAP NetWeaver Portal and planning for development. As such, the next topic to discuss is the blueprinting process and the process of designing the solution based on the blueprinting. This is the most important chapter from an implementation point of view; in most projects, the quality of the job done at the blueprinting level reflects directly on the implementation.

The most common problem that implementation teams face is getting the information they need from customers in order to accurately design the solution. Not asking the right questions leads to an incomplete understanding of the system and landscape, which results in inferior implementations. In this chapter, we provide a checklist of the most important considerations and questions the implementation team should address before choosing the architecture of the SAP NetWeaver Portal implementation.

We start by talking about *blueprinting*, which is the process of identifying the problems to solve and the features to implement. After the blueprinting is done, we are faced with the challenge of choosing the user interface (UI) technology on which to base the UIs. We will discuss the implementation process in detail as well as the factors that must be considered when choosing the right UI technology for the implementation.

5.1 Blueprinting

Blueprinting is the process of analyzing the business process and defining the system that needs to be implemented as part of the implementation process. In this section, we will explain the blueprinting process to make it easier for consultants. We will discuss various topics concerning SAP NetWeaver Portal that need to be discussed with the customer. In most of the implementations, customers will not be aware of the features and capabilities of SAP NetWeaver Portal. It is a consultant's responsibility to make the customer aware of these capabilities and determine how he wants the features to be implemented. Customer questionnaire topics such as "Objective of the Client's Portal Project" can have far-reaching effects on the portal implementation because the objectives will need to be considered in all of the important decisions you make during the implementation. What content will need to be created versus what existing content will need to be integrated will also drive the scope of the entire project. In this section, we discuss the important areas that should be covered by the consultant while blueprinting and the important questions that need to be answered.

5.1.1 Scoping Questionnaire

Asking the right questions can significantly simplify the blueprinting process. Before getting into the detailed requirements, it's helpful to ask the customer some important initial questions, such as the ones suggested here. The answers to these questions will form the basis for the next level of detailed questions and help identify the project requirements.

The following subsections categorize the various areas that you need to cover initially to get a feel for the implementation scope.

Objective of the Client's Portal Project

It's very important to determine whether the portal is implemented for employees, customers, or partners. The implementation approach is based on this answer. The following are the questions that need to be answered concerning the portal's objective:

▶ Is the client implementing a company portal for employees?

▶ Is the client implementing an external company portal for customers?

► Is the client implementing an external company portal for partners?

► Is the client implementing a portal for SAP applications?

► Is the client implementing a portal for non-SAP applications?

Because the UI standards for external and internal portals are different for many corporations, the requirements for the UI may change based on the overall objective of the client. The security requirements can vary based on the users of the portal.

Key Assumptions for the Project

Key assumptions reflect the guiding principles of the project. For example, some projects are implemented with an approach that excludes custom development, whereas some customers are more open to custom development that accommodates their requirements. The following are some other examples of key assumptions:

► **No modifications to SAP-delivered code should be done.**
SAP code modifications are sometimes avoided to make maintenance easier. In such scenarios, you need to look at other options such as enhancements, custom applications, and so on.

► **All UI development should be done using ABAP technology.**
Some customers are more comfortable with ABAP technology than Java. Your options are then limited to the ABAP stack.

► **The portal will be exposed to the Internet.**
When the portal will be exposed to internet, you have to start thinking about the whole landscape and consider security aspects.

Number and Skills of Available Resources

The resources that will be available for the project will affect its scope. The following roles are important for a successful portal implementation:

► Project manager

► Portal role administrator

► Systems administrator

► Web security administrator

► Web developer

► Content specialist

- ▶ Graphics specialist

- ▶ Extended team of business-process experts

- ▶ Backend systems expert

- ▶ Workflow developer

Client's Existing Technology

The client's existing network architecture is very important because SAP NetWeaver Portal normally has to fit into the client's existing network topology. The following are important considerations:

- ▶ Client's network architecture (firewalls, DMZ, etc.)

- ▶ Browsers and platforms used (including versions)

- ▶ Server platforms

- ▶ Databases

For example, if the client normally works on a Java platform, then he would probably be more inclined to keep long-term in-house maintenance in mind and therefore opt for Web Dynpro Java development.

Sizing and Scalability

The approximate sizing of the hardware depends on scalability requirements. One of the most important parameters is the number of concurrent users in peak load. In general, the following questions need to be answered:

- ▶ Is the portal expected to be available at all times?

- ▶ What is the peak number of concurrent users the client expects the portal to handle, and how many web requests does the client expect every day?

- ▶ How many different roles does the client expect to issue?

- ▶ Does the client plan on making the portal available to more users in future phases?

- ▶ To how many locations will the client make the portal available now and in future phases?

- ▶ How many documents will be stored in the portal?

- ▶ Will indexing be needed in the portal?

Security

SAP NetWeaver Portal has to be configured for the security policies of the enterprise and to comply with the single sign-on (SSO) policies for the client. Many customers want to seamlessly access the portal from their existing intranet portals, which requires that an SSO system be established between them. To understand the security requirements, you will need to gather the following information from the client:

▶ The authentication method that the client plans to use to authenticate the user, for example:

 ▶ Digital certificate

 ▶ Windows NT/2000 authentication

 ▶ Netegrity SiteMinder authentication

▶ If the client is going to use user ID and password authentication, you need to check the type of authentication required:

 ▶ **HTTP basic authentication**
 Before the portal user enters the portal, the browser prompts the user for an ID and a password.

 ▶ **Form-based logon**
 The portal displays an initial start page to the user. The page contains entry fields where the user can enter a user ID and password.

▶ If the client plans to use digital certificates, what certification authority (CA) will issue certificates? The following are the options:

 ▶ **SAP Trust Center Service**
 The SAP Trust Center Service can issue security certificates.

 ▶ **External certification authority**
 External certification authorities such as VeriSign can be used for certificates.

▶ Will Secure Sockets Layer (SSL) be used for encryption?
 If the client is going to use SSL, then you will need to understand where SSL will terminate. If the SSL will terminate at the portal, then you will need to configure the portal to handle SSL. If the SSL terminates at the load balancer or the proxy, then you may not need to configure the portal for SSL.

▶ Would the client like to provide anonymous access to the portal?
 If the client wants to provide anonymous access to the portal, you will need to create anonymous content and configure anonymous access.

- For which backend systems is SSO required?
  - SAP systems (specific versions)
  - Internet/extranet web servers
- Does the client require any custom development?
  Sometimes the security requirements involve some custom development. For example, some authentication and SSO systems may have special requirements that lead to custom development on the portal side.

User Management and Roles

The User Management Engine (UME) needs to be configured for the type of user management that the client wants to use. You need to know the following:

- Does the client already have user and identity management processes in place?
- Does the client plan to import roles from R/3 systems into the Portal Content Directory (PCD)?
- Has the client deployed a corporate LDAP directory to store users?
- If the client is already using a corporate LDAP directory to store users, which schema is used for the directory?
- Ask the client for a general description of the directory architecture. Is one server used for the entire organization (a tree)? Are multiple servers (a forest with referrals between servers) being used?
- Ask the client for a general description of how the directory stores users. Is a user stored directly beneath the group? Are users stored in one branch and groups in another?
- Ask the client for a description of how roles are defined in the corporate directory.
- What LDAP directory server product does the client use or plan to use?
- iPlanet Directory Server
- Novell NDS eDirectory
- Microsoft Active Directory Service
- Other

▸ Are roles already defined in the corporate LDAP?

▸ Will the client integrate user management with SAP systems?

▸ Does the client currently use SAP Central User Administration (CUA)?

▸ Will the client use CUA and its LDAP synchronization function?

▸ Is a self-registration function for users needed? If so, will users be able to decide whether (and when) they want to become registered portal users with personalized content?

Branding and Personalization

Every client wants the SAP NetWeaver Portal to be branded to align with their corporate standards. In this regard, you will need to acquire the following information from the client:

▸ Can the client provide visuals and examples of the branding for the portal (such as screenshots)?

▸ Does a website (intranet or extranet) exist to be used as a template or guide for branding the portal?

▸ Describe the requirements for look and feel. Are these consistent across users, or will the client require a different look and feel depending upon the user, project phase, and so on?

▸ Will the client require one consistent header or multiple headers? What determines multiple headers?

Content Integration

As the name suggests, *content integration* defines what content will be integrated into SAP NetWeaver Portal. Existing web content from other systems can be consumed inside the SAP NetWeaver Portal so that the latter becomes the central point of entry for all of the systems. Custom applications can also be developed and deployed on SAP NetWeaver Portal. In order to develop the content integration plan, you will need to know the following:

▸ Will the client develop custom iViews? If so, what type(s) (URL-based, Java, etc.)?

▸ Will the content be accessed from disparate systems?

- Does the client plan to develop Web Dynpro applications?

- Does the client plan to use Visual Composer to create applications for the portal?

- Does the client have an existing intranet that needs to be integrated with the SAP NetWeaver Portal?

- Which content management systems that the client already has will need to be integrated?

  - Interwoven

  - Documentum

  - Convera

Knowledge Management (KM)

Knowledge management refers to the management of structured and unstructured knowledge available within an enterprise. Knowledge Management (KM) can be configured to give a structured view for the unstructured knowledge available. To assess the KM requirements of the client, you need to get answers to the following questions:

- What document management systems does the use client currently?
  Based on this, you will need to start looking into the integration options with SAP NetWeaver Portal. You might want to discuss with the client the feasibility of replacing the client's existing document management system with KM.

- What content management systems does the client currently use?
  Based on this, you may want to talk to the client about centralizing the content management with SAP NetWeaver Portal or integrating with the existing content management system

- Does the client use a search engine?
  If the client currently uses a search engine, you may want to make use of that search engine within SAP NetWeaver Portal if an integration is possible. Or you may want to discuss using an SAP TREX (Text Search and Classification Engine) system implementation if search functionality is needed.

- What KM components will the client use?
  This answer will help you plan your KM folder structure and taxonomies.

▶ Does the client want to support collaborative authoring scenarios?
This will help you understand what kind of workflows will be needed for document publishing.

▶ Does the client have existing document management guidelines (naming conventions, documentation duties, etc.)?

▶ Does the client want to replicate metadata or content from external repositories to the web content management system?
If the client wants to replicate content or metadata from external repositories to the content management system, you will need to start looking into content replication tools and options.

▶ What other services and features does the client want to use from KM (retrieval, classification, web authoring, version control, workflow, etc.)?
This will help you analyze the scope of the KM implementation for the project.

Collaboration

The collaboration features of SAP NetWeaver Portal enable users to collaborate with others by means of virtual rooms, groupware integration, real-time collaboration (RTC), and other resources. During the blueprinting process, you should gather information about the following:

▶ Does the client use company-wide instant messaging?
If yes, find out which instant messaging tool is used.

▶ Does the client want to integrate instant messaging with SAP NetWeaver Portal?
In this case, you will need to look at the feasibility of integrating the instant messaging tool with SAP NetWeaver Portal.

▶ Does the client want to integrate groupware (Microsoft Outlook, Lotus Notes, etc.) with SAP NetWeaver Portal?

Components

Because SAP NetWeaver Portal is typically the gateway to a host of backend systems, it is important to determine both the SAP and non-SAP systems that need to integrated by asking the following questions:

▶ Which SAP systems does the client plan to integrate? For example, SAP ERP, SAP Customer Relationship Management (SAP CRM), or SAP NetWeaver Business Warehouse (SAP NetWeaver BW)?

▶ Which non-SAP systems, for example, a .NET system or a J2EE system, does the client plan to integrate with SAP NetWeaver Portal?

▶ Are all of the external systems in the client's intranet, or are some of them on the Internet?

Content–Business Packages

SAP NetWeaver Portal provides business packages, which are predefined portal content with access to backend SAP business functions. The following are examples of some of the business packages provided by SAP:

▶ Employee Self-Service (ESS)

▶ Manager Self-Service (MSS)

▶ Customer Relationship Management (CRM)

▶ Supplier Relationship Management (SRM)

Implementation of each of these business packages is a project in itself and is outside the scope for this discussion. However, it's important to identify how much customization will be needed in the delivered business package to meet the customer's requirements.

Internationalization and Languages

In any global project involving users in multiple countries, you need to support multiple languages. Gather answers to the following questions:

▶ What languages would your client like the portal to support?

▶ What languages do your client's browsers support?

▶ What languages does your client prefer for the administration of the portal?

▶ Does your client have portal users in different time zones?

In this section, we have discussed the important points that need to be considered during the blueprinting for an SAP NetWeaver Portal project. Appendix A offers a sample spreadsheet of these questions (which is also available for download from the book's website at *www.sap-press.com*). This should serve as a guideline for a consultant working on any SAP NetWeaver Portal implementation project.

5.1.2   Sizing

Sizing is the task of determining how much hardware capacity is needed to satisfy the load requirements of your software implementation project. Hardware capacity is usually defined by characteristics of the server landscape configuration, such as the following:

- Number of computers
- Type and number of CPUs
- Clock rates
- Amount of RAM
- Amount of hard disk or other external storage
- Network interface bandwidth

Depending on the kind of software application, there are different ways to define sizing requirements. Different approaches for hardware sizing directly lead to the different ways to define requirements for your load tests:

- **Based on transaction volume**
  This approach is mostly used for SAP ERP applications, where the term "transaction" is clearly defined.

- **Based on number of concurrent users**
  This approach is also used for SAP ERP applications when you know how many people are using a software application but not how many transactions are carried out.

- **Based on number of requests/hour**
  This approach is traditionally used for web applications. Because HTTP is stateless by nature, the transaction and concurrent user are hard to define. Measurements such as requests/second, however, are easy to measure on the web server or application server.

Because SAP NetWeaver Portal is a web-based application, the requirements for your load tests are best defined with the requests/hour (req/h) approach, which has the following advantages:

- ▶ Requests/hour requirements are more web-like and intuitive.
- ▶ Requests/hour requirements can be directly measured on legacy systems based on a web server. This information can be very valuable when defining requirements for a new SAP enterprise portal landscape.
- ▶ No think time and concurrent user requirement definitions are needed.
- ▶ Goals and requirements become somewhat independent of the special scenario definitions.
- ▶ Requests/hour load is always directly proportional to CPU load.

After obtaining information about their users, consultants can generate initial sizing information using SAP's online sizing tool, the Quick Sizer, which is available at *http://service.sap.com/quicksizer*. The Quick Sizer tool calculates the sizing and hardware configuration based on customer input. It provides an estimated hardware requirement to match the business needs of the portal users.

In the Quick Sizer tool, you need to create a project to start sizing for your project. If you have already created a project, you can display or change the project, or you can see a list of projects (Figure 5.1).

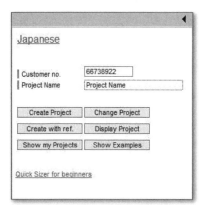

Figure 5.1 Quick Sizer Landing Screen

After you select the project, you will come to the customer information section where you will fill in a questionnaire. For SAP NetWeaver Portal implementations, you will be asked questions such as average number of users, peak number of users, peak load time, and so on. Information such as number of iViews, pages, roles, and so on are also needed to do the sizing. Figure 5.2 shows an example questionnaire.

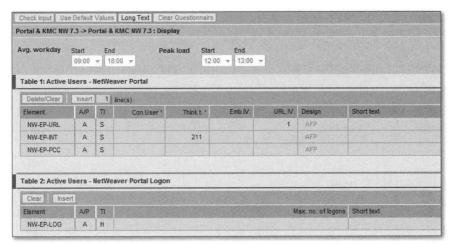

Figure 5.2 Sizing Questionnaire

After you have filled in the questionnaire, you can click the CALCULATE RESULT button to get the sizing results. This gives you the recommended sizing results according to the answers you entered in the questionnaire. The results screen looks like Figure 5.3.

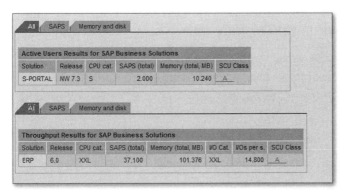

Figure 5.3 Quick Sizing Result

Because CPU consumption is highly dependent on the chosen platform, SAP created SAPS — a hardware-independent unit used to describe the CPU-related performance characteristics of a given hardware configuration. A detailed discussion of SAPS is beyond the scope of this book; for more information, go to *www.sap.com/benchmark*, and choose MEASURING IN SAPS.

5.2 Choosing the Technology

In the previous sections, we saw how to gather requirements from the client regarding your SAP NetWeaver Portal implementation. Your next step in the implementation is to see what technologies to consider for implementing any custom UI that needs to be developed. In this section, we will discuss the options available and the advantages and disadvantages of each option.

5.2.1 Custom Development

Various options need to be considered for custom development of applications to be deployed in SAP NetWeaver Portal. In general, the following UI options are available to the implementation team:

► Web Dynpro Java

► Web Dynpro ABAP

► Portal Development Kit (PDK) portal components

► Business Server Pages (BSPs)

The following are important factors that should be considered before arriving at the preferred UI development technology for SAP NetWeaver Portal:

► **Availability of skilled resources**
The development of applications in the chosen platform requires the availability of developers skilled in that platform.

► **Development time**
Some platforms provide tools and wizards that reduce the development time. These options should be evaluated before choosing the development technology.

► **Maintenance**
Because the maintenance after implementation continues for many years, we recommend that you choose a platform that provides for easy and cheap maintenance.

▶ **Infrastructure setup**

Consider how much time and effort it takes to set up the development infrastructure.

Of course, the decision to use a particular technology is never an isolated one, and most often it also needs to be aligned with the rest of the project. The next section elaborates on the pros and cons of each UI option.

Web Dynpro Java

Web Dynpro Java is a programming model of the SAP NetWeaver platform for designing UIs for business applications. It is based on the model view controller programming paradigm that separates the presentation logic from business logic. The development for Web Dynpro applications is done in the Web Dynpro perspective of SAP NetWeaver Developer Studio (NWDS), as shown in Figure 5.4.

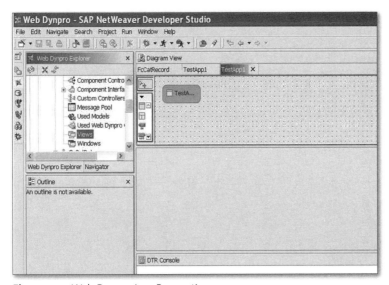

Figure 5.4 Web Dynpro Java Perspective

The following are the advantages of Web Dynpro Java:

▶ Ensures platform independence with the meta-model approach. When the application is designed, the Web Dynpro framework generates the metadata in the form of XML files, and the system then creates classes at runtime based on the XML.

▸ Minimizes the implementation effort through the declarative programming approach, in which the application can be designed by using drag and drop and configurations of the UI elements, thereby reducing the development time.

▸ Supports a structured design process by applying the model view controller paradigm. Web Dynpro Java enforces the model view controller approach by way of views, controllers, and models.

▸ Easily componentizes and reuses Web Dynpro applications, which leads to a better design and architecture of the overall application.

▸ Provides graphical tools for designing the whole application, including components, applications, windows, views, and other elements.

▸ Provides SAP NetWeaver Developer Infrastructure (NWDI), which acts as the source code repository and build and change management system for Web Dynpro Java code.

Web Dynpro Java was initially hugely successful because of the advantages it offered. However, Web Dynpro Java also has a few disadvantages:

▸ Requires that users have a separate NWDI set up to maintain and build the Web Dynpro Java code. In comparison, the rest of the project's ABAP code is maintained on the ABAP system.

▸ Requires that clients maintain ABAP transports as well as the NWDI transports.

▸ Not integrated with the ABAP Workbench. Consequently, every backend call to the SAP system needs development of a remote function call (RFC).

▸ Does not provide some of the ABAP features, such as ABAP List Viewer (ALV).

Web Dynpro ABAP

Web Dynpro ABAP is the standard SAP UI for developing web applications in the ABAP environment. It provides graphical tools for developing applications and is integrated with the ABAP Workbench (Transaction SE80), as shown in Figure 5.5. Conceptually, Web Dynpro ABAP is similar to Web Dynpro Java and provides similar tools and functions.

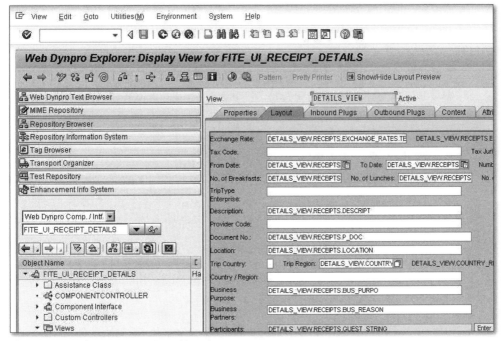

Figure 5.5 Web Dynpro ABAP Workbench

Web Dynpro ABAP is the strategic UI technology of SAP. Because Web Dynpro ABAP came after Web Dynpro Java, it has addressed some of the latter's pain points. The following are advantages of using Web Dynpro ABAP:

▶ The use of declarative and graphical tools significantly reduces the implementation effort. The tools are similar to Web Dynpro Java but are integrated with the ABAP Workbench (Transaction SE80).

▶ There is strict separation between layout and business data because Web Dynpro ABAP follows the model-view-controller (MVC) design pattern.

▶ Like Web Dynpro Java, Web Dynpro ABAP applications can be divided into reusable components, which aids in better application design.

▶ The layout and navigation are easily changed using the Web Dynpro tools.

▶ Stateful applications are supported — that is, if the page is changed, the required data remains intact so that you can access it at any time throughout the entire application context.

▶ Stateless applications are not possible.

▶ Automatic data transport between multiple views and components can be done using the data binding concept.

▶ Many utilities that reduce the development time, such as automatic input check and table filtering and sorting, are provided by the Web Dynpro framework.

▶ Full integration with the ABAP Workbench and ABAP transports means easier maintenance of code.

However, there are some disadvantages of Web Dynpro ABAP, not compared to Web Dynpro Java, but to other Web UI technologies:

▶ The look and feel of a Web Dynpro application is a little restrictive, and it does not allow building a rich UI application. Because Web Dynpro does not allow HTML editing for layout, it's sometimes difficult to achieve an application that appears smooth.

▶ It does not allow for JavaScript support. Because Web Dynpro does not support client-side scripting, client-side validations cannot be done.

Business Server Pages

The Business Server Pages (BSPs) server-side scripting technology is provided by SAP Web AS. BSP is like any other server page technology such as Java Server Pages (JSPs) and Active Server Pages (ASPs). HTML code is written to render the view, and server-side scripting is done in ABAP to make use of the SAP function modules, dictionary objects, and other modules. BSP development tools are integrated with the ABAP Workbench (Transaction SE80), as shown in Figure 5.6.

BSP provides the following advantages over other UI technology that SAP provides, such as Web Dynpro Java, Web Dynpro ABAP, and others:

▶ Fully integrated into the ABAP Workbench, which ensures that a BSP application has access to all of the ABAP objects (such as function modules, dictionary objects, etc.).

▶ Fully integrated into ABAP transports. Transport of BSP objects is done along with the other ABAP objects using the Change and Transport System (CTS/CTS+). This means that no separated infrastructure is needed for BSP development.

▶ Provides a MVC framework that the developer can use.

▶ Provides the ability to develop both stateful and stateless applications, which the Web Dynpro technology cannot. Using Web Dynpro, you can only create a stateful application.

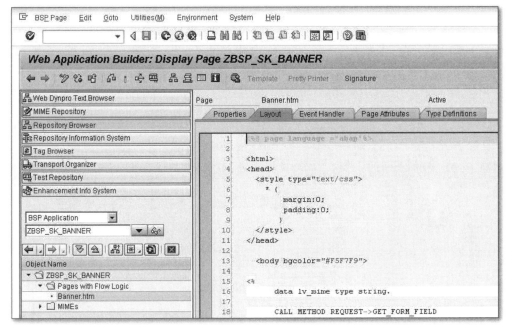

Figure 5.6 BSP Development Workbench

- ▸ Provides better control to the developer over the look and feel of the application due to required HTML development.

- ▸ Allows client-side scripting using JavaScript. This provides the ability to do client-side validations, which is not possible in Web Dynpro.

The following are disadvantages related to BSP:

- ▸ Lacks a graphical tool for automatic code generation. All of the code needs to be written by the developer.

- ▸ No drag and drop mechanism for developing the UI.

- ▸ Longer development time in comparison with Web Dynpro because BSP's lack of tools and wizards.

PDK-Based Components

PDK-based portal components are based on Java and provide an HTML-based UI on the web browser. PDK-based portal components are based on the Java servlet and JSP programming models, and are deployed on the portal as enterprise archive (EAR) files.

SAP NetWeaver Portal 7.3

PDK-based components were earlier deployed as portal archive (PAR) files instead of EAR files. However, beginning with SAP NetWeaver Portal 7.3, all Java-based applications are deployed as EAR files.

PDK-based portal components are developed using NWDS in the Enterprise Portal perspective, as shown in Figure 5.7.

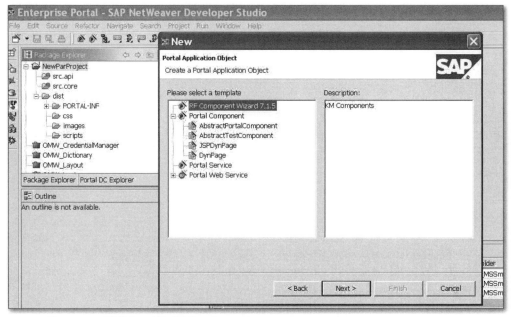

Figure 5.7 PDK-Based Portal Development

The following are advantages of PDK-based portal development:

▶ Follows well established Java servlet and JSP-based development, providing for MVC-based development.

▶ Provides the developer with full control over the UI look and feel because the UI is generated from the HTML code written in the servlets and JSPs.

▶ Allows client-side scripting, such as JavaScript, to be used for client-side validations.

▶ Integrates well into the Portal Runtime (PRT), so you can access the Portal Runtime Container.

▶ Easier to integrate with third-party and open-source libraries and applications because it is based on Java.

The following are disadvantages of PDK-based portal development:

▶ More difficult and time consuming to call the backend ABAP functions because there is no direct integration with the ABAP Workbench.

▶ NWDI is needed for code maintenance and versioning because it's Java code, and no integration with CTS/CTS+ for transporting code. Transport has to be done either manually or by using NWDI.

▶ Development times are usually longer compared to Web Dynpro applications because there are no tools and wizards available for automatic generation of code.

5.2.2 Maintenance and Supportability

When making any decision regarding technology and architecture, keep maintenance and supportability of the implementation in mind. For example, if considering Web Dynpro Java for a new development, remember that it requires maintaining NWDI, which involves a considerable amount of effort.

Also consider the support from SAP for a particular technology. From time to time, SAP phases out technologies that have completed their lifecycles, so customers should be careful of using technologies that are not in SAP's long-term support plan. For example, SAP has said that Web Dynpro Java has reached its maturity level and in future no more features will be added to Web Dynpro Java. This raises questions of long-term supportability from SAP, even though SAP has not confirmed anything about long-term support for Web Dynpro Java. Web Dynpro ABAP, on the other hand, currently has full commitment from SAP and will have more chances for long-term support and future additions of new features from SAP. If you follow the trend within SAP, you will find that most of the products that were earlier based on Web Dynpro Java are being converted to Web Dynpro ABAP. As a general rule, it's always better to take the direction in which SAP is moving.

5.2.3 Designing the Solution

So far, we have discussed the blueprinting requirements and weighed the options for development technology for any custom application. At the end of the blueprinting process, you should understand the overall portal implementation architecture and be able to identify the various integrations needed with the SAP NetWeaver Portal. Figure 5.8 provides a sample of such architecture.

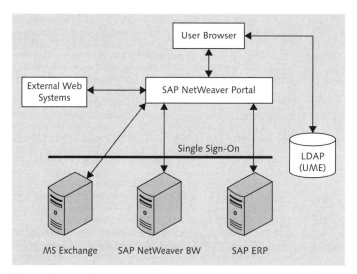

Figure 5.8 Architecture

In Figure 5.8, the SAP NetWeaver Portal connects to SAP ERP and SAP NetWeaver BW for SAP content. It uses an LDAP as the UME store, integrates with a Microsoft Exchange server, and makes use of SSO across all of these systems. After a user logs on to the portal, he can access all of the other systems seamlessly without authenticating again. An important end result of the blueprinting process is the arrival at one such architecture for your implementation.

5.3 Summary

This chapter was dedicated to learning the blueprinting process for an SAP NetWeaver Portal implementation, which complements the discussions of portal architecture, installation, and configuration in previous chapters. You now understand all of the basic information you need to know for implementing a SAP NetWeaver Portal solution. The next chapters will build on this foundation and jump in to actual implementation steps.

This chapter explains the main tasks related to SAP NetWeaver Portal content development and assigning different roles to different users. This chapter also explains how different layouts and themes can be applied to different groups of users.

6 Portal Content Development

In the previous chapters, we have covered preparatory topics related to SAP NetWeaver Portal, such as how to install it, how to perform initial configurations, and how to use the basic administration tools. In Chapter 5, we discussed how to blueprint for SAP NetWeaver Portal implementations and how to decide between various development technologies. All of these steps essentially prepare the SAP NetWeaver Portal and the consultant for starting the portal content development.

SAP NetWeaver Portal content development refers to developing the actual content that will make the framework of the user interface (UI) for the users. In other words, *portal content* defines what a specific user sees when he logs into SAP NetWeaver Portal. There are various types of content that typically need to be developed in an SAP NetWeaver Portal implementation. The following are the most important types of content:

▶ iViews

▶ Pages

▶ Worksets

▶ Roles

▶ Layout templates

▶ Framework pages

▶ Systems

These objects are organized and linked together to provide role-based views to the users. In this chapter, we will discuss these objects and see how they are created and organized in SAP NetWeaver Portal. We will also explain how to translate these objects for multi-lingual implementations.

Another important skill in portal content development is *portal branding*; this refers to aligning the look and feel of SAP NetWeaver Portal with the corporate standards of a company. There are various activities involved in this, from including the company logo and color schemes to using the right fonts and font colors. This chapter will discuss the concept of themes, which are most widely used in adapting the look and feel of SAP NetWeaver Portal. We will see how themes are created, edited, and applied to the user groups.

Portal implementations are also significantly affected by how you integrate SAP NetWeaver Portal with SAP and non-SAP systems—since, in many cases, it will be the single point of access for a wide variety of SAP and non-SAP systems. To this end, we will discuss some of the integration options available with SAP NetWeaver Portal.

Finally, we will wrap up the chapter by discussing the implementation of *business packages,* which are an essential component of portal development. A business package is predefined portal content that provides some functionality in SAP NetWeaver Portal. Although you can also develop your own business packages, SAP provides a lot of predefined business content that uses the functionality of SAP systems. Some of the most widely used examples of business packages are Employee Self-Service (ESS) and Manager Self-Service (MSS).

6.1   Roles, Worksets, Pages, and iViews

Before we get into SAP NetWeaver Portal content development, it is important to understand the different parts of an SAP NetWeaver Portal UI. The layout and content of the UI in SAP NetWeaver Portal is defined by a page called a *framework page*. The framework page defines what components are visible to the user and in what sequence and layout. Figure 6.1 shows the various parts of an SAP NetWeaver Portal framework page. Each part in the framework page is either a page or an iView.

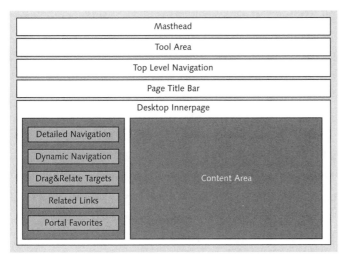

Figure 6.1 Framework Page

The following are the details of the parts that make up the framework page as shown in Figure 6.1:

▶ MASTHEAD
MASTHEAD is for displaying a personalized welcome message and other portal links, such as HELP, PERSONALIZE, and LOG OFF.

▶ TOOLS AREA
TOOLS AREA is generally just below the MASTHEAD and contains a search input field that is used with Knowledge Management (KM). By default, this area is hidden in the framework page and can be made visible from the framework page.

▶ TOP LEVEL NAVIGATION (TLN)
TOP LEVEL NAVIGATION (TLN) displays the top levels of the navigation hierarchy. By default, the hierarchy is two levels deep, which can be changed by configuring the TLN iView. The following are key properties of the TLN:

▶ **Hovering**
In hovering mode, the user can hover over a first-level node, and this node's second-level nodes are displayed.

▶ **Number of display levels**
By default, the TLN shows two root levels of the navigation hierarchy. If this attribute is 0, the TLN is not shown, and the hierarchy is displayed in the

detailed navigation (DTN). If this attribute is 1, the TLN contains one level, and the rest of the navigation hierarchy is displayed in the DTN.

> **Personalize portal page**
> The Portal Content Directory (PCD) location of the personalization portal page. By default, the portal personalization dialog page is used.

▶ PAGE TITLE BAR

PAGE TITLE BAR displays links for page-related functions, such as refreshing the page or opening the page in a new window.

▶ DESKTOP INNERPAGE

While all the preceding components were iViews, the DESKTOP INNERPAGE is a page and is part of the framework page below the PAGE TITLE BAR. DESKTOP INNERPAGE is the container for the actual application content and some other iViews that are listed next.

▶ DETAILED NAVIGATION (DTN)

DETAILED NAVIGATION (DTN) displays the portal navigation hierarchy. By default, it displays the navigation hierarchy from the third level. The first level to be displayed in the DTN iView depends on what is displayed in the TLN. For example, if the TLN displays one level, the DTN should start from the second level. The START AT LEVEL attribute specifies the start level in the DTN.

▶ DYNAMIC NAVIGATION

DYNAMIC NAVIGATION displays navigation iViews assigned to the current content.

▶ DRAG AND RELATE TARGETS

DRAG AND RELATE TARGETS displays a list of iViews related to the current content and for which drag and relate actions can be performed. A content administrator can select iViews and pages to associate with the current content, and drag and relate links to these iViews and pages are displayed in the drag and relate iView.

▶ RELATED LINKS

RELATED LINKS displays a list of iViews related to the current content. A content administrator can select iViews and pages to associate to the current content, and links to these iViews and pages are displayed in the See Also iView (also known as the Related Links iView).

▸ PORTAL FAVORITES

PORTAL FAVORITES displays a list of links to pages and iViews that the user has chosen as favorites.

Now that we have seen the various components of a framework page, let's look at a page from SAP NetWeaver Portal and determine the various components, as shown in Figure 6.2.

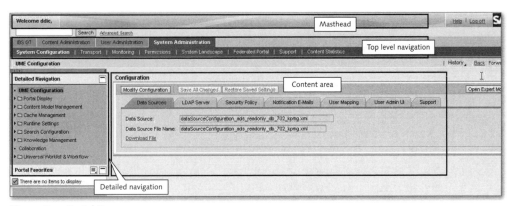

Figure 6.2 Portal Page

Before we go any deeper, it's important to understand the meaning and importance of various object types in SAP NetWeaver Portal. *iViews* are the lowest level of UI building blocks in SAP NetWeaver Portal. An iView typically represents an application window inside SAP NetWeaver Portal. iViews are also referred to as portlets in the portal world. A *page* is a collection of one or more iView(s), arranged in a predefined layout. Various page layouts, such as T layout, one column layout, two columns layout, and so on, have been provided by SAP to choose from. You can also create custom page layouts if needed. A *workset* is a collection of pages used to group together pages relating to similar functionality. A *role* is the highest level portal content object. A role is typically a collection of worksets that are assigned to a role. A role can be assigned to users or user groups and forms the basis for the separation of views between multiple roles. For example, a manager needs to be able to perform personnel actions (promotion, salary change, etc.) on his direct reports. So, all of the pages related to the personnel actions can be combined into one workset, which can be assigned to the manager role and not to the employee role. Thus any user who has the manager role will be able to see the personnel actions workset, and any other employee who is not a manager will not be able to see these pages.

Figure 6.3 shows the linking between various portal content objects.

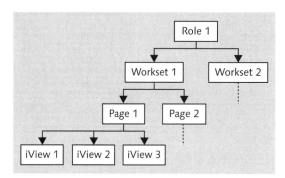

Figure 6.3 PCD Objects Linking

When a PCD object is added to another higher level object—like when an iView is added to a page—there are two ways in which it can be added:

▸ **Delta link**
In this case, only a reference to the object being added is stored. So, in the preceding example, if a change is made in the original iView, it reflects in the page too.

▸ **Copy**
If an iView is added to a page as a copy, a copy of the iView is made and added to the page. In this case, if you make any change to the original iView, it does not reflect in the page.

For creating portal content, log in to SAP NetWeaver Portal and navigate to the CONTENT ADMINISTRATION tab. In the PORTAL CONTENT section, you create all of the SAP NetWeaver Portal content. It is recommended that you create a folder for your project in the PORTAL CONTENT folder. It is also recommended that you create a subfolder inside the project folder for each type of object; for example, iViews, pages, worksets, roles, and so on.

To create a top-level folder for your project, right-click the PORTAL CONTENT folder, and click NEW • FOLDER as shown in the Figure 6.4.

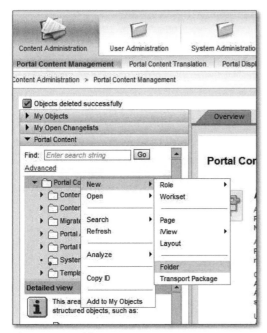

Figure 6.4 Folder Creation

After you enter a name and ID for the folder, the folder is created. For this example, we have created a folder named PROJECTABC. After you have created all of the subfolders too, the folder structure should look like the folder structure in Figure 6.5.

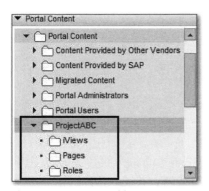

Figure 6.5 Project Folder

Next we'll see how content is developed and assigned to users. We'll start with the bottom-up approach by creating the iView first and then create the page, the workset, and a role.

6.1.1 Creating an iView

To create an iView, go to CONTENT ADMINISTRATION, and right-click the folder where you want to create the iView (in this example, the folder is IVIEWS inside the PROJECTABC folder). Select NEW • IVIEW • IVIEW FROM TEMPLATE. The resulting screen lists all of the SAP-provided templates available for creating the iView (Figure 6.6).

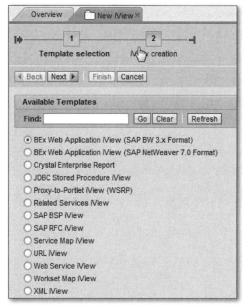

Figure 6.6 iView Creation

For our example, select the URL IVIEW and name the iView "Yahoo". In the next screen, you'll be asked to provide a URL because we have selected a URL IVIEW. Enter the URL as "*http://www.yahoo.com*", click NEXT, and then click FINISH. This creates the iView and gives a success message. You should now see an iView inside your iViews folder in the portal content. You can now right-click the iView and click PREVIEW (see Figure 6.7). This should launch the Yahoo! web page in a new window. This completes the creation of the iView.

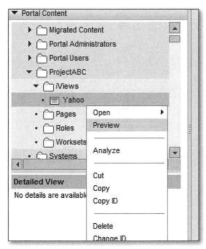

Figure 6.7 iView Preview

6.1.2 Creating a Page

Now let's look at the creation of a page. A page is a collection of one or more iViews arranged in a layout. SAP delivers many predefined layouts; however, in some cases, the layouts provided by SAP may not be sufficient. In these cases, you can create your own custom layouts. To create a page, right-click the folder in which you want to create it (for this example, the folder is PAGES inside the PROJECTABC folder), and select NEW • PAGE. You'll be asked to enter the name (for this example, the name is "News") and ID of the page; enter the information, and click NEXT.

In the next screen, you'll get a selection option between DEFAULT PAGE TEMPLATE and WEB DYNPRO PAGE templates. You should select the WEB DYNPRO PAGE template only if you plan to include only Web Dynpro iViews in this page. In our example scenario, we will select DEFAULT PAGE TEMPLATE because we are going to insert a URL iView into this page. Click NEXT.

Now you'll need to select the page layout. Figure 6.8 shows the page layouts delivered by SAP. The layout selected here will appear in the content area of the framework page. By default, the 1 COLUMN (FULL WIDTH) layout is included in the SELECTED LAYOUTS and also set as the DEFAULT LAYOUT at the bottom of the screen. You can change the layout of the page if needed.

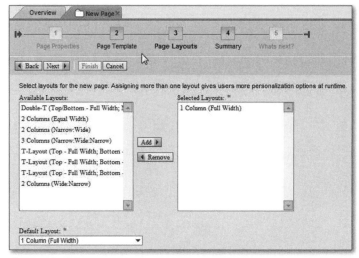

Figure 6.8 Page Layouts

For our example, we will leave the layout as 1 COLUMN (FULL WIDTH), click NEXT, and then click FINISH. This creates the page in the PAGES folder; close the new page wizard by clicking the CLOSE button.

Now that the page has been created, we need to add our iView to the page. To do this, right-click the PAGE in the PORTAL CONTENT, and select OPEN • PAGE. This opens up the PAGE CONTENT AND LAYOUT SETTINGS page. Now with this page open, expand the IVIEWS folder, right-click the iView created previously, and select ADD IVIEW TO PAGE • DELTA LINK as shown in Figure 6.9. This will add the iView YAHOO to the page NEWS. (The difference between a delta link and a copy was discussed earlier in Section 6.1).

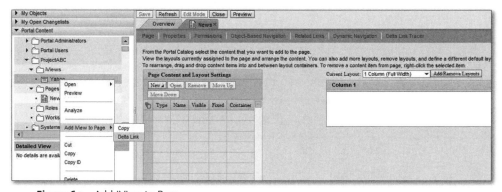

Figure 6.9 Add iView to Page

For this example, we have created one more URL iView named CNN for the website *http://www.cnn.com* and added it to the page we just created. The steps for creating the CNN iView are the same as the steps used for creating the Yahoo iView earlier. After both the iViews are added to the NEWS page, the page will look like Figure 6.10.

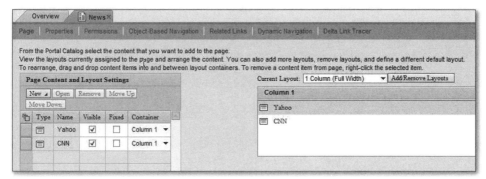

Figure 6.10   Page Layout

On the left side, you can see the iViews added to the page in the shown sequence. Here you can also select an iView from the PAGE CONTENT AND LAYOUT SETTINGS table and choose MOVE UP or MOVE DOWN to change the sequence of the iViews. Alternatively, you can also change the layout of the page from the right side section as shown in Figure 6.10. You can select an iView and drag and drop it to the desired location. After you do this, you will notice that the order of iViews on the left side table has also changed. From here, you also can add another layout to the page and change the default layout of this page. For this, you need to click ADD/REMOVE LAYOUTS BUTTON, which brings up a pop-up window with the available layouts, from which you can choose, add, and set a default layout for the page in the CURRENT LAYOUT section (see Figure 6.11).

Your page creation is complete. Now you can click the PREVIEW button to preview your page. In the preview of the page, you should see a page with two sections, one above the other; the first section should show you the Yahoo! web page, and the second section should show you the CNN web page (Figure 6.12).

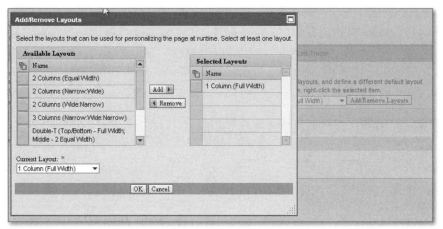

Figure 6.11 Changing the Page Layout

Figure 6.12 Page Preview

As you will notice in the preview, the two iViews in the page are laid out toward the top of the page, not taking the entire area of the web page and showing very little from both the websites. You would now want to increase the heights of both the iViews so you can see more content. To do this, go to the IVIEWS folder, right-click the iView (e.g., YAHOO iView), and select OPEN • PROPERTIES. Then go to the APPEARANCE – SIZE section, and change the FIXED HEIGHT (PIXELS) property to "300". You will need to click the MODIFY PROPERTIES button to change the property values. Save the iView, and repeat the same process for the CNN iView. Now you can preview the page again; you will see that the height of both the iViews has been increased, and you can see more content. Remember, we changed the height property in the iViews, and it is reflected in the page because we used the delta link while adding the iView to the page. Hence, any change we make in the iView is shown in the page too.

Along with the iView height property, another important property—height type—is often used. When you go to the APPEARANCE – SIZE section of the iView properties, you will notice the HEIGHT TYPE property (see Figure 6.13).

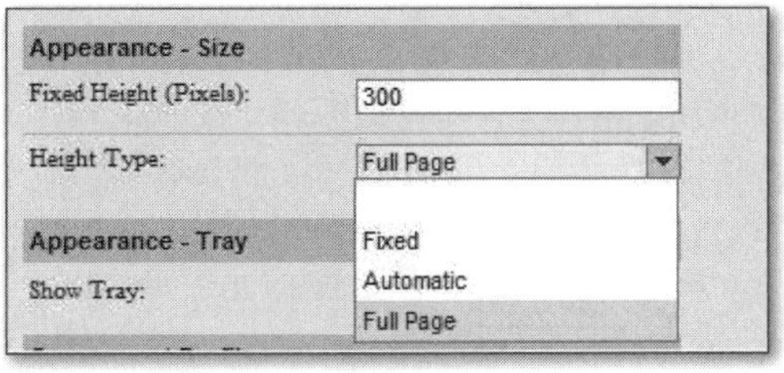

Figure 6.13 Height Type DropDown List

This field has a dropdown list, which has the following values:

▶ FIXED
This property lets you fix the height of an iView on the page in terms of pixels. If the value of this dropdown is set to FIXED, then the pixel value from the property FIXED HEIGHT (PIXELS) is considered, and the height of the iView is set to this pixel value. We saw an example of this earlier by setting the heights of the Yahoo! and CNN iViews to 300 pixels.

▶ AUTOMATIC
When the value of the dropdown is set to AUTOMATIC, the height of the iView is determined by the height of the content within that iView. The iView expands as the height of the content in the iView increases. You would set this value when you want to avoid vertical scrolling within the iView.

▶ FULL PAGE
When the value of the dropdown is set to FULL PAGE, the iView takes up the height of one full page on the browser. In this case, if the height of the content of the iView is bigger than a page, a vertical scrollbar appears within the iView frame.

This completes the discussion on creation of a page and various important aspects associated with it. Next we will discuss the creation of a workset.

6.1.3 Creating a Workset

A workset, as we have seen earlier, is a collection of pages with similar functionality. To create a workset, you select the folder in which you want to create it (in our example, the folder is named WORKSETS), right-click, and select NEW • WORKSET. In the next screen, enter the name and ID of the worksets, and click NEXT and then FINISH. After creating the workset successfully select OPEN THE OBJECT FOR EDITING. This will open the screen where you can add content to the workset. Now go to the page in the portal content that you want to add to the workset; in our example, we will add the NEWS page from our pages folders to the workset. To do this, right-click the page, and select ADD PAGE TO WORKSET • DELTA LINK. Now that the page has been added to the workset, save the entry, and the workset should look like Figure 6.14.

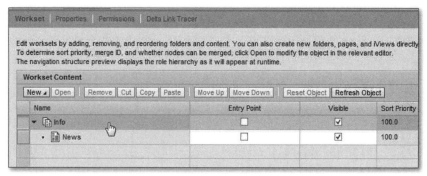

Figure 6.14 Workset Content

6.1.4 Creating a Portal Role

We have created the content that needs to be shown to the user. Now the next step is to assign this content to a user. The only SAP NetWeaver Portal content that can be assigned to a user or user group or a UME role is a portal role.

To create a role, go to the folder where you want to create the role (in our example, the ROLES folder inside the PROJECTABC folder). Right-click the folder, and select NEW • ROLE • FREESTYLE ROLE. Enter the name and ID of the role that you want to create; in our example, we will create a role named "Employee". You will see that the new role has been created in the ROLES folder in the portal catalog. To add our content to this new role, right-click the role EMPLOYEE, and select OPEN • ROLE. Now right-click the workset that you want to add to the role (in our example, the workset is INFO), and select ADD WORKSET TO ROLE • DELTA LINK. After the workset has been added, the role content will look like Figure 6.15.

| Role | Properties | Permissions | Delta Link Tracer | | | | |

Edit roles by adding, removing, and reordering folders and content. You can also create new folders, pages, and iViews directly in the role. To determine sort priority, merge ID, and whether nodes can be merged, click Open to modify the object in the relevant editor. The navigation structure preview displays the role hierarchy as it will appear at runtime.

Role Content

New ▲ | Open | Remove | Cut | Copy | Paste | Edit Connection | Move Up | Move Down | Reset Object
Refresh Object

Name	Entry Point	Visible	Sort Priority	Merge
▼ 🗐 Employee	☑	☑	100.0	Yes*
▼ 🗂 Info	☐	☑	100.0	Yes*
• 🗐 News	☐	☑	100.0	Yes*

Figure 6.15 Role Creation

This role will be assigned to a UME user, user group, or user role, and all of the content assigned to this portal role here will be visible for those users. Before we discuss the role assignment part, let's discuss another important point here. In Figure 6.15, you'll see a column with the ENTRY POINT checkbox. The entry points determine the navigation hierarchy that will be shown to the user. If you select the EMPLOYEE role as the entry point, the navigation hierarchy starts with the EMPLOYEE node. You can also select the WORKSET INFO as the entry point instead of the role EMPLOYEE, in which case, the hierarchy in the portal will start with the workset info. As you select the ENTRY POINT, the navigation hierarchy that will be applicable appears on the right side of the same screen as shown in Figure 6.16.

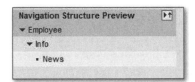

Figure 6.16 Navigation Structure Preview

We will see examples of how changing the entry point affects the navigation hierarchy, but before that, let's first see the assignment of the portal role to a UME user. To do that, go to the USER ADMINISTRATION tab, search for the user that you want to assign this role to, and then select the row from the result table. Details of the user should appear with multiple tabs containing various information about the user. Go to the ASSIGNED ROLES tab, and click MODIFY. The screen will split into two sections: AVAILABLE ROLES and ASSIGNED ROLES (see Figure 6.17).

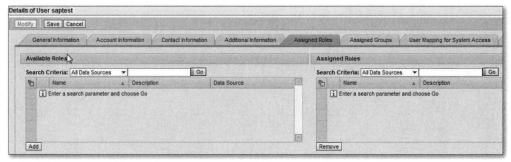

Figure 6.17   Role Assignment

Search for the portal role "Employee" that we created earlier in the AVAILABLE ROLES section (see Figure 6.18)

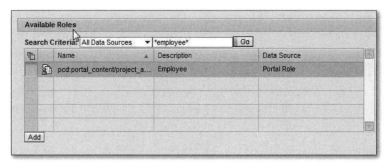

Figure 6.18   Searching a Role

Select the appropriate role, and then click the ADD button. This will add the selected role on the ASSIGNED ROLES side. Now click the SAVE button to the role assignment for the user. The role has been added to the user, so let's now try logging in with the user to which we assigned the role. Go to the SAP NetWeaver Portal URL (*http://<host>:<port>/irj*), and log in with the user to which we assigned the role. You should see the EMPLOYEE role with all of its content assigned to this user, as shown in Figure 6.19.

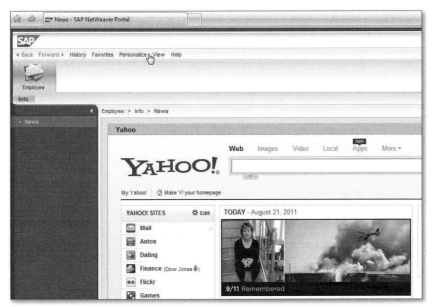

Figure 6.19 Role Assignment

This completes the process of creating the content and assigning the content to users. An important point to note here is that just as we searched for a user and assigned the role to the role, we can also search for a user group or role and assign the SAP NetWeaver Portal role. In that case, the SAP NetWeaver Portal role will be assigned to all of the users that are part of the user group selected or the role selected. To search for a user group or UME role, you need to select the appropriate entry from the SEARCH CRITERIA dropdown list.

Before we complete this section, let's revisit the concept of entry points that we were discussing earlier. Let's go back to the portal catalog and open the EMPLOYEE role. Now in the role hierarchy, uncheck the ENTRY POINT checkbox for the EMPLOYEE role, and select the checkbox for the INFO workset as shown in Figure 6.20.

Role Content

New ▲	Open	Remove	Cut	Copy	Paste	Edit Connection	Move Up	Move Down	Reset Object

Refresh Object

Name	Entry Point	Visible	Sort Priority	Merge	
▼ Employee	☐	☑	100.0	Yes*	
▼ Info	☑	☑	100.0	Yes*	
• News	☐	☑	100.0	Yes*	

Figure 6.20 Entry Point Property

Now, when you log in to the portal again with the user that is assigned the employee role, you will find that the navigation hierarchy does not start with the EMPLOYEE role; it starts with the INFO workset. This is because we assigned the INFO workset as the entry point (see Figure 6.21).

Figure 6.21 Entry Point Change

6.2 Portal Content Translation

When you are implementing an SAP NetWeaver Portal that will be used by multiple countries, you will probably need to make your content multi-lingual. SAP NetWeaver Portal provides tools for translating iViews, pages, roles, worksets, etc. You can find the tools related to translation by navigating to CONTENT ADMINISTRATION • PORTAL CONTENT TRANSLATION (Figure 6.22).

Portal content translation is performed in the following two areas:

▶ TRANSLATION WORKLIST COORDINATION
This is used for translation worklist creation and adding content.

▶ WORKLIST TRANSLATION
This area is for the actual translation.

The steps for translation are shown in Figure 6.23.

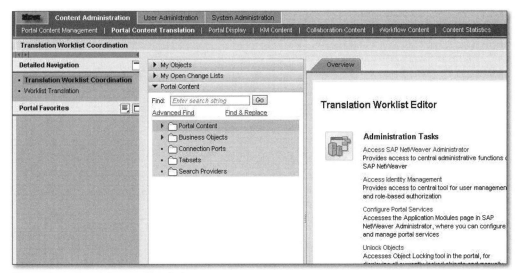

Figure 6.22 Portal Content Translation

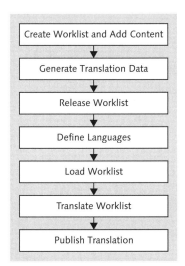

Figure 6.23 Translation Steps

Next we discuss the details of how portal content translation worklists are created and how translation is performed. For the example scenario (Figure 6.24), we will use an employee role that has a News workset. The News workset has a News page that holds a Company News iView.

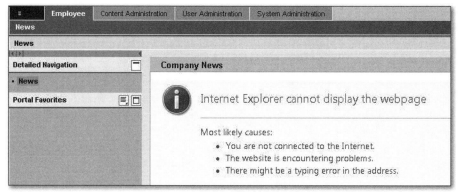

Figure 6.24 Example Content for Translation

6.2.1 Creating a Translation Worklist

To create the translation worklist, follow these steps:

1. Navigate to CONTENT ADMINISTRATION • PORTAL CONTENT TRANSLATION • TRANSLATION WORKLIST COORDINATION.

2. Right click on the folder where you want to create the translation worklist and choose NEW • TRANSLATION WORKLIST as shown in Figure 6.25.

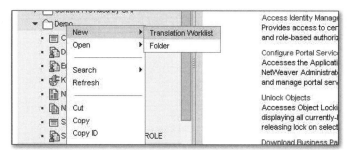

Figure 6.25 Creating a Translation Worklist

3. Enter the properties for the translation worklist, such as name, ID, etc. Click NEXT and then click FINISH as shown in Figure 6.26.

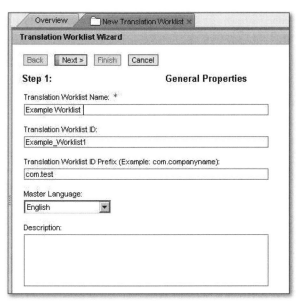

Figure 6.26 Translation Worklist Creation

6.2.2 Adding Content and Releasing a Translation Worklist

Now let's add the content we want to translate. With the translation worklist open, right-click on each element of portal content that you want to translate and choose Add Object to Translation Worklist (Figure 6.27). You can also add all objects of a folder at once.

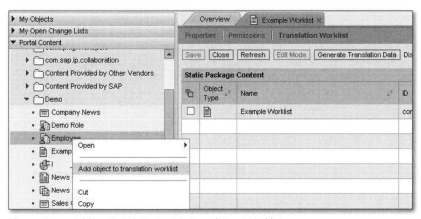

Figure 6.27 Adding Portal Content to Translation Worklist

After you have added all the objects to the translation worklist, you are ready to generate the translation data. In the translation worklist, click on the GENERATE TRANSLATION DATA button. This prepares the worklist for translation. Next, you have to release the worklist so that it can be translated; click on the RELEASE FOR TRANSLATION button located toward the bottom of the translation worklist (Figure 6.28).

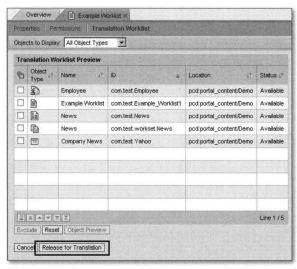

Figure 6.28 Releasing Translation Worklist

You will get a success message saying the worklist has been released for translation, as shown in Figure 6.29. At this point, you cannot add new objects to the translation worklist.

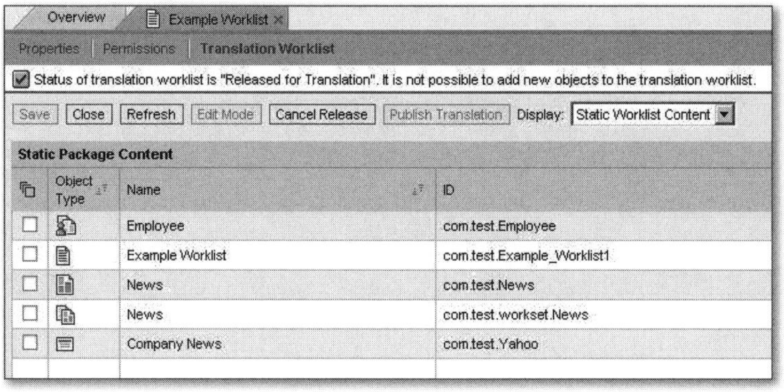

Figure 6.29 Translation Worklist Released

6.2.3   Loading and Translating a Translation Worklist

The worklist is now prepared for translation, so the next step is to translate the objects. Follow these steps:

1. Navigate to CONTENT ADMINISTRATION • PORTAL CONTENT TRANSLATION • WORKLIST TRANSLATION.

2. Search for the translation worklist that you just created and select the worklist from the search result, as shown in Figure 6.30.

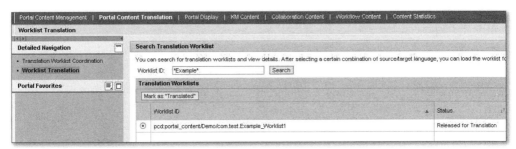

Figure 6.30   Selecting a Worklist for Translation

3. Toward the bottom of the same screen, you will see a section to select the source and target languages. Select the source language as ENGLISH and a target language (FRENCH, for this example) and click on the LOAD FOR TRANSLATION button. Figure 6.31 shows the source and target language selection screen.

Figure 6.31   Loading the Worklist for Translation

4. In the next screen (Figure 6.32), select one row at a time and enter the target text in the TARGET TEXT section at the bottom. The target texts appear in the TARGET TEXT column above.

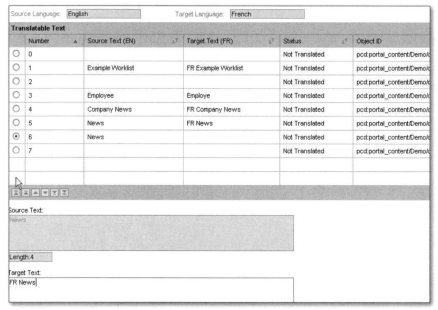

Figure 6.32 Translating the Text

5. When you are done, save the translation and click on CLOSE. This will bring you back to the worklist search screen.

6. Select your worklist and click on the MARK AS TRANSLATED button. You will see the status of the worklist change to TRANSLATED, as shown in Figure 6.33.

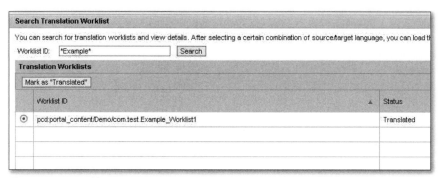

Figure 6.33 Worklist Status Set to Translated

6.2.4 Publishing and Testing a Translation Worklist

The translation has now been completed, but it will not be visible to users until you publish the translation. To do this, go back to the TRANSLATION WORKLIST COORDINATION area and open your worklist. Click on the PUBLISH TRANSLATION button (Figure 6.34).

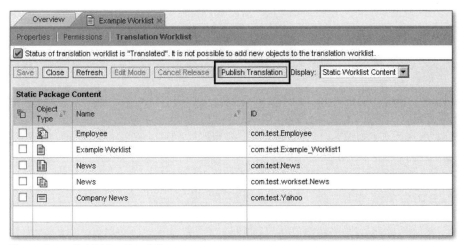

Figure 6.34 Publishing Translation

Close the translation worklist after publishing the translation; the translation process has now completed.

Next, you need to test the translation. Change the browser language to the target language you had selected (French, for this example). To change the language for Internet Explorer, go to TOOLS • INTERNET OPTIONS • GENERAL and click on LANGUAGES. Add the French language and make sure that this is the first language in the sequence (Figure 6.35).

After changing the browser language to French, load the portal page again. You should now see the translated content in the target language, as shown in Figure 6.36.

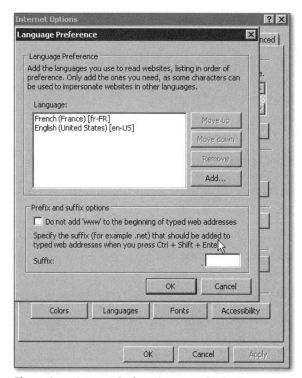

Figure 6.35 Internet Explorer Language Settings

Figure 6.36 Translated Portal Content

6.3 Portal Branding

Companies that implement SAP NetWeaver Portal will want to customize the look and feel of SAP NetWeaver Portal so that it aligns with their corporate branding guidelines. Branding of SAP NetWeaver Portal can be done in various places; the most important are the logon page, the framework page, and the themes. These are the types of branding customizations that are most frequently needed by corporations. In this section, we will look at how to perform these types of customizations.

6.3.1 Logon Page

There are two levels of logon page customization: changing just the branding image on the logon page, and revamping the whole logon page to look completely different. Here we will look at both levels.

Changing the Logon Page Branding Image

To change the logon page branding page logo, log in to the SAP NetWeaver Administrator page by going to *http://<host>:<port>/nwa*, where *<host>* is the hostname of the SAP NetWeaver Portal server, and *<port>* is the HTTP port of the SAP NetWeaver Portal server.

Once inside SAP NetWeaver Administrator, go to CONFIGURATION • AUTHENTICATION AND SINGLE SIGN-ON. Then click PROPERTIES (Figure 6.37) to bring up the screen where you can modify the UME properties.

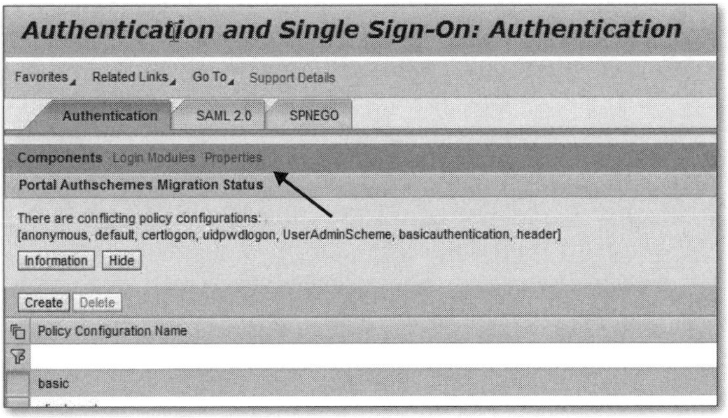

Figure 6.37 Link to UME Properties

Click the MODIFY button to enable the fields for changing the parameter values. On this screen, you will find the property PATH OR URL TO THE BRANDING IMAGE (UME.LOGON.BRANDING_IMAGE). This property should be pointed to the URL of the image that you want to use on the logon page; this can be a URL on the same SAP NetWeaver Portal server or an external URL. If you use an external URL, make sure that the URL will be accessible for the client browsers; the browser will make a request to this URL directly, without going through SAP NetWeaver Portal.

As an example, let's try to replace the default branding image of SAP NetWeaver Portal to an image from the *google.com* website. Right-click the image on Google's website, and click PROPERTIES to get the URL of the image.

Next, configure this URL as the logon branding image for the SAP NetWeaver Portal. On the UME PROPERTIES page, change the value of the PATH OR URL TO THE BRANDING IMAGE (UME.LOGON.BRANDING_IMAGE) field to the URL of the image from Google's website as shown in Figure 6.38.

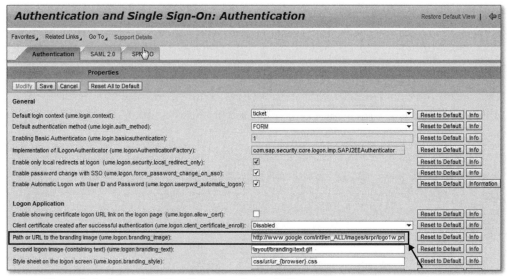

Figure 6.38 Logon Page Branding Image Customization

Now save your changes and try to access SAP NetWeaver Portal again. You will see that the branding image on the logon page has been replaced by the image from Google's website (Figure 6.39).

Figure 6.39 Logon Page Branding Image Customized

Changing the branding image on the logon page did not require any coding, just a configuration change. However, sometimes the changes needed in the logon page are much more complex than just changing the branding image. In such cases, you will need to do some development in your NWDS. Let's look at that scenario next.

Customizing the Logon Page via NWDS

Customizing the logon page is much more involved and requires development using NWDS. This explanation assumes that you have NWDS installed and are familiar with it. If you don't have NWDS, visit the following link for downloading and installation instructions:

https://nwds.sap.com/swdc/downloads/updates/netweaver/nwds/nw/730/

To customize the logon page, you must first get the WAR file delivered by SAP for the logon page, import it in the NWDS, and then customize it.

> ### PAR and WAR Files in SAP NetWeaver 7.3
>
> Until SAP NetWeaver 7.3, portal applications were deployed as PAR (portal archive) files, which is an SAP proprietary format for deploying web applications on SAP NetWeaver Portal. But in the SAP NetWeaver 7.3 version, SAP no longer supports the PAR format, in favor of the web archive (WAR) and enterprise archive (EAR) formats, which are standard Java EE formats used in the Java world. SAP also provides a utility called the PAR Migration Tool that you can use to migrate your existing PAR applications to run on the SAP NetWeaver Portal 7.3 version. You can access this tool by going to SYSTEM ADMINISTRATION • SUPPORT • PAR MIGRATION TOOL (Figure 6.40).

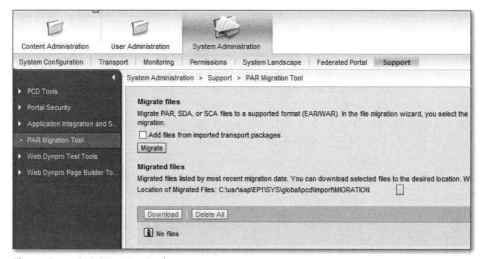

Figure 6.40 PAR Migration Tool

In our example, the WAR file is available because it is part of the portal installation; as such, we don't need to use the PAR Migration Tool for customizing the logon page. You can find the logon page WAR file from the file system of the SAP NetWeaver portal server at the following path:

<drive>:\usr\sap\EP1\J00\j2ee\cluster\apps\sap.com\com.sap.security.core.logon\ servlet_jsp\logon_ui_resources

In this location, you will find the file named *tc~sec~ume~logon~ui.war*. You need this WAR file to customize the logon page. Now start NWDS, and import the WAR file by going to FILE • IMPORT • WEB • WAR FILE.

Select the WAR file that you want to import from your local file system (Figure 6.41).

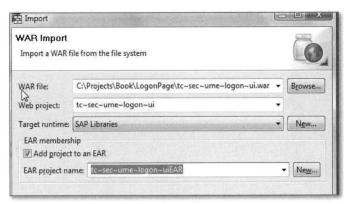

Figure 6.41 Logon WAR File Import

Because the only format of application that can be deployed in a Java EE application server is the EAR format, we also need to create an EAR project. To do this, check the ADD PROJECT TO AN EAR checkbox, and specify a name for the EAR project in the EAR PROJECT NAME field as shown in Figure 6.41. NWDS suggests a name base on the WAR project name, so you can either leave the default or change it to something else. Click FINISH to create both the WAR and EAR projects in NWDS. The WAR project depends on the JAR (Java Archive) file *tc~sec~ume~logon~logic_api. jar*. You can locate this JAR file from this location:

<drive>:\usr\sap\EP1\J00\j2ee\cluster\apps\sap.com\com.sap.security.core.logon\ servlet_jsp\logon_app\root\WEB-INF\lib

Copy this file to the *WebContent\WEB-INF\lib* folder of the imported WAR application. Also, add this JAR file to the Java build path of the WAR application. To do this, right-click the WAR project, and select BUILD PATH • CONFIGURE BUILD PATH. This will bring up the JAVA BUILD PATH screen. On this screen, go to the LIBRARIES tab, and click ADD EXTERNAL JARS. Now select the JAR file *tc~sec~ume~logon~logic_api. jar* from the local file system, and click on the ADD button. After adding the JAR file, the JAVA BUILD PATH screen will look like Figure 6.42.

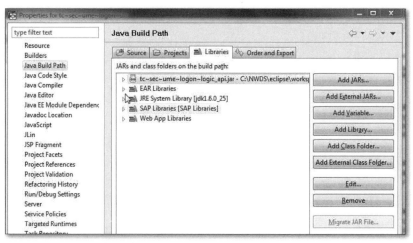

Figure 6.42   Java Build Path Screen

Now make sure that you are in the Java EE perspective, and expand the WAR project. Expand the WEBCONTENT folder, and double-click the file LOGONPAGE.JSP. This is the JSP file that renders the logon page. You can now change the layout of the logon page by changing the JSP file (Figure 6.43).

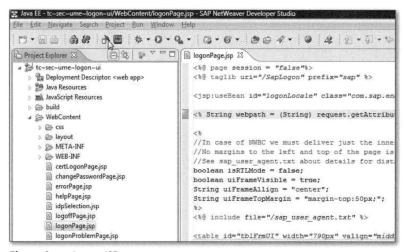

Figure 6.43   Logon JSP

After you are done changing the layout and look and feel of the JSP, right-click the WAR project, and select JAVA EE TOOLS • UPDATE EAR LIBRARIES. This will make sure that the compiled WAR is updated in the EAR project so that when you generate the EAR file, it picks up the latest changes that you made in the *logonPage.jsp* file.

Now expand the EAR project, and double-click the APPLICATION-J2EE-ENGINE.XML file. This file is the SAP-specific deployment descriptor of an EAR application. When this file opens, enter a name in the PROVIDER NAME field, which is typically the domain name of the company for which this is being developed. For our example, let's name it "test.com".

Next we need to add a reference to the standard application *com.sap.security.core. logon*. To do this, right-click REFERENCES, select ADD, and then click the CREATE NEW button. Add the following entries in the fields that are provided:

▶ REFERENCE TARGET: com.sap.security.core.logon

▶ REFERENCE TYPE: hard

▶ REFERENCE TARGET TYPE: application

▶ PROVIDER NAME: sap.com

The *application-j2ee-engine.xml* file should now look like Figure 6.44.

Figure 6.44 application-j2ee-engine.xml File

Figure 6.44 represents an easier UI for the XML file that gets generated in the background. If you select the SOURCE tab, you will be able to see the actual XML source, which should look like Listing 6.1.

```xml
<?xml version="1.0" encoding="UTF-8" standalone="no"?>
<application-j2ee-engine
    xmlns:xsi="http://www.w3.org/2001/XMLSchema-instance"
    xsi:noNamespaceSchemaLocation="application-j2ee-engine.xsd">
    <reference
        reference-type="hard">
        <reference-target
            provider-name="sap.com"
            target-type="application">com.sap.security.core.logon
        </reference-target>
    </reference>
    <provider-name>test.com</provider-name>
</application-j2ee-engine>
```

Listing 6.1 application-j2ee-engine.xml file

After configuring the *application-j2ee-engine.xml*, you need to configure another deployment descriptor: *application.xml*. The *application.xml* file is a deployment descriptor provided by the Java EE standards, so any Java EE-compliant application needs to support the *application.xml* deployment descriptor.

Double-click the *application.xml* file from the WAR project to open the editor for this XML file. Go to the MODULES tab, and select the WAR module TC~SEC~UME~LOGON~UI. WAR. Change the CONTEXT ROOT field value to a new name, for example, "test_logon". The *application.xml* should now look like Figure 6.45.

Again, the screenshot shown in Figure 6.45 is just an easier UI for the XML file; the actual source of *application.xml* can be seen by going to the SOURCE tab. The source should now look like Listing 6.2.

```xml
<?xml version="1.0" encoding="UTF-8" standalone="no"?>
<application
    xmlns="http://java.sun.com/xml/ns/j2ee"
    xmlns:xsi="http://www.w3.org/2001/XMLSchema-instance"
    id="Application_ID"
    version="1.4"
    xsi:schemaLocation="http://java.sun.com/xml/ns/j2ee http://java.sun.
com/xml/ns/j2ee/application_1_4.xsd">
    <display-name>tc~sec~ume~logon~uiEAR</display-name>
```

```
<module
    id="WebModule_1313956418913">
    <web>
        <web-uri>tc~sec~ume~logon~ui.war</web-uri>
        <context-root>/test_logon</context-root>
    </web>
</module>
</application>
```

Listing 6.2 application.xml file

Figure 6.45 application.xml

All of the development needed for the logon page customization has been completed. Now it's time to build and deploy the application. Right-click the EAR project, and select EXPORT • SAP EAR FILE. This will create a deployable EAR file that will appear in the hierarchy of the EAR project. Right-click the EAR file, and select RUNS AS • RUN ON SERVER. Choose a server on which you want to deploy, and then enter the credentials to be able to deploy. A success message appears after successful deployment.

After the customized logon screen application has been deployed, you need to tell the SAP NetWeaver Portal server to use the new application for the logon screen instead of the SAP-delivered logon application. You do that by changing a UME property with the following steps:

1. Log in to SAP NetWeaver Administrator as described earlier in this section.

2. Go to CONFIGURATION • AUTHENTICATION AND SINGLE SIGN ON.

3. Click PROPERTIES (as shown earlier in Figure 6.37) to bring up the screen where you can modify the UME properties.

4. Click the MODIFY button to open the properties in edit mode.

5. Change the property UME.LOGON.APPLICATION.UI_RESOURCES_ALIAS to point to the customized application that you deployed (Figure 6.46): UME.LOGON.APPLICATION.UI_RESOURCES_ALIAS = /TEST_LOGON.

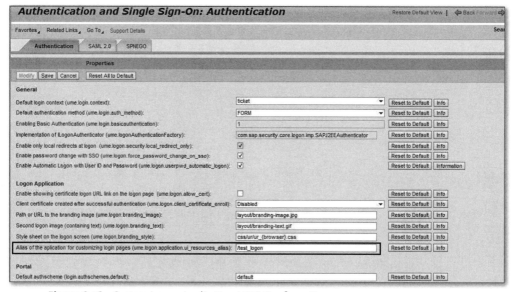

Figure 6.46 Custom Logon Application UME Configuration

This will make the SAP NetWeaver Portal launch the custom application with the customized look and feel instead of the SAP-delivered application. You will need to restart the server for the change to take effect.

6.3.2 Framework Page

As we have seen earlier, a framework page is the overall container of all the iViews and pages that get rendered on a web page. SAP provides standard framework pages that you can copy and customize for your own implementations. Framework pages are assigned to users by assigning them to a portal desktop, as we will see later in Section 6.3.4. You will find the framework pages provided by SAP in the PCD in this location: PORTAL CONTENT • CONTENT PROVIDED BY SAP • END USER CONTENT • STANDARD PORTAL USERS. SAP provides the following types of framework pages:

▶ **AJAX framework page**
The AJAX framework page is a new framework page that SAP has started providing with the newer versions of SAP NetWeaver Portal. This page is AJAX based and gives an enhanced user experience. The AJAX framework page is implemented using JavaScript, which makes use of asynchronous communication between the client and server and moves activities to the client side, giving users a flicker-free experience on the web pages. The AJAX framework page is located in PORTAL CONTENT • CONTENT PROVIDED BY SAP • END USER CONTENT • STANDARD PORTAL USERS • AJAX FRAMEWORK CONTENT • AJAX FRAMEWORK PAGE. Figure 6.47 shows the contents of the AJAX framework page.

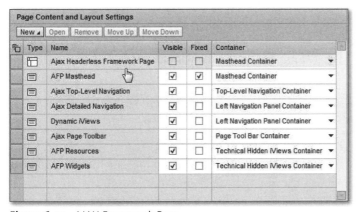

Figure 6.47 AJAX Framework Page

The following are the various components of the AJAX framework page as shown in Figure 6.47:

▶ AJAX HEADERLESS FRAMEWORK PAGE: The headerless framework page supports the headerless navigation.

▶ AFP MASTHEAD: This is the masthead of the AJAX framework page.

▶ AJAX TOP-LEVEL NAVIGATION: This is the top level navigation iView that is part of the AJAX framework page.

▶ AJAX DETAILED NAVIGATION: This is the detailed navigation iView that is laid out on the left side and gives navigation to the next level in the hierarchy after top level navigation.

▶ DYNAMIC IVIEWS: This is the iView for dynamic navigation for the AJAX framework page. In the AJAX framework page, the dynamic navigation iView opens in a new window next to the navigation pane.

▶ AJAX PAGE TOOLBAR: The AJAX page toolbar is the iView that provides the breadcrumb navigation for the pages.

▶ AFP WIDGETS: The AFP widgets iView generates a widget library in JavaScript. This library can be used by other iViews on the client side.

▶ **Classic Framework Page**
This is the standard framework page that SAP has provided since its earlier versions. Figure 6.48 shows the classic framework page.

With SAP NetWeaver 7.3, SAP has made the AJAX framework page the default framework page in SAP NetWeaver Portal. You can easily set the rules regarding which framework page should be loaded for which user or user group, as you'll see later. However, if you want to see the SAP NetWeaver Portal in the classic framework page without changing the rules, you can go to *http://<host>:<port>/ irj/portal/classic.*

With SAP NetWeaver Portal 7.3, SAP has introduced a new tool called the Framework Page Configuration tool, which you can use to customize the framework pages (Figure 6.49). You can launch the Framework Page Configuration tool by going to CONTENT ADMINISTRATION • PORTAL DISPLAY • FRAMEWORK PAGE CONFIGURATION.

Figure 6.48 Classic Framework Page

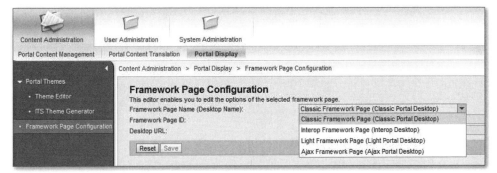

Figure 6.49 Framework Page Configuration

As you can see in Figure 6.49, the Framework Page Configuration tool gives you an option to select the framework page that you want to customize. Here you can customize the SAP-delivered CLASSIC FRAMEWORK PAGE and AJAX FRAMEWORK PAGE, as well as create your own custom framework pages by copying and modifying the predelivered pages. When you select a framework page, you are given the various properties that you can customize. For example, if you choose CLASSIC FRAMEWORK PAGE, you will be able to customize the following properties (Figure 6.50):

- ▶ MASTHEAD
  - ▶ LOG ON/LOG OFF
  - ▶ ADD TO PORTAL FAVORITES
  - ▶ NEW SESSION
  - ▶ PERSONALIZE
  - ▶ HELP
  - ▶ TITLE
  - ▶ DESKTOP TITLE
- ▶ TOOLBAR
  - ▶ BREADCRUMB
  - ▶ HISTORY LIST
  - ▶ ADD TO BROWSER FAVORITES OPTION
  - ▶ BACK/FORWARD LINKS
- ▶ TOP LEVEL NAVIGATION
  - ▶ NUMBER OF LEVELS IN TLN

Figure 6.50 Configuring Masthead with Framework Page Configuration Tool

Similarly, you can customize properties for the other framework pages in the Framework Page Configuration tool.

6.3.3 Themes

In most of the SAP NetWeaver Portal implementations, customers would want to adapt the look and feel of the portal. An important part of the look and feel is the color combination used for various UI elements, font sizes, images, and so on. SAP

NetWeaver Portal themes defines these characteristics for the portal UI elements. SAP provides a Theme Editor to edit the theme characteristics. You can launch the Theme Editor by going to CONTENT ADMINISTRATION • PORTAL DISPLAY • THEME EDITOR. When you go to the Theme Editor, you will see the SAP-delivered themes as shown in Figure 6.51.

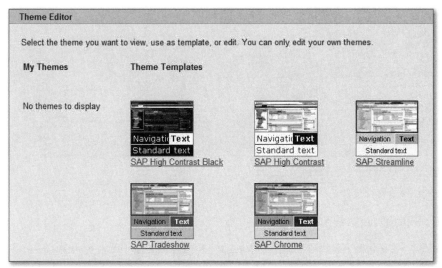

Figure 6.51 Theme Editor

You cannot change an SAP-delivered theme, but you can copy an SAP-delivered theme, save it as a custom theme, and make changes. When you open an SAP-delivered theme, you will see the SAVE AS button. You can use this option to save a theme in your customer name and use this theme for storing all of your changes (Figure 6.52). By default, all themes are stored in the PORTAL CONTENT • THEMES folder, so your newly created theme should be saved there as well.

As shown in Figure 6.52, all of the UI elements are listed on the left side, and you can change the properties of the selected UI element on the right side. There is also a section to preview the changes you make to the theme; the changes are reflected immediately in the preview area.

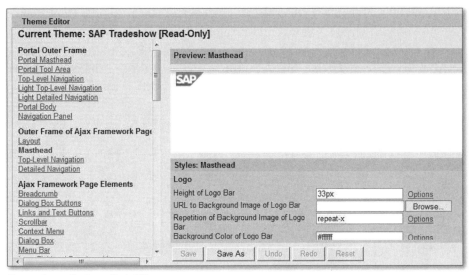

Figure 6.52 Saving a Portal Theme

6.3.4 Portal Desktop

The SAP NetWeaver Portal desktop defines the structural layout as well as the look and feel on a page on SAP NetWeaver Portal. A portal desktop is a combination of a framework page and a theme. The portal desktop can be assigned to users, user groups, or roles and can be used to differentiate between the views of different users. Assume, for example, a company has many divisions, and each division wants to have a different color combination on the pages and a different masthead showing a division-specific banner. You can create multiple themes and multiple framework pages for those divisions and then assign them to different portal desktops. You can then assign a different portal desktop to each user of each division.

To create a portal desktop, go to SYSTEM ADMINISTRATION • SYSTEM CONFIGURATION • PORTAL DISPLAY • DESKTOPS & DISPLAY RULES. Then go to the folder in which you want to create the portal desktop. Right-click the folder, and select NEW • PORTAL DESKTOP. Enter the name and ID, and click NEXT. You need to select a framework page to add to the portal desktop. Navigate to the framework page in the PORTAL CONTENT list on the left side, then right-click, and select ADD FRAMEWORK PAGE TO PORTAL DESKTOP (Figure 6.53).

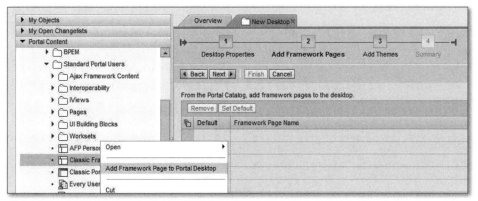

Figure 6.53 Add Framework Page to Portal Desktop

For this example, let's add the classic framework page. Click NEXT, and now you need to add a theme to the portal desktop. Navigate to the theme that you want to add to the portal desktop, right-click, and select ADD THEME TO PORTAL DESKTOP. Click NEXT and then FINISH, and your new portal desktop is saved.

Now when you open the portal desktop for editing, you will see that it contains the framework page and the theme that you added, as shown in Figure 6.54.

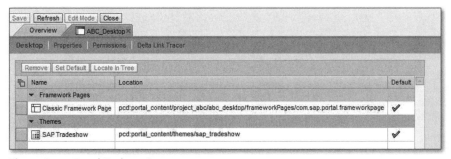

Figure 6.54 Portal Desktop Components

You can add multiple framework pages and multiple themes to a portal desktop. But at any one time, you can have only one framework page and one theme as default. To change the default framework page or the default theme, select the row, and click the SET DEFAULT button. You will see a tick mark in the DEFAULT column changing as you change the default framework page or theme.

Now that the portal desktop has been created, the only step remaining is to assign the portal desktop to a user. To do this, go to SYSTEM ADMINISTRATION • SYSTEM CONFIGURATION • PORTAL DISPLAY • DESKTOPS & DISPLAY RULES, and then go to PORTAL CONTENT • PORTAL ADMINISTRATORS • SUPER ADMINISTRATORS • MASTER RULE COLLECTION. Right-click the master rule collection, and select OPEN • RULE COLLECTION. This brings up the rule collection screen as shown in Figure 6.55.

Figure 6.55 Master Rule Collection

To add a new rule, click ADD IF EXPRESSION. Add this rule:

```
IF User = saptest
THEN Portal Desktop = pcd:portal_content/every_user/general/
defaultDesktop
```

Save the rule by clicking the SAVE button. After saving, the rule collection should look like Figure 6.56.

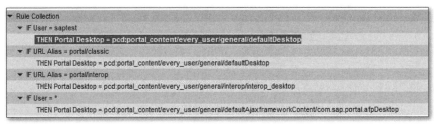

Figure 6.56 Master Rule Collection Change

This completes the portal desktop assignment to a user. Now if you log in with the user to which you assigned the new portal desktop, you will see that the framework page and theme assigned to this portal desktop apply to the user.

6.4   Integrating SAP and Non-SAP Content

Now that you are familiar with the basic functionality of SAP NetWeaver Portal, you know that its main purpose is to integrate various SAP and non-SAP content, thereby providing a single and seamless point of entry to a company's information resources. Using SAP NetWeaver Portal, content from different internal and external sources can be combined in one central access point, the portal browser.

You can integrate SAP and non-SAP systems with SAP NetWeaver Portal in two different ways:

▶ Content integration

▶ Single sign-on (SSO)

These two levels of integration ensure that users are able to access all of the internal, external, SAP, and non-SAP applications (content integration) from one point of access without having to log in to each system separately (SSO).

> **SSO**
>
> We do not discuss SSO in this section, since it is covered in Chapter 4; instead, we focus on just content integration.

Content integration can be done at the following levels:

▶ **Full page integration**
In this type of integration, the web page of the third party is fully integrated with SAP NetWeaver Portal. It can be displayed inside an iView, such as a URL iView, or a link can be provided in SAP NetWeaver Portal that provides a redirection to the third-party system.

▶ **Custom iView integration**
In this type of integration, a custom iView is developed that calls the third-party system to get and send data. This type of iView can take full advantage of the SAP NetWeaver platform, including security, user management, and so on.

▶ **Repository manager integration**
In this type of integration, an online connector integrates repositories such as file systems, web servers, WebDAV servers, Lotus Notes, and Microsoft Exchange Server.

▶ **Knowledge Management integration**
This type of integration makes use of the Knowledge Management (KM) services and integrates external services into the KM services framework.

Figure 6.57 shows the various ways in which SAP system content can be integrated with SAP NetWeaver Portal. Most of the SAP applications can be integrated with SAP NetWeaver Portal by means of iView integration.

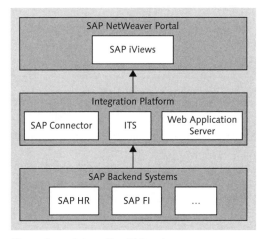

Figure 6.57 Integrating SAP systems

There are three ways in which SAP backend systems are most commonly integrated with SAP NetWeaver Portal:

▶ **SAP Connector**
An example of SAP connection is the SAP Java Connector (SAP JCo). It's possible to develop SAP NetWeaver Portal applications that use SAP JCo calls to interact with SAP systems by making remote function calls (RFCs). These SAP NetWeaver Portal applications can then be exposed via an iView and rendered to the user. Such applications can take full advantage of the user management, security, and SSO features of SAP NetWeaver Portal.

▶ **Internet Transaction Server (ITS)**
Using ITS, SAP transactions can be directly accessed from SAP NetWeaver Portal. SAP GUI for HTML can be used for rendering SAP backend transactions in HTML and can be accessed from SAP NetWeaver Portal.

▶ **Web Application Server**
Web Application Server (Web AS) is part of the backend ABAP stack and provides the runtime for Web Dynpro ABAP and Business Server Pages (BSP) applications. SAP NetWeaver Portal provides iView templates for creating Web Dynpro ABAP and BSP iViews and can connect to the Web AS to access these applications. These applications execute inside SAP NetWeaver Portal iFrames and take advantage of the SSO feature provided by SAP.

Non-SAP content is integrated into SAP NetWeaver Portal in a variety of ways. When integrating a non-SAP web-based application with SAP NetWeaver Portal, we need to look at the capabilities of the external system. In general, there are various ways to achieve integration with non-SAP systems:

▶ **Web Services**
If the external system does not have a web interface and it supports Web Services, you can create portal applications that call the Web Services for accessing the remote functions. These applications can then be wrapped as an iView on SAP NetWeaver Portal.

▶ **URL iView**
This is the most common form of integration with non-SAP web-based applications.

▶ **Link**
Links to the external system can be provided on SAP NetWeaver Portal that redirect the users from SAP NetWeaver Portal to the third-party system.

6.5 Implementing Business Packages

A *business package* refers to predefined SAP NetWeaver Portal content that can be deployed in the portal; it is a collection of iViews, pages, worksets, and roles that provide a specific functionality. SAP provides many business packages that can be deployed and used out of the box or can be customized to suit customer requirements; for example, Employee Self-Services (ESS), Manager Self-Services (MSS). Because business packages already include most of the functionality needed in the specific application areas, it greatly speeds up the implementation process for the customers.

Business packages are normally provided by SAP in the SCA (software component archive) formats. You can deploy the business package using the deployment tool. Once deployed, the portal content related to the business package will appear in the PCD. You can copy the roles provided by the business package to your customer folder and start making changes. You can then assign these modified portal roles to your user groups as appropriate.

You can see a list of available business packages by going to the PREDEFINED PORTAL CONTENT INTEGRATION page on SAP Developer Network (SDN) at *http://www.sdn. sap.com/irj/sdn/portal-content-portfolio*. Here you can see business packages provided by SAP as well as those provided by other vendors (Figure 6.58).

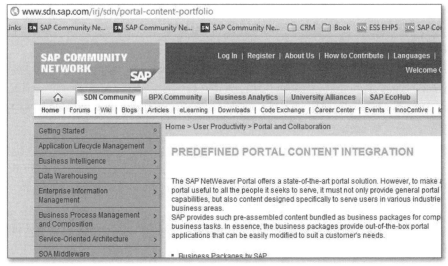

Figure 6.58 Portal Content Portfolio

To install and configure business packages, follow these steps:

1. Download the business package from the SAP Service Marketplace and deploy it on SAP NetWeaver Portal.

2. Configure the system landscape in SAP NetWeaver Portal for the backend systems that the business package will access.

3. Assign the portal roles delivered by the business package to the desired users or user groups.

4. Configure the backend system as needed for the business package (the specific business package vendor normally provides the documentation relating to all of the configurations needed for the business package to work).

In general, the business packages are downloaded and installed using SAP Solution Manager. For specific steps regarding a business package you should refer to the documentation provided by the business package vendor.

6.6   Summary

Creation of portal content forms the core of the portal implementation process for any SAP NetWeaver Portal project. In this chapter, we discussed in detail various steps for creating iViews, pages, worksets, and roles, along with some of the finer points to keep in mind when developing the portal content. Then we looked at the creation of framework pages and portal desktops and how these portal desktops are assigned to users. We also described how different themes can be applied for different groups of users based on the concept of portal desktops. After reading this chapter, you should understand how portal content is organized, how roles are organized, and how different layouts can be assigned to different sets of users.

In the next chapter, you will see how to develop applications for SAP NetWeaver Portal using various technologies.

When you need to develop custom content for SAP NetWeaver Portal, many technologies for designing the user interface are available to you. This chapter provides an overview of development in various technologies and the factors to consider when choosing which technology to use.

7 Development for SAP NetWeaver Portal

In the previous chapters, we have seen various SAP NetWeaver Portal implementation steps, from blueprinting to portal content development. All of these steps will help you develop portal content based on applications already existing somewhere; however, we have not yet seen how to develop custom SAP NetWeaver Portal applications from scratch. Within SAP NetWeaver Portal, you might have seen many different types of applications running, and all of these applications do not necessarily have to run on the same SAP NetWeaver Portal. You can develop a variety of applications on different platforms and still integrate with SAP NetWeaver Portal by using suitable iViews. Some of the most common user interface (UI) technologies used for developing applications for consumption by SAP NetWeaver Portal are:

▶ **Portal component applications**
UI is developed in the form of portal components.

▶ **Web Dynpro Java**
UI is developed in the form of Web Dynpro components in Java.

▶ **Web Dynpro ABAP**
UI is developed in the form of Web Dynpro components in ABAP.

Your choice of the UI technology will depend on a lot of factors, which have been discussed in Chapter 5. In this chapter, we will go through each UI development technology for SAP NetWeaver Portal. Instead of an exhaustive guide for any particular technology, this chapter discusses the important concepts of each technology and provides examples to help you understand how these UI technologies work and how, as an SAP NetWeaver Portal consultant, you can help your customers with the right technology in the right way. After reading this chapter, you should be aware of how each technology works and interacts with SAP NetWeaver Portal, and you should be able to develop some basic applications using these technologies.

In this chapter, we will first start with an introduction to portal component development, where we will also discuss important aspects of the NWDS, which is the single Integrated Development Environment (IDE) for all Java development for SAP. We will then discuss the steps in performing development for SAP NetWeaver Portal components. Finally, we will discuss developing UI applications using Web Dynpro Java and Web Dynpro ABAP.

7.1 Introduction to Portal Component Development

Portal components are developed using a Portal Development Kit (PDK), which is embedded into the SAP NetWeaver Developer Studio (NWDS). NWDS is an Integrated Development Environment (IDE) provided by SAP. NWDS is based on the open-source IDE Eclipse (*www.eclipse.org*) and has been extended by SAP-based plug-ins needed for various types of Java development within SAP. NWDS is the development environment that you will need for all SAP Java developments, so this section begins by introducing you to NWDS. Then we will look into the structure of a portal component application (a deployable application that is used to generate a UI) and the relationship between a portal application project and a portal component. During this discussion, we will also focus on *portalapp.xml*, which is the deployment descriptor portal component.

7.1.1 SAP NetWeaver Developer Studio

In the previous chapter, we touched on NWDS when we were looking at how to customize the logon page; however, we did not discuss the NWDS tool in detail. As said earlier, NWDS is based on open-source Eclipse and has been enhanced with SAP-specific plug-ins. You can download SAP NetWeaver Developer Studio 7.3 from this location:

https://nwds.sap.com/swdc/downloads/updates/netweaver/nwds/nw/730/

You will need an S-User ID from SAP to download NWDS and at least JDK 1.6 installed on the machine where you are going to install NWDS. You will also need to install NWDS on a machine from which the SAP NetWeaver Portal server is reachable so that after you develop the applications, you can deploy them to the portal from within NWDS.

After you have installed NWDS, go to the folder where you installed it, and locate the executable file named *SapNetweaverDeveloperStudio.exe*. Execute this file to launch NWDS. You should create a desktop shortcut for this executable so that you can launch NWDS easily in the future.

When you launch it for the first time, you must select the workspace for NWDS (Figure 7.1).

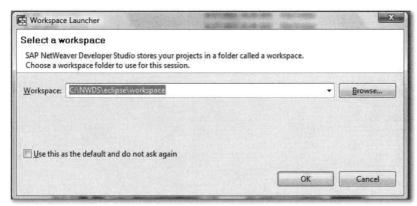

Figure 7.1 SAP NetWeaver Developer Studio Workspace

A workspace for NWDS sets the default folder where the applications that you will create using NWDS are stored. You can change this location for each application when you create the application. After the workspace has been set, NWDS loads. If this is the first time you've loaded NWDS after installation, you will see the welcome page; otherwise, you will be taken to the application that you were last working on. The welcome page of NWDS is shown in Figure 7.2.

The welcome page gives links to various guides for development using NWDS. NWDS gives the development tools in the form of *perspectives*, and each perspective provides the tools for working with a type of development. For example, the ENTERPRISE PORTAL perspective, shown selected in Figure 7.3, provides all of the related tools for developing SAP NetWeaver Portal applications that run inside the Portal Runtime (PRT). Similarly the Web Dynpro perspective provides the set of tools for developing and deploying Web Dynpro Java applications. To open a perspective, go to the menu item WINDOWS • OPEN PERSPECTIVE • OTHER. This will give you a list of all of the perspectives in NWDS (Figure 7.3).

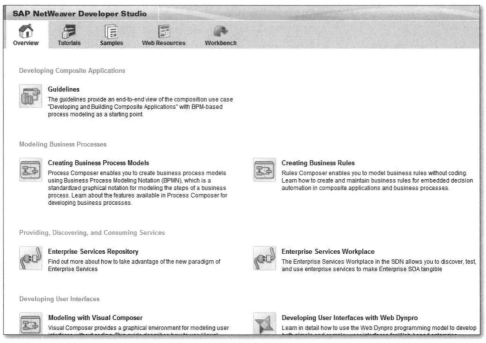

Figure 7.2 SAP NetWeaver Developer Studio Welcome Page

Figure 7.3 Perspectives in SAP NetWeaver Developer Studio

When you choose a perspective and click OK, all of the tools related to that perspective are loaded. For example, the ENTERPRISE PORTAL perspective is selected, and as you can see in Figure 7.4, enterprise portal development-related and deployment-related tools have been loaded.

Figure 7.4 Enterprise Portal Perspective

At the top-left side, just below the menu items, there are tools for creating a portal application project, exporting a portal application archive, and so on.

When you develop the portal applications using NWDS, you will also need to deploy the application on SAP NetWeaver Portal, which means you must configure your NWDS to do so. To do that, navigate to WINDOWS PREFERENCES SAP AS JAVA. Here you need to add the server where you will deploy your applications (Figure 7.5).

Click the ADD button, enter the host name and instance details, and click OK. After you have entered the correct entries, your server should be listed as the configured server for the NWDS as shown in Figure 7.6.

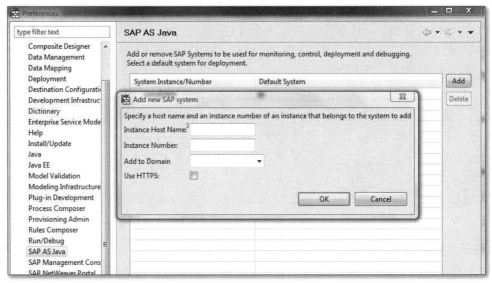

Figure 7.5 SAP AS Java Configuration

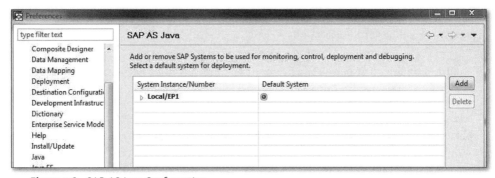

Figure 7.6 SAP AS Java Configuration

You can add multiple servers to NWDS configuration; however, at any one time, you can have only one default system. The default system will be used for deploying the applications from the development perspective. You can choose the radio button in the DEFAULT SYSTEM to set a system as the default as shown in Figure 7.6. After configuring AS Java, you should be able to see the system in the SERVERS view of NWDS. You can open this view by going to WINDOWS • SHOW VIEW • OTHER • SERVER • SERVERS. From this view, you can also start, stop, and restart the server. You can also perform many other activities from here as shown in Figure 7.7.

Figure 7.7   Servers View in NWDS

After you have configured NWDS, you are ready to start the development.

7.1.2   Portal Application Structure

To develop a portal application using NWDS, you need to go to the menu FILE • NEW • PROJECT • PORTAL APPLICATION • CREATE A PORTAL APPLICATION PROJECT. Click NEXT, and enter a name for the portal application project and the location of the file system where the folder for the project should be created. After you enter those details and click FINISH, you will see that the project has been created, and a folder hierarchy will be created in the PACKAGE EXPLORER view on the left side as shown in Figure 7.8.

You can also create a portal application project by clicking the quick launch button located just below the menu in NWDS.

Because SAP NetWeaver Portal runs on AS Java, which is compliant with Java EE 5, all applications deployed on the portal need to be in the EAR (Enterprise Archive) format. EAR is an archive format that is used by all J2EE containers. NWDS packages the portal application into an EAR file before deploying to the server.

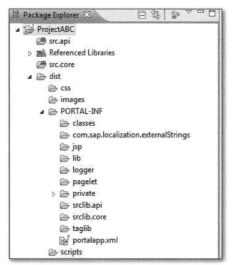

Figure 7.8 Portal Application Project Folder Structure

Let's now consider the structure of a portal application project. The following are the important folders (shown in Figure 7.8) that need to be understood for developing SAP NetWeaver Portal applications:

▶ CSS
This folder contains the cascading style sheets (CSS) files needed by your application.

▶ IMAGES
This folder contains the images used by your application.

▶ CLASSES
This folder contains all classes that are referenced by this application and can also be referenced by external applications.

▶ LIB
This folder contains JAR files that are referenced by this application and can also be referenced by external applications.

▶ PRIVATE/CLASSES
This folder contains the classes that are referenced only by this application.

▶ PRIVATE/LIB
This folder contains the JAR files that are exclusively used by this application.

As shown in Figure 7.8, the project also contains an XML file named *portalapp. xml*. This file is the deployment descriptor for the portal application and contains configuration information for all applications. When you double-click the XML file, it opens up with four tabs. The OVERVIEW tab shows all of the components and services that have been developed as part of this application in a graphical user interface (GUI) as shown in Figure 7.9. So far, we haven't created any components or services in the application, so it doesn't show any components and services. We will revisit this after we have created portal components or services.

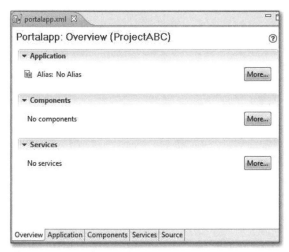

Figure 7.9 portalapp.xml

You can also see the actual source of the *portalapp.xml* file by going to the SOURCE tab. The source for the empty project without any components looks like this:

```
<?xml version="1.0" encoding="ISO-8859-1"?>
<application>
<application-config/>
<components/>
<services/>
</application>
```

After the creation of components or services, this XML gets updated, which you'll see later in Section 7.1.2. The *portalapp.xml* file has the following important elements:

▶ `<Application-Config>`

This defines the configuration for the entire application. It defines parameters such as the security zone and whether the application should be started as soon as it is deployed or when a request comes for the application.

▶ `<Components>`

This node is for defining components that are part of this application. Each application can have multiple components, and all of the components will be listed here. There are configuration subelements within this element too.

▶ `<Services>`

This node is for defining services that are part of this application. Each application can have multiple services, and all of the services will be listed here. There are configuration subelements within this element too.

▶ `<Registry>`

This element defines entries in the portal registry.

In the screen shown in Figure 7.9, you can go to the COMPONENTS and SERVICES tabs to manage the components and services individually. You can also create the components and services directly from here.

Listing 7.1 provides an example of a complete *portalapp.xml* file with one component and one service.

```
<application>
  <application-config>
   <property name="releasable" value="true"/>
 </application-config>
  <components>
   <component name="Comp1">
     <component-config>
       <property name="ClassName" value="com.test.comp1 "/>
     </component-config>
     <component-profile>
       <property name="diplayHistory" value="10"></property>
         <property name="plainDescription" value="This is comp1">
         </property>
     </component-profile>
   </component>
  </components>

  <services>
```

```
    <service name="Service1">
      <service-config>
        <property name="startup" value="true"></property>
        <property name="className" value="com.test.service1">
        </property>
      </service-config>
      <service-profile>
        <property name="value1" value="100"></property>
      </service-profile>
    </service>
  </services>
</application>
```

Listing 7.1 portalapp.xml File

7.2   Creating a Portal Component

One portal application project can contain many components. Each component is normally a fully functional application that can run independently, and an SAP NetWeaver Portal iView can be created (except for portal services) for it. The following are the five main types of components that you can create:

▶ **AbstractPortalComponent**
Makes use of Java code to render the HTML UI.

▶ **AbstractTestComponent**
Used for creating testing components. This type of component is very rarely used in portal development, so we will not discuss this component in detail in this chapter.

▶ **DynPage**
Also makes use of Java code to render the UI, but it uses the HTMLB (HTML for Business) class library for that. Since the introduction of JSPDynPage (discussed below), the use of DynPage is uncommon, because its class-based approach for generating UIs is cumbersome and difficult to maintain. We will not spend much time on this component in this chapter. JSPDynPage provides a more elegant way to generate UIs for SAP NetWeaver Portal.

▶ **JSPDynPage**
Makes use of JSP to render the HTML UI.

▶ **Portal services**

Global services that can be deployed into SAP NetWeaver Portal and can be accessed by multiple components. Unlike other types of components, this does not generate any UI, so no iView can be created for portal services.

In this section, we will see how to create different types of portal components in NWDS and how they are executed in SAP NetWeaver Portal. We will first see how Java-based components are created using AbstractPortalComponent, and then we will look at creating JSP-based portal components using JSPDynPage and native JSP. (In the case of native JSP, a SAP NetWeaver Portal application is created using a JSP that does not use either HTMLB tags or the HTMLB class library; it instead uses HTML tags.) Finally, we will discuss *portal services*.

7.2.1 Creating an AbstractPortalComponent

To create an AbstractPortalComponent component, follow these steps in NWDS:

1. Choose FILE • NEW • OTHER • PORTAL APPLICATION • CREATE A NEW PORTAL APPLI-CATION OBJECT.

2. You will be asked to choose a portal application project in which you want to create this component. Choose the project that you had earlier created.

3. You will now need to choose the type of portal component that you want to create (Figure 7.10). For this example, choose ABSTRACTPORTALCOMPONENT, and click NEXT.

4. You will now be asked to enter or choose the following information as shown in Figure 7.11:

   ▶ NAME: This is the name of the portal component. This must be unique within the portal application project.

   ▶ LOCATION: The location can have two values: CORE and API. CORE means this class is private and can only be accessed within this component. API means that this class is public and can be accessed by other components of this portal application project as well.

   ▶ CLASS NAME: Name of the class that will be created for this AbstractPortal-Component.

   ▶ PACKAGE NAME: Name of the Java package to which this component will belong.

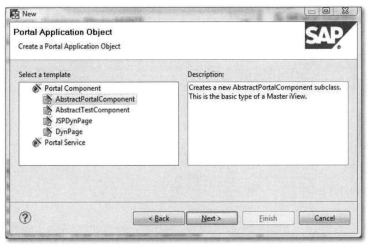

Figure 7.10 Creating a Portal Application Component

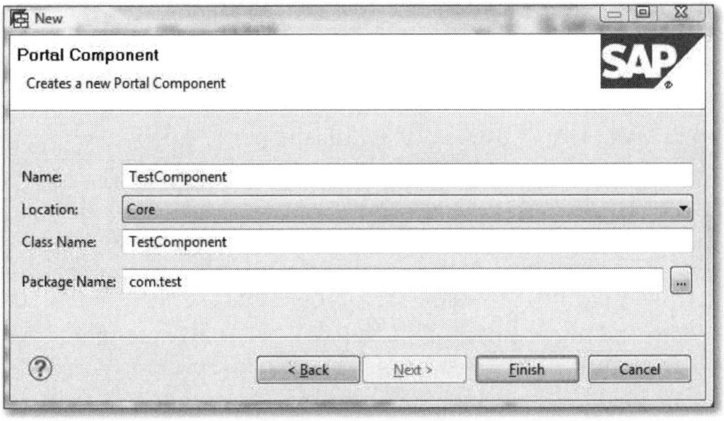

Figure 7.11 Creating an AbstractPortalComponent

5. When you click FINISH, the component is created. Figure 7.12 shows the new component. You can see that the Java file *TestComponent.java* was created in the *src.core* folder because we had selected the location as CORE. Also, the Java class `TestComponent` extends the Java class AbstractPortalComponent. AbstractPortalComponent provides the base implementation of the IPortalComponent interface.

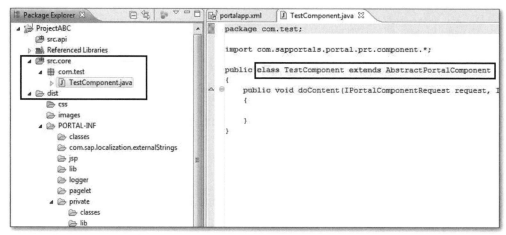

Figure 7.12 New AbstractPortalComponent

The AbstractPortalComponent class implements the IPortalComponent interface and the method of this interface. There are two other important interfaces that are used most often: IPortalComponentRequest and IPortalComponentResponse. We will discuss these next, and then provide an example of an AbstractPortalComponent. Finally, we will show you how to create an iView for the portal component.

IPortalComponent Interface

The portal component can be compared to a servlet in its capabilities of handling client requests and providing an HTML-based response to the clients. The IPortal-Component is the central abstraction of the SAP NetWeaver Portal components. All components implement this interface either directly or indirectly. You can either extend the abstract class AbstractPortalComponent or you can directly implement the IPortalComponent interface.

The IPortalComponent interface has the following hook methods that are called by the PRT during a component's lifecycle:

▶ init()
   Method called during the initialization of the component.

▶ service()
   Method called to handle the client requests. This method responds to the user's requests.

▶ `destroy()`

Method called when the component is unloaded from the memory. This method is mainly used to do cleanups to free up the memory being used by the component.

AbstractPortalComponent Class

AbstractPortalComponent is an abstract class that implements the IPortalComponent interface. It contains the following methods:

▶ `doContent()`

Method used to generate and render response to the client requests.

▶ `doEdit()`

Method used to provide the personalization dialog to the users.

▶ `doHandleEditData()`

Handler method for personalization. (A handler method is a method that is called by the runtime and handles various events in the portal request and reponse cycle.)

▶ `doBeforeContent()`

Handler method for the `BEFORE_CONTENT` event.

▶ `doAfterContent()`

Handler method for the `AFTER_CONTENT` event.

▶ `doRequestEvent()`

Handler method for a client-raised event that is not handled in any event handlers.

IPortalComponentRequest Interface

The IPortalComponentRequest interface provides the object that encapsulates the request object and is used in retrieving information about the client request. IPortalComponentRequest is an abstraction of the `HTTPServletRequest` class. It provides the following important methods:

▶ **For retrieving the context information:**

```
request.getComponentContext().getProfile()
request.getPrivateResourcePath()
request.getPublicResourcePath()
```

▶ **For retrieving resources:**

```
request.getResource(IResource.IMAGE, filename)
```

▶ **For retrieving request parameters:**

```
request.getParameter("Username")
```

▶ **For accessing the underlying HTTPServletRequest object:**

```
request.getServletRequest()
```

IPortalComponentResponse Interface

The IPortalComponentResponse interface provides the object that encapsulates the response object and is used in sending a response to the client request. IPortalComponentResponse is an abstraction of the `HTTPServletResponse` class. It provides the following important methods:

▶ `response.write()`
Method used to write the response to the client, which is most often an HTTP client.

▶ `response.getWriter()`
Method used to get a handle to the writer object that writes to the response stream.

▶ `response.addResource()`
Method used to add a resource to the output.

▶ `response.setContentType()`
Method used to set the content type of the response. Most frequently, you will need to set the response type as text/HTML.

▶ `response.addCookie()`
Method used to set a cookie to the user's browser.

▶ `response.getStatus()`
Method used to get the status of the response.

Example AbstractPortalComponent

Now that we've seen the important APIs of the portal components, let's look at creating an example component. We earlier saw an example of creating the `TestComponent`. We will now code a response from the component that will be displayed on the browser. In the `doContent()` method of the `TestComponent` we will write the following code to output "Hello World":

```
response. Write("Hello World");
```

Your program should now look like Figure 7.13.

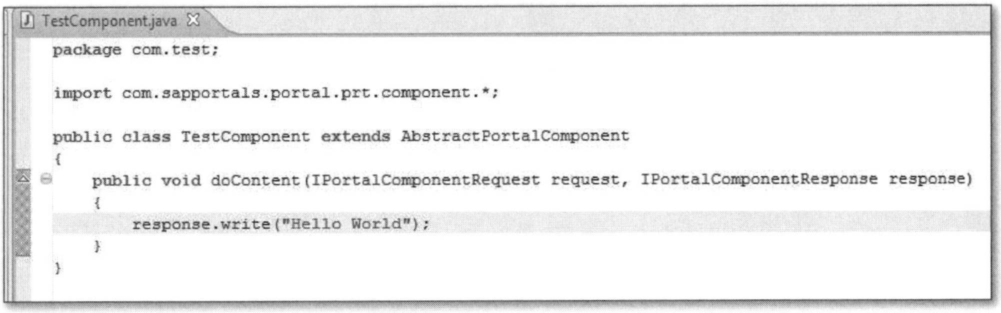

```
TestComponent.java

    package com.test;

    import com.sapportals.portal.prt.component.*;

    public class TestComponent extends AbstractPortalComponent
    {
        public void doContent(IPortalComponentRequest request, IPortalComponentResponse response)
        {
            response.write("Hello World");
        }
    }
```

Figure 7.13 Hello World Example for AbstractPortalComponent

The "Hello World" program is not complete; we now need to build and deploy this program to see the output of this component.

To build the application, follow these steps:

1. Right-click your project, choose EXPORT • SAP NETWEAVER PORTAL • EAR FILE, and click NEXT.

2. Select your portal application project from the list that appears, and click NEXT.

3. You will be asked to enter the name for the EAR file and the location where the EAR file should be generated. You will then use this EAR file to deploy it to the server. Click FINISH after entering the details.

You will see that the EAR file has been generated in the location that you provided. You will also see the EAR file appear in the portal application project hierarchy.

To deploy the EAR file, follow these steps:

1. Open the DEPLOY VIEW in NWDS. If this view is not visible on NWDS, you can open the view by going to WINDOW • SHOW VIEW • OTHER • DEPLOY VIEW • DEPLOY VIEW.

2. Chose the WORKSPACE DEPLOYABLE ARCHIVES node, right-click, and choose ADD (Figure 7.14).

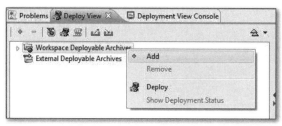

Figure 7.14 Adding an EAR File to Deploy

3. You will be presented with the list of EAR files that are associated with the projects in NWDS. Select the EAR file that you want to deploy, and click OK (Figure 7.15).

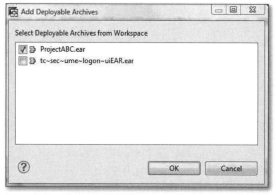

Figure 7.15 Select an EAR File to Add

4. The EAR file you selected is added to the Workspace Deployable Archives node. Select the EAR file you want to deploy, right-click, and select Deploy (Figure 7.16).

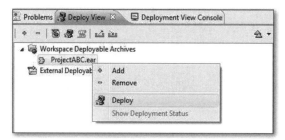

Figure 7.16 Deploying an EAR File

After you get the message that the deployment has completed successfully, your component has been deployed. You can now try to access the component in a web browser. You can execute the application by going directly to *http://<server>:<port>/ irj/servlet/prt/portal/prtroot/<APP_NAME>.<COMP_NAME>* where *<APP_Name>* is the name of your project, and *<COMP_NAME>* is the name of your component. For example, if your application project name is ProjectABC, and the component is TestComponent, the URL will be *http://<server>:<port>/irj/servlet/prt/portal/prtroot/ ProjectABC.TestComponent.*

After you authenticate, the browser should output the "Hello World" response returned by the component, as shown in Figure 7.17.

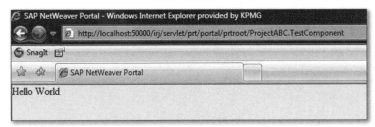

Figure 7.17   Hello World Response

Creating an iView for the Portal Component

As we discussed earlier, a component is an independent unit that can be executed, and an iView can be created based on the component. In this section, we will see how an iView can be created for the portal component that we just created.

Follow these steps to create an SAP NetWeaver Portal iView for the portal component:

1. In CONTENT ADMINISTRATION, expand the PORTAL APPLICATIONS node, go to your application project, and select the component for which you want to create the iView.

2. Right-click the component, and select COPY (Figure 7.18).

3. Navigate to the folder where you want to create the iView for the copied component, right-click, and choose PASTE AS PCD OBJECT (Figure 7.19).

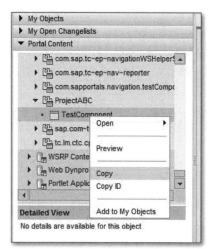

Figure 7.18 iView for the Portal Component

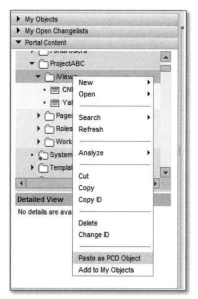

Figure 7.19 Paste as PCD Object

4. Enter the name and ID details for the iView. When you enter all of the details and finish, you will see that the iView has been created.

5. Right-click the new iView created, and select PREVIEW. This opens a new window with the preview of your component. This should show the same "Hello World" text that we saw earlier.

You should now understand how to create a Java-based portal component based on AbstractPortalComponent. In the next section, we will see how to create a JSP-based portal component using JSPDynPage.

7.2.2   Creating a JSPDynPage

In the previous section, we saw how to create a portal component using an Abstract-PortalComponent. An AbstractPortalComponent development, as discussed earlier, is like a servlet development: It has the same problems that are inherent in a servlet way of developing an HTML response. First, it's difficult to create a complex HTML UI using the servlet style programming because the HTML tags are embedded inside Java code. Second, it creates a code that is very difficult to maintain. To overcome these difficulties, SAP has provided the HTMLB (HTML for Business) set of controls.

HTMLB provides the following types of elements:

▶ Forms

▶ Controls

  ▶ Layout controls

  ▶ Visible controls

  ▶ Nonvisible controls

▶ Container

▶ Events

The controls can be accessed and manipulated using HTMLB to render and HTML UI to handle the user events. HTMLB controls can be accessed by the following:

▶ A Java class using the HTMLB class library (classlib)

▶ A JSP using the tag library (taglib)

In this section, we will see an example of how the HTMLB tag library can be used in a JSP for rendering the HTML UI on a web browser. To create a JSPDynPage component, follow these steps:

1. Go to FILE • NEW • OTHER • PORTAL APPLICATION • CREATE A NEW PORTAL APPLI-CATION OBJECT.

2. Select the project in which you want to create the component. You can select the same project in which we created the AbstractPortalComponent earlier.

3. Select the type of the component you want to create. In this case, choose JSP-DYNPAGE (Figure 7.20).

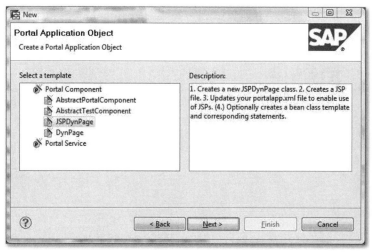

Figure 7.20　Creating a JSPDynPage

4. You will need to enter the following details (Figure 7.21):

   ▶ NAME: Name of the `JSPDynPage` component.

   ▶ LOCATION: Location can be CORE or API as discussed earlier.

   ▶ JSPDYNPAGE PACKAGE NAME: A package name in which the classes will be created.

   ▶ JSP FILE NAME: The name of the JSP file that will be created.

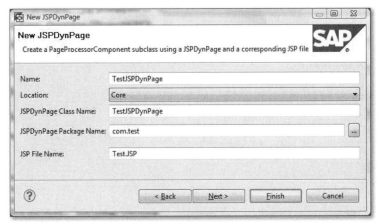

Figure 7.21 JSPDynPage Details

5. Click FINISH after entering the details. The following files are created or updated:

▶ A JSP file (Figure 7.22) with the name that you had provided. This JSP file is used to render the HTML response to the client. You can use the HTMLB tags in this JSP.

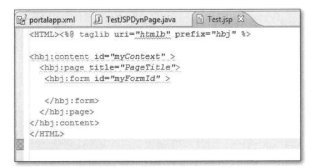

Figure 7.22 JSP File for JSPDynPage

▶ A Java class (Figure 7.23) with the name that you had provided for the JSP-DynPage class name. Here you will find that your JSPDynPage component extends the PageProcessorComponent class, and the class name you provided extends the JSPDynPage class. Also notice that the method doProcessBefore-Output() sets the name of the JSP that will be rendered by this method:

```
this.setJspName("Test.jsp");
```

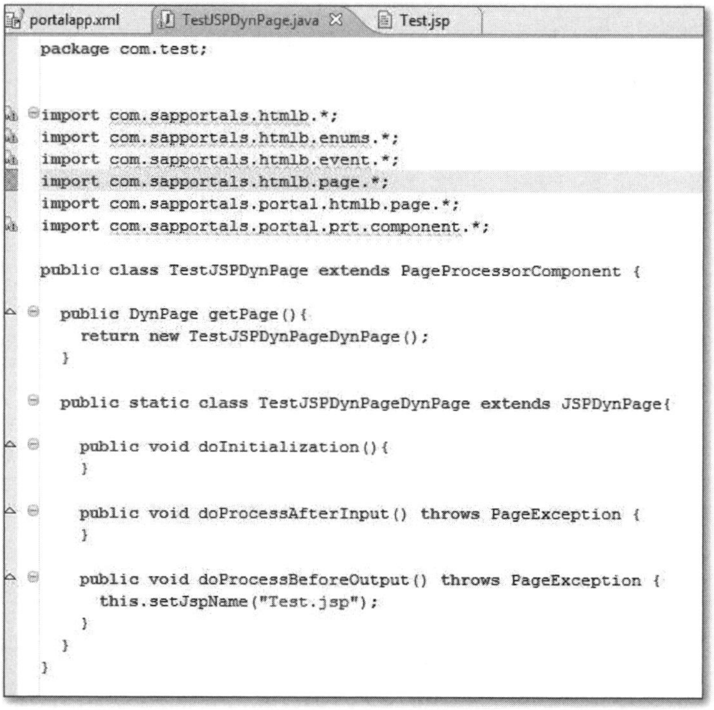

```
portalapp.xml        TestJSPDynPage.java ✕        Test.jsp

    package com.test;

 ⊖import com.sapportals.htmlb.*;
  import com.sapportals.htmlb.enums.*;
  import com.sapportals.htmlb.event.*;
  import com.sapportals.htmlb.page.*;
  import com.sapportals.portal.htmlb.page.*;
  import com.sapportals.portal.prt.component.*;

  public class TestJSPDynPage extends PageProcessorComponent {

 ⊖  public DynPage getPage(){
      return new TestJSPDynPageDynPage();
    }

 ⊖  public static class TestJSPDynPageDynPage extends JSPDynPage{

 ⊖    public void doInitialization(){
      }

 ⊖    public void doProcessAfterInput() throws PageException {
      }

 ⊖    public void doProcessBeforeOutput() throws PageException {
        this.setJspName("Test.jsp");
      }
    }
  }
```

Figure 7.23 JSPDynPage Java Class

▶ The *portalapp.xml* file is changed. As highlighted in Figure 7.24, you will see that the details of the new component have been added to the same *portalapp. xml* file.

Please note the following property:

```
<property name="htmlb" value="/SERVICE/htmlb/taglib/htmlb.tld"/>
```

This property in the component profile enables the component to find the tag library (*htmlb.tld*) to be used in the JSP. The component reads the tag library from the HTMLB service running in SAP NetWeaver Portal. To access the HTMLB service, the *portalapp.xml* file needs to declare that it refers to the HTMLB service, which is done by the following property inside the `<application-config>` tag of the *portalapp.xml* file (Figure 7.24).

```
<property name="SharingReference" value="com.sap.portal.htmlb"/>
```

```
portalapp.xml ⊠   TestJSPDynPage.java    Test.jsp
<?xml version="1.0" encoding="UTF-8" standalone="no"?>
<application>
  <application-config>
    <property name="SharingReference" value="com.sap.portal.htmlb"/>
  </application-config>
  <components>
    <component name="TestComponent">
      <component-config>
        <property name="ClassName" value="com.test.TestComponent"/>
      </component-config>
      <component-profile/>
    </component>
    <component name="TestJSPDynPage">
      <component-config>
        <property name="ClassName" value="com.test.TestJSPDynPage"/>
        <property name="SecurityZone" value="com.test/low_safety"/>
      </component-config>
      <component-profile>
        <property name="htmlb" value="/SERVICE/htmlb/taglib/htmlb.tld"/>
      </component-profile>
    </component>
  </components>
  <services/>
</application>
```

Figure 7.24 The portalapp.xml File

All of the files needed are now created, so let's modify the JSP page to render something on the browser. In this example, we will add a button to the JSP. After modifying, the code will look like Listing 7.2.

```
<HTML><%@ taglib uri="htmlb" prefix="hbj" %>

<hbj:content id="myContext" >
  <hbj:page title="PageTitle">
   <hbj:form id="myFormId" >
   <hbj:button id="myButton"
           text="click here"
           onClick="click"
           tooltip="click" />
   </hbj:form>
  </hbj:page>
</hbj:content>
</HTML>
```

Listing 7.2 JSP Page

In Listing 7.2, an HTMLB button has been added with the text "click here."

Now create an archive, and deploy the application following the same steps used to work with the AbstractPortalComponent. After the deployment has been completed, you can access the JSPDynPage by accessing *http://<server>:<port>/irj/servlet/prt/portal/prtroot/<APP_NAME>.<COMP_NAME>* where *<APP_NAME>* is the name of your application project, and *<COMP_NAME>* is the name of your component.

Figure 7.25 shows the output of the JSPDynPage component. As shown in Listing 7.2, it created the button with the text "click here."

Figure 7.25 Output of JSPDynPage

On the click of the button, the `onClick()` method of the JSPDynPage class is called. So to handle the event, you will need to implement this method as shown in Listing 7.3.

```
Public void onClick(Event event) throws PageException {
IPortalComponentRequest request = (IPortalComponentRequest) this.
getRequest();
...
...
}
```

Listing 7.3 onClick() Method of JSPDynPage Class

7.2.3   Using Native JSP

We have seen how to use an AbstractPortalComponent for generating HTML responses. We have also seen how to use HTMLB controls in a JSP using the tag library in the JSPDynPage component. Sometimes, however, you don't want to be limited by the HTMLB controls, and you want to use native JSP by using HTML controls. You can integrate a native JSP with an AbstractPortalComponent by calling a JSP as a resource.

Follow these steps to integrate a native JSP with SAP NetWeaver Portal:

1. Create a JSP file. The following is an example:

```
<html>
<body>

    Hello World

</body>
</html>
```

2. This JSP prints the "Hello World" text on the browser. Put the JSP in the *pagelet* folder of your project.

3. Create an AbstractPortalComponent component in your portal application project.

4. In the `doContent()` method of the Java file that is generated, call the JSP as a resource using the following sample code:

```
public class NativeJSPExample extends AbstractPortalComponent
{
     public void doContent(IPortalComponentRequest request,
IPortalComponentResponse response)
     {
        IResource res = request.getResource("jsp", "pagelet/Example.
JSP");
        response.include(request, res);
     }
}
```

In the preceding example, the first statement creates a resource object for the JSP file:

```
IResource res = request.getResource("jsp", "pagelet/Example.JSP");
```

In the second statement, the JSP resource is served as the response of the request:

```
response.include(request, res);
```

This leads to the JSP rendering the response to the client. For the code to compile, you need to add the following import so that the compiler is able to find `IResource`:

```
import com.sapportals.portal.prt.resource.*;
```

When you build and deploy the application project and access this new component in the browser, you will find that now the native JSP is served by the component, as shown in Figure 7.26.

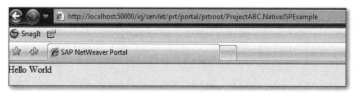

Figure 7.26 Native JSP Example

7.2.4 Portal Services

The portal service portal component includes services to provide commonly used functionality across applications. Portal services can be accessed by any component running in the PRT. These services are usually used to implement common functionalities that are needed by many applications and are not specific to any particular application logic. Portal services just provide an API for accessing the functionality and don't provide any UI, so no iViews are created for portal services. Other components can access portal services directly from within SAP NetWeaver Portal by using its public API, whereas external systems can access portal services using Web Services.

In this section, we will see how portal services are created using NWDS and how other applications can access a portal service deployed on SAP NetWeaver Portal.

Creating a Portal Service

To build a new portal service, you need to implement the `IService` interface. The creation, load and destroy, or portal services are handled by the PRT. The following hook methods are called by the PRT to manage the lifecycle of a portal service:

▶ `init()`
Method called when the portal service is loaded into memory.

▶ `afterInit()`
Method called after the INIT method.

▶ destroy()

Method called when the portal service is being unloaded from memory.

To create a new portal service, follow these steps:

1. Create a new portal application project as described in Section 7.2.1.

2. Choose FILE • NEW • OTHER • PORTAL APPLICATION • CREATE A NEW PORTAL APPLI-CATION OBJECT from the menu in NWDS.

3. Choose the new portal application project that you created for the portal service.

4. Choose PORTAL SERVICE for the type of object to be created, as shown in Figure 7.27.

Figure 7.27 Creating a Portal Service

5. Enter the service name, the Java class name, and the package name, and click FINISH.

6. You will see the following three files:

▶ **Interface file:** A Java interface is created that extends the IService interface (Figure 7.28). In the interface file, you need to provide a value for the KEY. This should be a fully qualified name that includes the name of the application, a period, and the name of the service. For example, if the name of the application is TestService, and the name of the service is also TestService, the KEY should be "TestService.TestService".

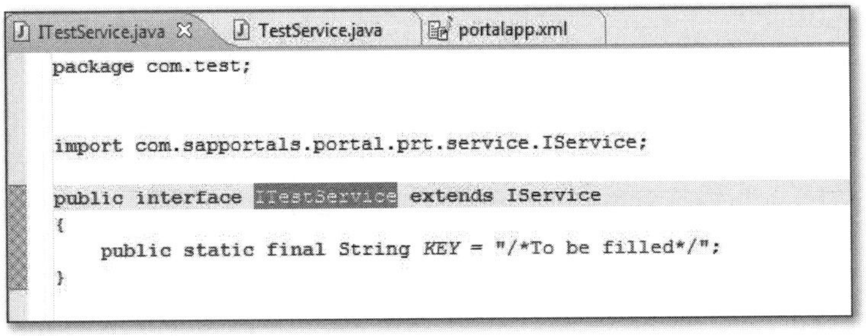

Figure 7.28 Interface File for Portal Service

▶ **Java class:** A Java class with the name you specify is created. This Java class implements the preceding interface (Figure 7.29).

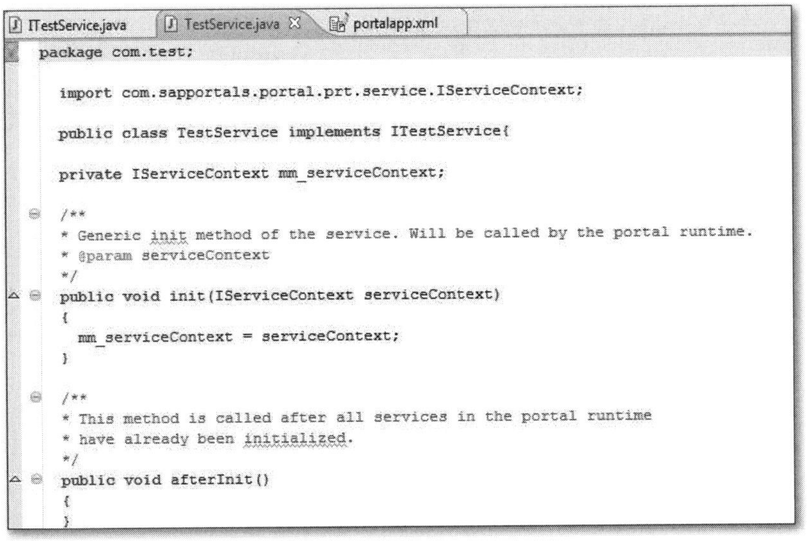

Figure 7.29 Portal Service Java File

▶ **portalapp.xml:** The *portalapp.xml* file contains the details about the portal service. The sample *portalapp.xml* file is shown here:

```xml
<?xml version="1.0" encoding="utf-8"?>
<application>
  <application-config/>
  <components/>
  <services>
```

```
<service name="TestService">
  <service-config>
    <property name="className" value="com.test.TestService"/>
  </service-config>
  <service-profile/>
</service>
</services>
</application>
```

7. You will want your custom service to implement custom methods that can be called by other applications. To do this, define a custom method in the generated interface. For example:

```
public String getValue(String key);
```

When you define this method in the interface, you will need to provide the implementation for this method in your Java class. This implementation will be executed when the client applications call this service.

Here is an example of the implementation of this method:

```
public String getValue(String key) {
return "Hello World";
}
```

8. You can now export the EAR file for the application and deploy as before. After the successful deployment, the service is available in the PRT.

Accessing a Portal Service

In the previous section, we saw how to create a portal service. In this section, we discuss how to access the portal service. The portal service must have already been deployed to SAP NetWeaver Portal.

To develop a portal application to access a portal service, you must do the following:

► Add a SharingReference in the deployment descriptor *portalapp.xml* file. This is the declaration that this application will be accessing the portal service.

► Add the API library of the portal service to your project. You will get the API library in the form of a JAR file from the portal service application project.

► Write the code to access the portal service. This involves the following steps:

- ▶ Import the package of the portal service.
- ▶ Get the handle to an instance of the portal service.
- ▶ Call the methods exposed by the service.

Follow these steps to create an application to access the portal service:

1. Create a portal application project and an AbstractPortalComponent component as discussed in Section 7.2.1.

2. Add a `SharingReference` property in the application configuration of the *porta-lapp.xml* file. This will tell the PRT that this application accesses the portal service defined in the file. After you have defined the `SharingReference` property, the file should look like this:

```xml
<?xml version="1.0" encoding="utf-8"?>
<application>
  <application-config>
   <property name="SharingReference" value="TestService" />
  </application-config>
  <components>
   <component name="CallService">
     <component-config>
       <property name="ClassName" value="com.test.CallService"/>
     </component-config>
     <component-profile/>
   </component>
  </components>
  <services/>
</application>
```

3. After the `SharingReference` has been defined, you need to add the API JAR file from the portal application into this project. To do that, right-click the project folder of the application, and choose Build Path • Add External Archives (Figure 7.30).

4. Select the *api.jar* file from the portal service project. You can extract the API JAR file from the WAR file of the portal service project, but the WAR file first needs to be extracted from the EAR file; you can use a utility such as WinZip or WinRAR for this. After you have added the JAR file, it should get listed in the Referenced Libraries section of your project, as shown in Figure 7.31.

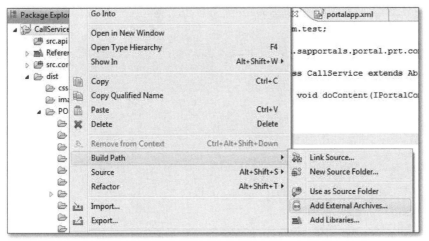

Figure 7.30 Add External Archives

Figure 7.31 Referenced Libraries

5. Write the code to access the portal service by following these steps:

▶ Add the import for the package of the portal service, for example:

```
import com.test.*;
```

▶ Add the import for the `PortalRuntime` class:

```
import com.sapportals.portal.prt.runtime.PortalRuntime;
```

▶ Get the instance of the portal service, and call the method:

```
public class CallService extends AbstractPortalComponent
{
    public void doContent(IPortalComponentRequest request,
IPortalComponentResponse response)
    {
        IPortalRuntimeResources res = PortalRuntime.
getRuntimeResources();

        IService serv = res.getService(com.test.ITestService.KEY);

        com.test.ITestService myService = (com.test.ITestService)
serv;

        String val = myService.getValue("Key");

        response.write(val);
    }
}
```

6. Export the portal application and deploy it, as discussed earlier.

7. When you now access this application in the browser, the application should call the portal service's getValue() method and display the returned value in the browser.

7.3   Web Dynpro Java

We've seen how to develop portal components for developing web-based UIs on SAP NetWeaver Portal. The problem with portal component development, though, is that it does not provide any modeling tool to design the UIs. SAP Web Dynpro Java is a technology for developing UIs and provides many tools to generate the UI and code.

The Web Dynpro programming model for designing UIs does the following:

▶ Defines an event-driven model based on an MVC (model-view-controller) design pattern

▶ Provides a set of tools for UI design

▶ Generates code in the form of metadata

▸ Provides a runtime (Web Dynpro Runtime) for running the Web Dynpro applications

Figure 7.32 shows the development process for Web Dynpro.

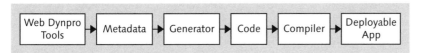

Figure 7.32 Web Dynpro Development Cycle

The various steps in Web Dynpro Java development are listed here:

1. Using Web Dynpro Java tools, you generate the Web Dynpro metadata.

2. Using the metadata, the code generator generates the code. The code generated is a code skeleton, with empty implementations. It can also generate the actual code for some actions such as firing a plug (as you'll see later).

3. You then write your custom code in the code skeleton generated by the code generator. The generated code and custom code together make the whole application.

4. The compiler then compiles the whole application to create a deployable application that can be deployed on SAP NetWeaver Portal.

This section is aimed at familiarizing you with the basic concepts of Web Dynpro Java so that you can get started with this technology. Because Web Dynpro Java is heavily dependent on the use of NWDS features provided in the Web Dynpro perspective, we start with an introduction to the Web Dynpro perspective in NWDS. After that, we will move to the basic concepts of Web Dynpro. Finally, we will create, enhance, deploy, and run a sample Web Dynpro application on the server.

To get started, open the Web Dynpro perspective in NWDS by going to WINDOW • OPEN PERSPECTIVE • OTHER • WEB DYNPRO (Figure 7.33). This opens the Web Dynpro perspective in NWDS, as shown in Figure 7.34. Here you can see the Web Dynpro projects that are available in the current workspace of NWDS.

Figure 7.33 Opening Web Dynpro Perspective

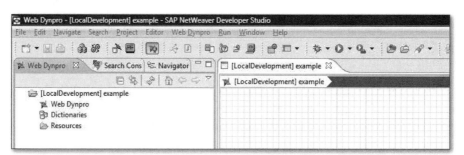

Figure 7.34 Web Dynpro Perspective

7.3.1 Web Dynpro Java Concepts

Let's start with a sample Web Dynpro application created in NWDS to understand the different concepts of Web Dynpro. Figure 7.35 shows a sample Web Dynpro Java application that has been already created in NWDS.

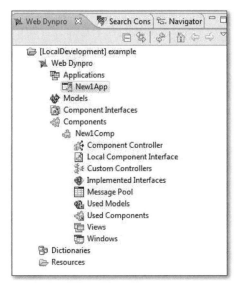

Figure 7.35 Sample Web Dynpro Application

A Web Dynpro project consists of the following parts, which we discuss in more detail next:

▶ Web Dynpro component

▶ Web Dynpro window

▶ Web Dynpro view

▶ View controller

▶ Component controller

▶ Navigation plugs

▶ Web Dynpro application

Web Dynpro Component

A Web Dynpro project can consist of one or more components. A component is an independent self-contained unit that provides a functionality that can run on its own or can be used by another Web Dynpro component. Figure 7.36 shows the relationship between a Web Dynpro application and a Web Dynpro component.

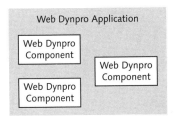

Figure 7.36 Web Dynpro Component

A component can contain multiple windows, multiple views, and multiple controllers; data flow can be defined between these. At any point, you can see the whole data flow between the parts of the component by opening the data modeler. To open the data modeler for a component, right-click the component, and select OPEN DATA MODELER. This opens the data modeler of the selected component as shown in Figure 7.37. We'll look at a data modeler in detail when we create our own Web Dynpro example.

Figure 7.37 Data Modeler of the Web Dynpro Component

The palette on the right side of the data modeler shows all of the types of objects that can be created for the Web Dynpro component.

Web Dynpro Window

A Web Dynpro *window* is a container of Web Dynpro views. One Web Dynpro window represents one browser window at runtime, and a Web Dynpro component can have only one window as the default window at any time. As shown in Figure 7.38, you will see that views can be arranged in a window. If multiple views are embedded in a window, you can set one view as the default one that will be loaded initially when the window is loaded on the browser.

You can also arrange multiple views in one window by using ViewSets. A *ViewSet* is a container that provides for the layout of multiple views on one window. There are various layouts of ViewSets provided by default, as you can see in Figure 7.38.

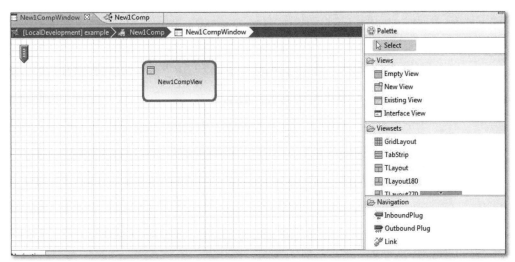

Figure 7.38 Web Dynpro Window

Figure 7.39 shows a T Layout ViewSet with the views embedded into the view areas of the ViewSet. A ViewSet is divided into view areas where the views can be embedded. Each view area can have multiple views embedded, but only one view can be set as the default view in each view area.

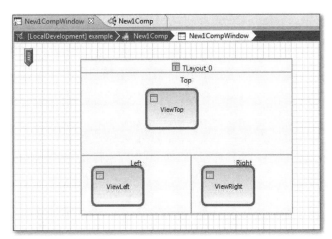

Figure 7.39 ViewSet

Web Dynpro View

A *Web Dynpro view* is an independent layout of UI controls that can be loaded in the web browser. Web Dynpro provides many UI controls that can be used to design a UI, but one of the most powerful of these is drag and drop; this feature allows you to create simple Web Dynpro applications without writing even a single line of code.

Figure 7.40 shows the designing of the layout in the Web Dynpro view.

Figure 7.40   Web Dynpro View

On the left side of Figure 7.40, you can see the palette that provides various types of UI controls for dragging and dropping onto the canvas. After dropping, you can arrange the layout on the canvas. Whenever you select a UI element on the canvas, the properties of the element appear in the properties window below the canvas. Here you can change various properties of each UI element (Figure 7.41).

All of the UI elements added to a view are also shown in the outline view. You can also add, remove, and organize the UI elements directly from the outline view. To add a UI element using the outline view, right-click ROOTELEMENT in the outline view, and choose INSERT CHILD.

In a popup window (Figure 7.42), you will see a list of all UI elements that the tool provides and can be added to the view. The UI elements are categorized, and you can filter based on the category or library to choose the UI element. You can also provide an ID for the UI element here.

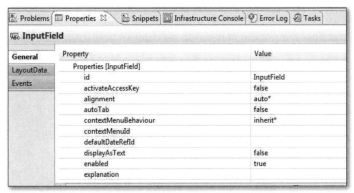

Figure 7.41 User Interface Element Properties

Figure 7.42 Adding a UI Element from Outline View

View Controller

Every Web Dynpro view also contains a view controller that is part of the view. The purpose of a *view controller* is to handle user events and to manage the transfer of data from one controller to another. A view controller consists of context, methods, and event handlers. To open the Java code that contains the methods and event handlers, you can right-click the view and choose OPEN • JAVA EDITOR (Figure 7.43).

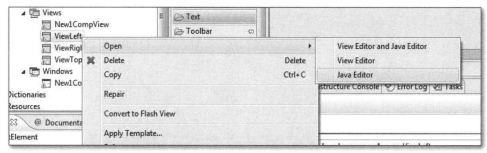

Figure 7.43 Opening the Java Editor

A *context* is a structure that holds the data of the application at runtime. The context of a view consists of nodes and attributes and is part of the view (Figure 7.44). The context at design time defines the template of the data that will be available at runtime. At runtime, instances of the node are created, and each instance of a node is called an *element*. A node can have one or more elements depending on the cardinality of the node defined at design time.

You can go to the context of a view by opening the view editor and going to the CONTEXT tab from the PROPERTIES view. As shown in Figure 7.44, you can define the data type for each attribute.

Component Controller

A *component controller* is a global controller for the whole component. Like a view controller, a component controller also contains context and Java code. The Java code in the component controller is used to make calls to the model or business logic of the Web Dynpro application. In NWDS, you can open either the modeler or the Java Editor. The CONTEXT tab is in the modeler of the component. To open the modeler, just double-click the component controller in the project hierarchy, or right-click the component controller, and choose OPEN • MODELER. After the modeler is opened, you can find the CONTEXT tab in the PROPERTIES view (Figure 7.45).

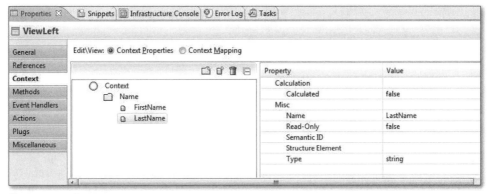

Figure 7.44 Context

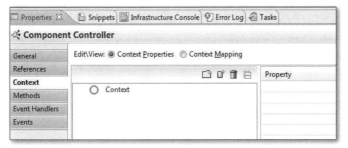

Figure 7.45 Component Controller Context

A component controller is the default controller of a Web Dynpro component. Web Dynpro also provides another type of controller, *custom controllers.* These are the same as the component controllers in terms of functionality and usage, but you need to create them manually as needed. The real use of custom controllers is in separating your application logically with each custom controller, grouping together similar types of functionality. The context of the component controller or a custom controller can be used to enable data flow across views in a Web Dynpro component. Because the component controller context is visible globally to all of the views, you can bind the context of the component controller to multiple views, thus enabling data sharing between those views.

Figure 7.46 shows the relationships among the view controller, component controller, and custom controllers.

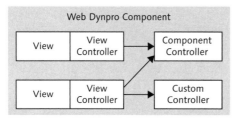

Figure 7.46 Relation between Controllers

Navigation Plugs

Navigation plugs are another set of important components of a Web Dynpro application. Navigation plugs enable navigation between views in a Web Dynpro application. To define navigation between two Web Dynpro views, you need to define the exit and entry points, and then you need to link these points to enable navigation. *Inbound plugs* define possible entry points to a view, and *outbound plugs* define exits from a view. To enable navigation between two views, you need to connect the outbound plug of a view to the inbound plug of another view by using *navigation links*.

Figure 7.47 shows the navigation between two views where a navigation link has been created between the outbound plug of the view VIEWTOP and the inbound plug of the view VIEWRIGHT.

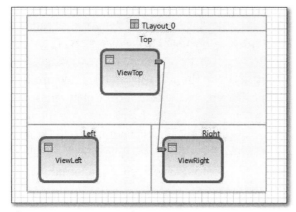

Figure 7.47 Navigation Plugs

Web Dynpro Application

An application in Web Dynpro is an entry point to a Web Dynpro component. It can be compared to context root in Java EE development where the context root provides an entry point to a web application. A Web Dynpro application always points to one — and only one — Web Dynpro component. And when the Web Dynpro application is launched, it executes this Web Dynpro component by default.

7.3.2 Creating and Enhancing a Web Dynpro Application

Now that we've seen the basics of Web Dynpro Java, let's create and enhance a Web Dynpro Java application.

Creating a Web Dynpro Application

Follow these steps to create a simple "Hello World" application:

1. First, create a Web Dynpro development component. To do so, in NWDS, choose FILE • NEW • PROJECT WEB DYNPRO • WEB DYNPRO DEVELOPMENT COMPONENT.

2. Select a software component in which your development component will be created. If you are connected to SAP NetWeaver Development Infrastructure (NWDI) , choose the appropriate software component. If you are not connected to NWDI, choose LOCALDEVELOPMENT • MYCOMPONENTS (Figure 7.48). This will create the new development component in a local software component provided by NWDS. Click NEXT after selecting the software component.

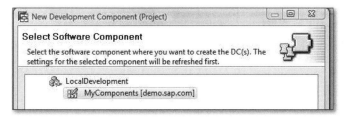

Figure 7.48 Selecting a Software Component

3. Enter the name of the Web Dynpro application that you want to create (Figure 7.49). Click NEXT and then FINISH. This will create the Web Dynpro project in your NWDS, and it will appear in your Web Dynpro explorer. Notice that the tool has created an empty container project with no applications and components

created. You now need to create the components, windows, views, applications, and so on to complete the Web Dynpro project.

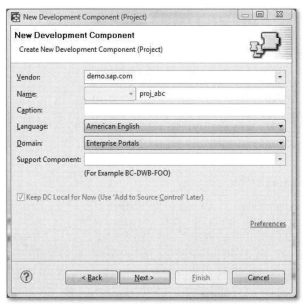

Figure 7.49 Creating a Web Dynpro Application

4. Select the APPLICATIONS node, right-click, and choose CREATE APPLICATION (Figure 7.50).

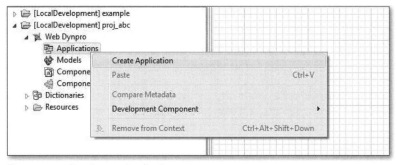

Figure 7.50 Creating an Application

5. Enter the name of the application and a package in which the application should be created. Click NEXT.

6. Choose a Web Dynpro component that this application should launch (Figure 7.51). Because we haven't created any components yet, we do not have any existing components in this project. Choose the CREATE A NEW COMPONENT OPTION, and click NEXT.

Figure 7.51 Choosing a Web Dynpro Component

7. Enter the component name and package (Figure 7.52). Notice that the checkbox DEFAULT WINDOW AND VIEWS is selected. With this option checked, a window and view will be created and set as the default window and view for this component.

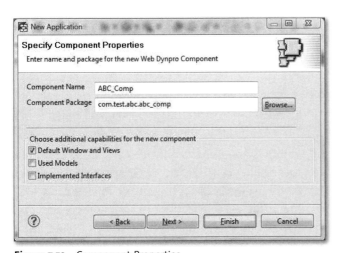

Figure 7.52 Component Properties

253

8. Now you will be presented with the proposed names for the default window and view that will be created (Figure 7.53). You can change the name and add views to the window from here. For each view added, you can select or deselect the checkboxes for EMBED and DEFAULT. Click FINISH after you have defined the properties.

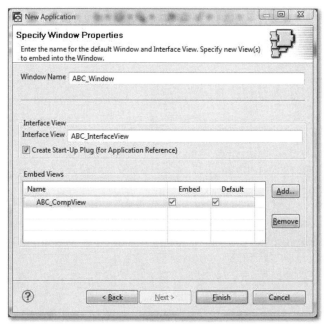

Figure 7.53 Creating the Default Window and Views

9. After clicking FINISH, NWDS generates the project structure with the application, component, window, and views created in the project. You can expand the project structure in Web Dynpro explorer to see this (Figure 7.54).

Notice that the views and windows are contained inside the component. You can double-click the project to view the *component modeler* that shows the project structure in a graphical way. It will show which application is connected to which component and which window is the default window in each component. Figure 7.55 shows the component modeler for the example project. One more component—TEST_COMP—has been created in this project to help explain the component modeler.

Figure 7.54 Web Dynpro Project Structure

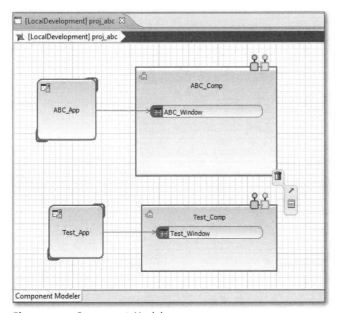

Figure 7.55 Component Modeler

10. Double-click the view ABC_COMP, and insert a UI element of type TEXTVIEW. This element can show a static text on the browser. You can find the TextView UI element under the TEXT category in the UI elements palette.

11. Select the new TEXTVIEW element, and in the PROPERTIES tab, go to the TEXT property, and enter the text "Hello World" as the value.

12. You have now completed the exercise to create a "Hello World" application; now you need to build and deploy this application to see the "Hello World" text on the browser. To do that, select the application ABC_APP, right-click, and select DEPLOY NEW ARCHIVE AND RUN (Figure 7.56).

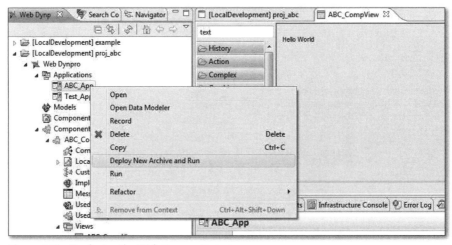

Figure 7.56 Deploying the Web Dynpro Project

This will first build the whole project and then deploy the application on AS Java. After the successful deployment, NWDS will launch a new browser to execute the application on the browser. Figure 7.57 shows the Web Dynpro application running in the browser.

Figure 7.57 Web Dynpro Application Running

The Web Dynpro application can also be run by launching this URL:

http://<HOST>:<PORT>/webdynpro/resources/<NAMESPACE>/<PROJ_NAME>/<APP_NAME>

In this URL, *<NAMESPACE>* is the namespace of the vendor that we specified while creating the Web Dynpro project (refer back to Figure 7.49). *<PROJ_NAME>* is the name of the Web Dynpro project, and *<APP_NAME>* is the name of the Web Dynpro application that you want to execute.

Enhancing a Web Dynpro Application

Now we will enhance our application by adding some more functionality. This example shows you how to navigate between views and how to use the context to transfer data across views. Our enhanced application will provide the following functionality:

▶ The first view will have an input field and a SUBMIT button.

▶ In the input field, you will enter your name and click SUBMIT.

▶ The application will navigate to the second view with a greeting.

▶ The second view will have a button to navigate back to the first view.

Follow these steps to achieve this functionality:

1. Open the project that you had created earlier to show the "Hello World" text.

2. Open the component controller, and create a context attribute to hold the user input. We will take the user's name as input, so let's create an attribute called "Name." Open the component controller's CONTEXT tab, select the CONTEXT node, and click NEW ATTRIBUTE. Select the radio button for MANUALLY, enter the name as "Name", and select the type as STRING (Figure 7.58). The component controller will now have the context attribute created.

3. In the first view, create an input field for the user's input, and create a SUBMIT button as shown in Figure 7.59.

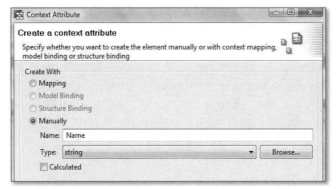

Figure 7.58 Creating a New Context Attribute

Figure 7.59 Creating User Interface Elements

4. Map the context attribute we created in the component controller to this view's context to ensure that the data will flow from the view controller to the component controller. In the view editor, go to the CONTEXT tab, and choose the radio button for CONTEXT MAPPING. On the right side corner, click the dropdown, and select ADD CONTROLLER REFERENCE. Select the component controller, and click OK to add the component controller's context for mapping to the view's context, as shown in Figure 7.60.

5. To do the context mapping, select the attribute from the component controller's context, and then drag and drop it on the view's context. The context mapping between the view controller and component controller is done, as shown in Figure 7.61.

Figure 7.60 Adding the Component Controller in View

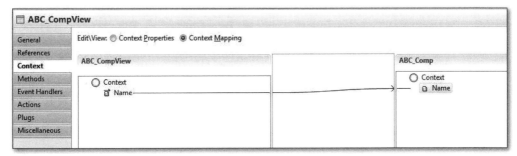

Figure 7.61 Context Mapping

6. Do the data binding for the input field so that whatever input the user enters into the input field gets transferred to the context. Go to the view layout, and select the input field. In the PROPERTIES tab, click the VALUE column for the VALUE property. A BIND button will appear; this is used to bind the input field's value to a context attribute. Click the BIND button, and select the NAME attribute from the popup. The input field is now bound to the context attribute, as shown in Figure 7.62.

inputPrompt		
length	20	
onEnterBehavior	default*	
passwordField	false	
readOnly	false	
state	normal*	
suggestValues	false	
textDirection	inherit*	
tooltip		
value	Name	Bind
visible	visible*	

Figure 7.62 Data Binding

7. Create one more view, VIEW2, and add both the views to the default window. The window should now look like Figure 7.63.

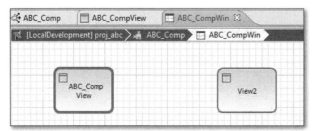

Figure 7.63 Web Dynpro Java Component Window

8. Add one inbound plug and one outbound plug to both views. Create a navigation link between the outbound plug for the first view and inbound plug for the second view. Similarly, create a navigation link between the outbound plug of the second view and an inbound plug for the first view. To create a plug, right-click the view, and select CREATE INBOUND PLUG or CREATE OUTBOUND PLUG. To create a navigation link, right-click an outbound plug, and select LINK. Then select the view and the inbound plug to which you are linking the outbound plug.

For this simple example, the plugs of the first view are named FIRSTIN and FIRSTOUT, and the plugs of the second view are named SECONDIN and SECOND-OUT. After the navigation plugs are created, your window should look like Figure 7.64.

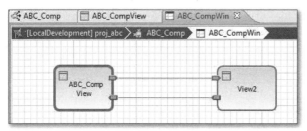

Figure 7.64 Navigation Plugs

9. Go back to the first view, and create an action that will be called when the user clicks on the SUBMIT button. Open the first view, and go to the EVENTS tab. Go to the VALUE column on the onAction property, and click the CREATE button to create an action (Figure 7.65).

Figure 7.65 Creating an Action

10. Define the action parameters. Figure 7.66 shows the various action parameters that you need to define. There are a couple of points to note here:

   ▸ A default handler is created with the name `onAction<ACTION_NAME>`. So if the action name you have specified is SUBMIT, the event handler created will be `onActionSubmit`.

   ▸ You can select the FIRE PLUG property and choose an outbound plug that you want to fire for navigating to a different view (Figure 7.66). If you choose this, the tool will generate the code for firing the plug automatically. If you don't select the FIRE PLUG property, you can still code firing the plug by going to the `onActionSubmit` method in the view's Java editor.

Figure 7.66 Action Parameters

If you now open the Java editor for this view, you will notice that a new method `onActionSubmit` has been created with the following implementation:

```
public void onActionSubmit(com.sap.tc.webdynpro.progmodel.api.
IWDCustomEvent wdEvent )
  {
    //@@begin onActionSubmit(ServerEvent)
    wdThis.wdFirePlugFirstOut();
    //@@end
  }
```

11. We have completed all that is needed for the first view. Now open the second view and map the context attribute from the component controller as we did for the first view. This will make sure that the data can flow from the context of the first view to the context of the second view via the context of the component controller. The context mapping should look like Figure 7.67.

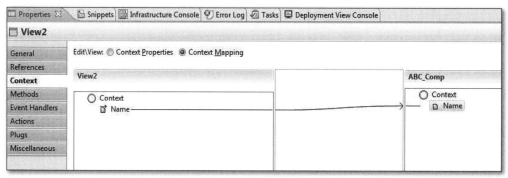

Figure 7.67 Context Mapping

12. Create two text views in the second view, assign the text "Hello" to the first text view, and, for the second text view, bind the property `Text` to the context attribute. With this, whatever name the user enters in the input will flow to this TextView via the context mapping.

Create a BACK button for going back to the first view. As we did in the first view, create an action named BACK, and assign this action to the BACK button. Choose to fire the outbound plug of the second view on the click event of this button. After this, the second view should now look like Figure 7.68.

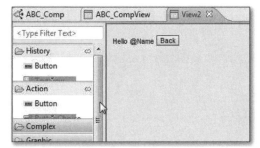

Figure 7.68   User Interface Elements for the Second View

You will notice that a method, onActionBack, has been created in the Java code for the second view, with the following implementation:

```
public void onActionBack(com.sap.tc.webdynpro.progmodel.api.
IWDCustomEvent wdEvent )
  {
    //@@begin onActionBack(ServerEvent)
    wdThis.wdFirePlugSecondOut();
    //@@end
  }
```

The application has now been completed. You can now build and deploy the application and execute it, as discussed before.

The first view initially loads with an input field and a Submit button. When you enter your name and click Submit, the application navigates to the second view and greets you with "Hello *Name*." The second view has a Back button that takes you back to the first view.

With this application, we complete our section on Web Dynpro Java development. Although Web Dynpro Java is a vast programming platform and cannot be explained fully in this chapter, the purpose here was to introduce you to the programming style of Web Dynpro Java and provide a few examples.

7.4   Web Dynpro ABAP

Web Dynpro ABAP is another flavor of the Web Dynpro technology provided by SAP. Web Dynpro ABAP was released by SAP after Web Dynpro Java and has been available since SAP NetWeaver Application Server 7.0. Most of the concepts of Web Dynpro ABAP are the same as Web Dynpro Java, so we will not discuss the architecture and design of Web Dynpro ABAP. We will, however, discuss some of the features that are different from Web Dynpro Java.

Web Dynpro ABAP development is done on the ABAP stack by going to Transaction SE80 as shown in Figure 7.69.

Figure 7.69   Web Dynpro Development Environment

To create or edit Web Dynpro ABAP applications, you need to click the REPOSITORY BROWSER button in the left side of the screen and select WEB DYNPRO COMP./INTF.

In this section, we will explain the steps needed to develop a Web Dynpro ABAP application (using the same example functionality that we developed using Web Dynpro Java). This will help you compare both the platforms. We will also explore some advanced features in Web Dynpro ABAP, such as integrating an ABAP List Viewer (ALV) and integrating an interactive Adobe form in Web Dynpro ABAP applications. In addition, because Web Dynpro ABAP runs on the ABAP stack and not on the portal platform, we will see how Web Dynpro ABAP applications are integrated into SAP NetWeaver Portal and how various integration features related to eventing are used.

7.4.1   Creating a Web Dynpro ABAP Application

In this example application, we will have two views with the following functionality.

- The first view will have an input field and a Submit button.

- In the input field, you will enter your name and click Submit.

- The application will navigate to the second view with a greeting.

- The second view will have a button to navigate back to the first view.

You will need to follow several steps to achieve this functionality; we discuss these steps next.

Creating the Web Dynpro Component

First, we start by creating the Web Dynpro component. To do this, follow these steps:

1. Navigate to Transaction SE80, and create a Web Dynpro ABAP component by entering a name and pressing Enter. If a component by that name does not exist, the system will offer to create that object (Figure 7.70). Choose Yes.

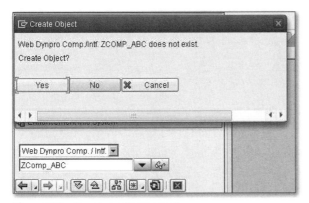

Figure 7.70 Creating a Component

2. The system will propose the names of a window and a view to be created along with the component. Keep the component name as COMP_ABC, the window name as ABC_W, and the view name as FIRST_V.

3. Enter a package in which you want to create this component. For this example, we will just choose the $TMP package, which means that this will be created as a local object and will not be transported to other systems. You can also click the Local Object button here to save it as a local object (Figure 7.71).

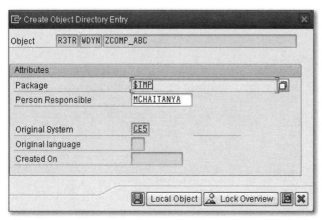

Figure 7.71 Assigning a Package

4. Right-click the component, and choose CREATE • WEB DYNPRO APPLICATION. Enter a name for the application, and save. As in the case of Web Dynpro Java, a Web Dynpro ABAP application is an entry point for a Web Dynpro component.

Creating the Views and Context

The next step is to create the views and context by following these steps:

1. Create one more view named VIEW2.

2. Open the component controller, and go to the CONTEXT tab. In the content, create a node called NAME, and inside that node, create an attribute called NAME. You can create a node by right-clicking the root context and selecting CREATE • NODE. In the code, keep the cardinality as 1..1, to make sure that only one element of this node exists at runtime. Figure 7.72 shows the various properties of node.

The important thing to note here is that when you set the cardinality of a node to 1..1, the runtime automatically creates an element of that node. After creating the node and attribute, the context of the component controller should look like Figure 7.73.

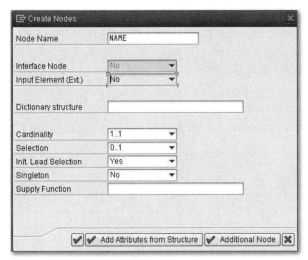

Figure 7.72 Creating a Node

Figure 7.73 Context of the Component Controller

3. Now map the context to the context of both the views. Open the first view MAIN, and go to the CONTEXT tab. Because the component controller is added to the view as a used controller by default, the context of the component controller is available for mapping with the view's context (Figure 7.74).

Figure 7.74 Context Mapping

267

4. Drag the context node NAME from the component controller's context, and drop it on the view controller's context. The same node and attribute will be created in the view's context, and it will be mapped to the component controller's context. This means that the data available in this node of the view's context will flow to the component controller's context. After the mapping, if you look at the properties of the node in the view, you will see the mapped path mentioned, and the node will have an arrow indicating that a mapping exists (Figure 7.75).

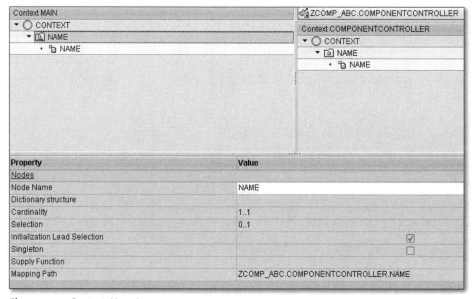

Figure 7.75 Context Mapping

5. Similar mapping needs to be done for the second view, VIEW2, so that this view will also have the NAME node created and mapped to the component controller's node.

Creating the Navigation Plugs and Navigation Links

Next, you must create the navigation plugs and links. Follow these steps:

1. We will now create the outbound and inbound plugs to enable navigation between the views. In the MAIN view, we will create an outbound plug MAIN_OUT and an inbound plug MAIN_IN. Similarly, in the VIEW2 view, we will

create an outbound plug VIEW2_OUT and an inbound plug VIEW2_IN. To create the plugs, go to the OUTBOUND PLUGS tab and the INBOUND PLUGS tab in the view. Figure 7.76 shows an outbound plug for the MAIN view.

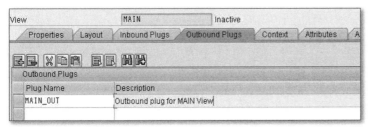

Figure 7.76 Navigation Plugs

2. Create navigation links between the plugs so that you can navigate from the MAIN view to VIEW2 and back. To create the navigation links, open the window ZCOMP_ABC, and navigate to the WINDOW tab. In the windows structure, you will find that the view MAIN is already added to the window; however, the second view is not added. This is because the MAIN view and the window were created together when the component was created, and the tool added the view to the window by default. To add the second view, right-click the window, and choose EMBED VIEW. Then in the popup, select the view (VIEW2) to be added, and press ⌷Enter⌷. Now the second view will be added, and the window should look like Figure 7.77.

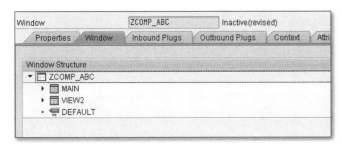

Figure 7.77 Adding a View to a Window

3. To create the navigation links, expand the view, and select the outbound plug. Right-click the outbound plug, and select CREATE NAVIGATION LINK (Figure 7.78).

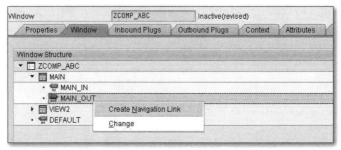

Figure 7.78 Creating a Navigation Link

4. Choose the destination view and the destination inbound plug for creating the navigation link (Figure 7.79). Press ⌊Enter⌋, and the navigation link will be created.

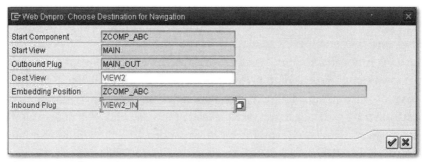

Figure 7.79 Selecting the Navigation Link Target

5. Similarly, create the navigation link from the second view to the first view so that you can navigate back to the first view from the second view. After creating both the navigation links, your window should look like Figure 7.80.

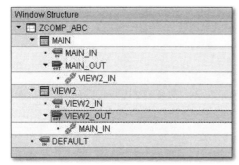

Figure 7.80 Navigation Links

We have created the contexts so that the data flow will take place across views. We have also created the navigation links, so we can trigger the navigation between the views. Next, we need to create the UIs.

Creating the Layout

You can create the layout by following these steps:

1. In the first view, MAIN, create an input field and a SUBMIT button. For this, go to the LAYOUT tab of the MAIN view, right-click ROOTUIELEMENTCONTAINER, and select INSERT ELEMENT. Enter a name, and select the type of UI element. Choose the type INPUTFIELD for creating the input field and the type BUTTON for creating the SUBMIT button. After creating the elements, the view should look like Figure 7.81.

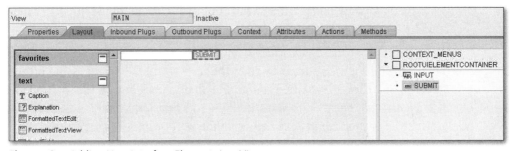

Figure 7.81 Adding User Interface Elements in a View

2. Map the value property of the input field to the NAME attribute from the context.

3. Create an action for the SUBMIT button's `onAction` event. When defining the action, you can also select the outbound plug that needs to be fired during this action. Figure 7.82 shows that the outbound plug MAIN_OUT has been chosen to be fired.

If we now look at the methods, we see that a new method, `ONACTIONSUBMIT`, has been created with the following implementation:

```
method ONACTIONSUBMIT .
  wd_this->fire_main_out_plg(
  ).
endmethod.
```

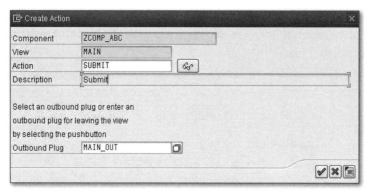

Figure 7.82 Creating an Action

Whenever you create an action, a method named ONACTION<ACTION_NAME> is created, where ACTION_NAME is the name of the action you defined while creating it. With this code, whenever the SUBMIT button is clicked, the MAIN_OUT outbound plug will be fired.

4. Now open the second view, VIEW2, and create two TEXTVIEW elements and a button. In this view, we want to greet the user who entered the name on the first view and clicked SUBMIT. The button will be a back button that on clicking will take the user back to the first screen. For the first TextView, provide the text as "Hello". For the second TextView, map the TEXT property to the context attribute, so that the name the user entered in the first screen will flow to this view. The layout of the second view will now look like Figure 7.83.

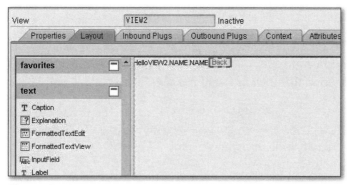

Figure 7.83 View Layout

5. Now we need to create an action for the BACK button so that we can navigate back to the first screen. Enter the action details and, as before, provide the outbound plug name (Figure 7.84) to be fired so that the code for firing the outbound plug is also automatically generated.

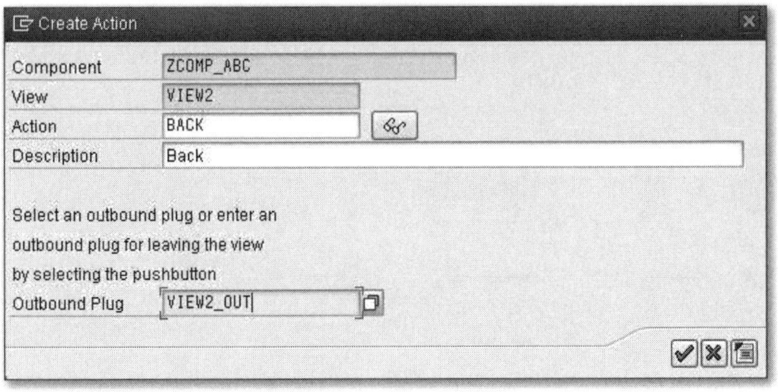

Figure 7.84 Creating an Action

You will see that a new method, ONACTIONBACK, has been created with the following implementation:

```
method ONACTIONBACK .
  wd_this->fire_view2_out_plg(
  ).
endmethod.
```

Executing the Application

With all of the previous steps, our application is complete. Now we can execute the application by right-clicking the application and choosing TEST, or by going to the following URL:

http://<host>:<port>/sap/bc/webdynpro/<NAMESPACE>/<APP_NAME>?sap-client=<CLIENT>&sap-language=<LANG>

In this URL, *<NAMESPACE>* is the namespace of the application, *<APP_NAME>* is the name of the Web Dynpro application, *<CLIENT>* is the client in which you want to run the application, and *<LANG>* is the language; for example, EN, FR, and so on.

When the application runs, it shows the first view as shown in Figure 7.85.

Figure 7.85 Executing the Application

When the user enters a name and clicks SUBMIT, the second screen is loaded with the greeting as shown in Figure 7.86.

Figure 7.86 Second Screen

If you now click the BACK button, it will take you back to the initial screen.

7.4.2 Creating a Web Dynpro ALV Application

The ABAP List Viewer (ALV) is a very popular tool that is used to display lists and tabular structures. It provides many common functions and can also be enhanced with custom functions. For Web Dynpro ABAP, SAP provides a component, SALV_WD_TABLE, that can be used within your Web Dynpro ABAP applications to provide ALV functionalities in a web application. The following functionalities are available with the standard ALV Web Dynpro component:

▶ Filtering

▶ Sorting across multiple columns

▶ Displaying calculations and subtotals

▶ Displaying information in SAP Crystal Reports with predefined SAP Crystal Reports layouts

▶ Configuring a print version in PDF format

▶ Exporting data to Excel

▶ Displaying tables hierarchically

When you include an ALV into your Web Dynpro application, you can also configure the ALV using the ALV configuration model; this allows you to decide which functionalities are available in your ALV.

In this section, we will look at each of the steps needed to integrate an ALV with your Web Dynpro ABAP application. For the purpose of this example, we will use the flight list sample data provided by SAP. This example will provide the functionality to search for a flight based on carrier ID and flight number.

Creating a Web Dynpro Component

By now you know how to create a Web Dynpro ABAP component by going to Transaction SE80 (Figure 7.87).

Figure 7.87   Creating a Web Dynpro ABAP Component

Creating Context Nodes and Attributes

In the component controller, create a context node FLIGHT based on the dictionary structure SFLIGHT, and choose fields CARRID and CONNID (Figure 7.88). These attributes will be used for storing the search criteria for searching the flights.

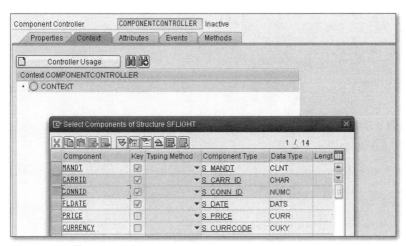

Figure 7.88   Choosing Fields

To create the attributes directly from the structure, you can right click on the context node and choose CREATE USING THE WIZARD • ATTRIBUTES FROM COMPONENTS OF STRUCTURE as shown in Figure 7.89. Make sure that the cardinality of the node is set to 1..1.

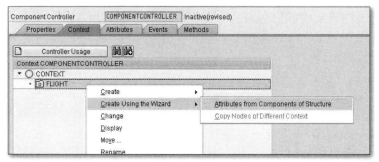

Figure 7.89 Choosing Fields from a Dictionary Structure

Since the node for the search fields is created, now you need to create a context node that will hold the data for the search results. For this, create a context node, FLIGHT_TAB, based on the SFLIGHT structure. Make sure that the cardinality for this node is selected as 0..n, because this node will need to hold the data for multiple flights. Figure 7.90 shows the creation of the node based on the SFLIGHT dictionary structure with cardinality 0..n.

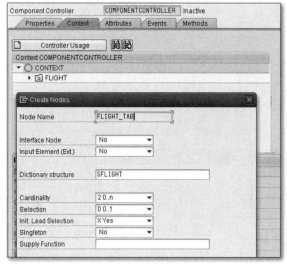

Figure 7.90 Creating Node for Flight Data

After creating the node, add the fields of the structure SFLIGHT to it. Figure 7.91 shows the process of choosing the required fields and adding these fields as attributes of the node FLIGHT_TAB.

Figure 7.91 Choosing Fields from Dictionary Structure

After the nodes and attributes are created, the context will look like Figure 7.92.

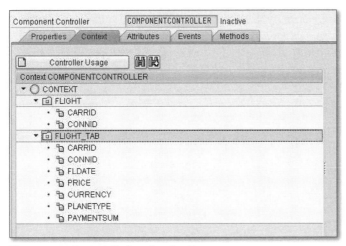

Figure 7.92 Context Nodes after Creation

277

Writing the Method for Searching Flights

The next step is to write the code to search for flights based on the search criteria entered by the user. For this we will create a method, SEARCH_FLIGHTS, in the component controller of the component. We will write the code to search the flights in this method.

Listing 7.4 shows the code for searching for flights based on the user search criteria.

```
* fill context node "node_flighttab"
  DATA:
    node_flight      TYPE REF TO if_wd_context_node,
    node_flighttab   TYPE REF to if_wd_context_node,
    elem_flight      TYPE REF TO if_wd_context_element,
    stru_flight      TYPE if_componentcontroller=>element_flight,
    ls_where(72)     TYPE c,
    lt_where         LIKE TABLE OF ls_where,
    lt_flights       TYPE TABLE OF sflight.
* navigate from <CONTEXT> to <NODE_FLIGHT> via lead selection
  node_flight = wd_context->get_child_node( name = 'FLIGHT' ).
* get element via lead selection
  elem_flight = node_flight->get_element(  ).
* get all declared attributes
  elem_flight->get_static_attributes(
    IMPORTING
      static_attributes = stru_flight ).
* create where condition
  IF NOT stru_flight-carrid EQ ''.
    CONCATENATE 'CARRID = ''' stru_flight-carrid '''' INTO ls_where.
    APPEND ls_where TO lt_where.
  ENDIF.
  IF NOT stru_flight-connid EQ '0000'.
    CONCATENATE 'CONNID = ''' stru_flight-connid '''' INTO ls_where.
    IF stru_flight-carrid NE ''.
      CONCATENATE 'AND' ls_where INTO ls_where separated by space.
    ENDIF.
    APPEND ls_where TO lt_where.
  ENDIF.
* read data
  select * from sflight into table lt_flights
    WHERE (lt_where).
```

```
* navigate from <CONTEXT> to <NODE_FLIGHT> via lead selection
  node_flighttab = wd_context->get_child_node( name = 'FLIGHT_TAB' ).
* fill context node
  node_flighttab->bind_table( lt_flights ).
```

Listing 7.4 Code to Search for Flights

The method SEARCH_FLIGHTS will be called from the view.

Creating the View Context and Layout

The next step is to map the context node FLIGHT from the component controller to the view's context. To do this, open the view's context tab and drag and drop the FLIGHT node from the component controller's context to the view controller's context. This will ensure that the search criteria entered by the user will flow from the view controller to the component controller. In the component controller, the method SEARCH_FLIGHTS uses these parameters to search for flights based on user input. The view's context will look like Figure 7.93 after the context mapping.

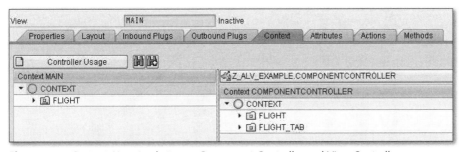

Figure 7.93 Context Mapping between Component Controller and View Controller

Now that you have created the context of the view, the next step is to create the layout. In the layout, add the fields for entering the airline code and the flight number and bind them to the CARRID and CONNID attributes of the FLIGHT node, respectively. Also include a search button to generate the event for search for flights.

After creating the UI elements, your layout should look like Figure 7.94.

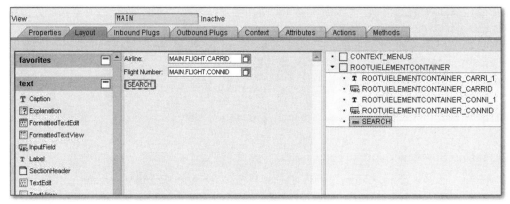

Figure 7.94 Layout for Flight Search

Create a SEARCH action and assign it to the `onAction` event of the SEARCH button. In the `ONACTIONSEARCH` method that gets generated, call the method `SEARCH_FLIGHTS` of the component controller. The code you will need to write is this:

```
wd_comp_controller->search_flights( ).
```

Now, add a UI element of type ViewContainerUIElement to the view. This view container will hold the data for the flights in an ALV format. After adding the view container for the result, the view should look like Figure 7.95.

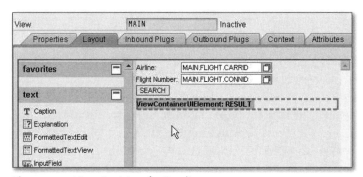

Figure 7.95 View Container for Result

Using the ALV Component

The next step is to use the ALV component provided by SAP to make use of the ALV features. To do so, double click on your component; in the USED COMPONENTS section add the component SALV_WD_TABLE. This defines that your component is going to use the ALV table component provided by SAP. You can name the component usage anything; in this example, we have named it "ALV_TABLE" (Figure 7.96).

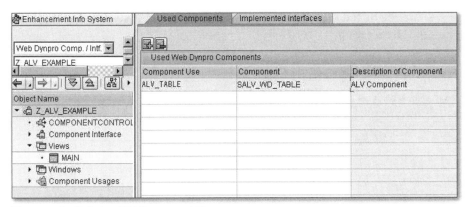

Figure 7.96 Defining ALV Component Usage

After defining the usage of the ALV component, we need to map the flight data from the component controller to the ALV component so that the data selected in the component controller is displayed in the ALV. To do so, go to COMPONENT USAGES • ALV_TABLE in the component and double click on INTERFACECONTROLLER_USAGE. Click on the controller usage button and select the component controller to define the controller usage so that you can do a context mapping between the component controller and the ALV component's interface controller. After adding the controller usage, the context of the component controller should get added to the right side of the ALV interface controller's context, as shown in Figure 7.97.

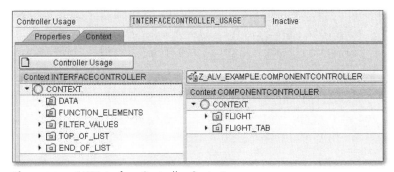

Figure 7.97 ALV Interface Controller Context

Now drag the FLIGHT_TAB context node of the component controller and drop it on the DATA node of the ALV interface controller. This maps the data of the FLIGHT_TAB node to the DATA node of the interface controller. After the mapping, the DATA node of the interface controller should have a bi-directional arrow, as shown in Figure 7.98.

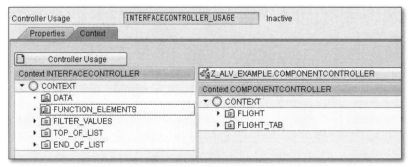

Figure 7.98 Mapped ALV Interface Controller Context

This mapping will make sure that whatever data has been filled in the FLIGHT_TAB node of the component controller will flow into the data node of the ALV component, and the ALV table will show that data.

Embedding the ALV View

We will now embed the TABLE view of the ALV component into our view where we want it to be displayed. We had created a view container RESULT in our view for this purpose, so we will add the ALV table view into the RESULT view container.

Double click on the Window tab and navigate to the view container where you want to embed the ALV table. Right click on the view container and select Embed View. From the pop-up, select the TABLE view of the SALV_WD_TABLE component, as shown in Figure 7.99.

Your component has been created, so now you can activate the whole component. Create a test Web Dynpro application to try out this application. When you execute the application, you will see the screen where you can search for flights based on the carrier ID and the connection ID. Figure 7.100 shows the ALV application running.

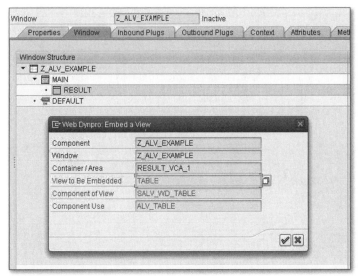

Figure 7.99 Using the TABLE View of the ALV Component

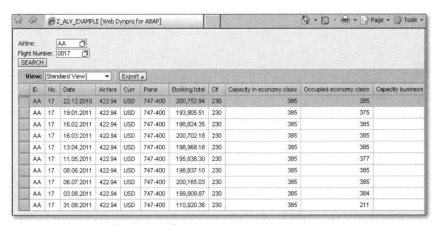

Figure 7.100 Testing the ALV Application

7.4.3 Integrating Adobe Interactive Forms with Web Dynpro ABAP

You can use SAP Interactive Forms by Adobe with Web Dynpro ABAP to create Adobe-form-based interfaces. This is helpful in many scenarios; for example:

▸ Printing non-interactive forms where user input is not required

▸ Creating interactive forms where user input is required

▶ Creating offline forms that can be stored offline and uploaded into the system using Web Dynpro for ABAP

In this section, we explain how to create a Web Dynpro ABAP application that integrates with Adobe Interactive Forms and updates data in SAP tables. Figure 7.101 shows a sample SAP table that we will update from an Adobe form running with a Web Dynpro ABAP application.

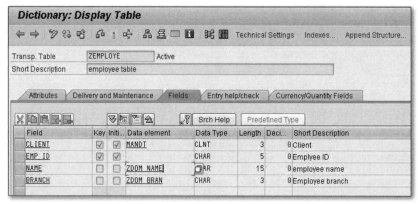

Figure 7.101 SAP Table

Creating a Web Dynpro Component

To start building the Web Dynpro ABAP component, go to Transaction SE80 and create a component named "Z_ADOBE_EXAMPLE". After the component is created, your screen should look like Figure 7.102.

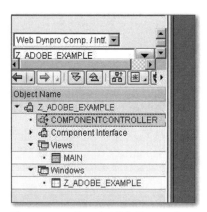

Figure 7.102 Sample Web Dynpro Component

Creating the Context

Open the default view that got created with the component and go to the CONTEXT tab. Create a node named "ADOBE" in the view's context, as shown in Figure 7.103, and make it a singleton node by marking YES in the SINGLETON field.

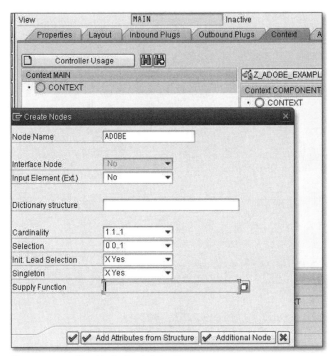

Figure 7.103 Top Node for Adobe Form

Inside the ADOBE node, create another node named "EMPLOYEE". Use the ZEM-PLOYE dictionary structure to choose fields for creating the attributes for this node, as shown in Figure 7.104.

Create another attribute named "PDF_SOURCE" under the CONTEXT root node and assign the type XSTRING to this attribute, as shown in Figure 7.105. This attribute will hold the form data in binary format.

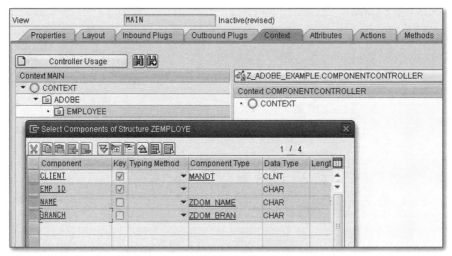

Figure 7.104 Creating Attributes from a Dictionary Structure

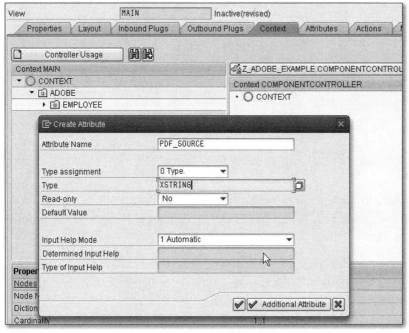

Figure 7.105 PDF_SOURCE Attribute

After all the nodes and attributes are created, the context of the view should look like Figure 7.106.

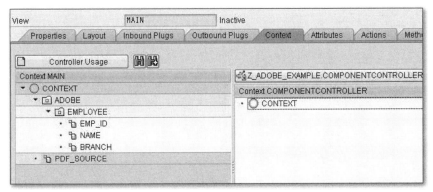

Figure 7.106 View Content after Nodes Creation

Creating the Layout

You have created the context nodes and attributes needed for the form; now you will create the view layout. In the view layout, insert an InteractiveForm element as shown in Figure 7.107.

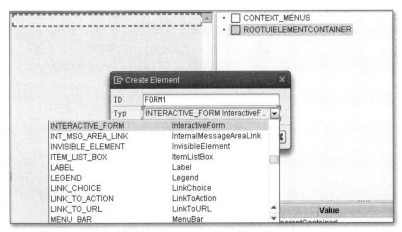

Figure 7.107 Inserting an InteractiveForm Element to View

You will see the new element created under the ROOTUIELEMENTCONTAINER in the view layout. Check the checkbox for the ENABLED attribute and set the height and width settings to 500px each. Also bind the PDFSOURCE property to the context attribute PDF_SOURCE that you created. After these attributes are set, the element properties should look like Figure 7.108.

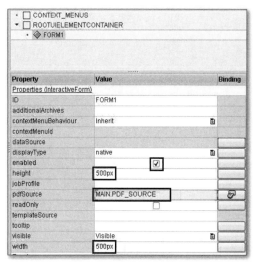

Figure 7.108 InteractiveForm Element Properties

Creating the Form

In the next step, we will provide a template source for the form and then create the form and the interface. In the InteractiveForm element properties, go to the TEMPLATESOURCE property and enter a template named "Z_ADOBE". When you hit Enter, you will see a message saying that the form does not exist, and that to create a form you need to specify an interface name. Specify the interface name as "Z_ADOBE". This process is shown in Figure 7.109.

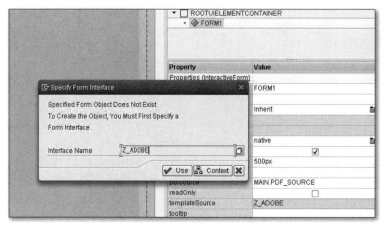

Figure 7.109 Creating a Template Source

Press the CONTEXT button to create the interface from the context node, and you will get a pop-up asking you to select the node for creating the interface. Select the node ADOBE and click CONTINUE (Figure 7.110).

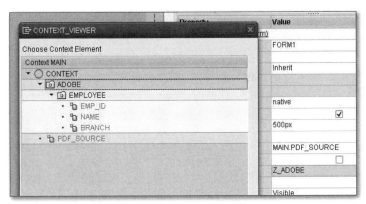

Figure 7.110 Creating Interface from Context Node

When you click CONTINUE, you will be prompted to save the view. After you save the view, you will be taken to the Form Builder, where you can design your form as shown in Figure 7.111.

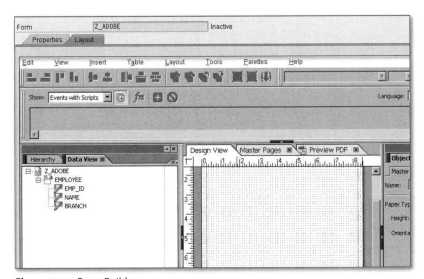

Figure 7.111 Form Builder

289

From the DATA VIEW tab on the form, drag the EMPLOYEE node and drop it on the form. You will see that fields for the attributes of the EMPLOYEE node are created on the form. Now open the library; from the group WebDynproActiveX, add the SUBMIT button to the form. After the fields and button have been added, the form should look like Figure 7.112.

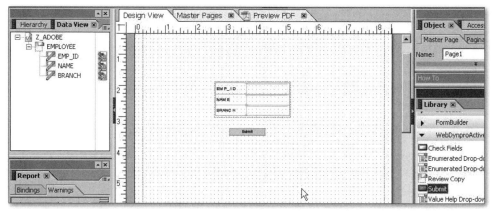

Figure 7.112 Adding Fields on the Form

Save and activate the form and the interface.

Handling the Submit Event in Web Dynpro

You have created the form and the form interface; the next step is to handle the event of the SUBMIT button. Go to the InteractiveForm element FORM1 that you just created. In the EVENTS section, click on the CREATE button and create an action named "SUBMIT". We now need to implement the ONACTIONSUBMIT method that was generated when you created the SUBMIT action. In this method we will write the code to read the values entered by the user on the form, and then insert these values into the SAP table.

Listing 7.5 provides the code to do this.

```
method ONACTIONSUBMIT .
  data:
    Node_Adobe          type ref to If_Wd_Context_Node,
    Node_Employee       type ref to If_Wd_Context_Node,
    Elem_Employee       type ref to If_Wd_Context_Element,
    Stru_Employee       type If_Main=>Element_Employee .
```

```
data wa_zemploye type zemploye.

* navigate from <CONTEXT> to <ADOBE> via lead selection
  Node_Adobe = wd_Context->get_Child_Node( Name = IF_MAIN=>wdctx_
Adobe ).

* navigate from <ADOBE> to <ZDEPT> via lead selection
  Node_Employee = Node_Adobe->get_Child_Node( Name = IF_MAIN=>wdctx_
Employee ).

* get element via lead selection
  Elem_Employee = Node_Employee->get_Element(  ).

* get all declared attributes
  Elem_Employee->get_Static_Attributes(
    importing
      Static_Attributes = Stru_Employee ).

  wa_zemploye-EMP_ID = Stru_Employee-EMP_ID.
  wa_zemploye-NAME = Stru_Employee-NAME.
  wa_zemploye-BRANCH   = Stru_Employee-BRANCH.

  insert into zemploye values wa_zemploye.

endmethod.
```

Listing 7.5 Read the Form Data and Insert into Table

Save and activate the Web Dynpro component.

Testing the Application

Our component is now ready to test. Create a Web Dynpro application called "Z_ADOBE_EXAMPLE" to launch this component, and launch the application. When the application loads into the browser, you will see that the Adobe form you created gets loaded. Figure 7.113 shows the Adobe interactive form loaded in the browser.

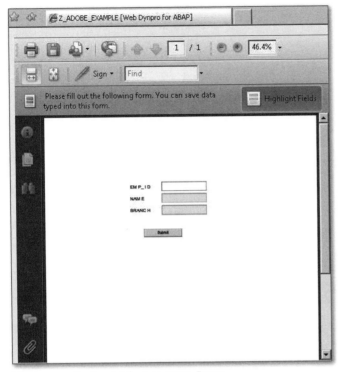

Figure 7.113 Testing Adobe Interactive Forms

Now, when you enter the data and click on the SUBMIT button, you will see that the entered data gets inserted into the SAP table.

7.4.4 Integrating a Web Dynpro ABAP Application with SAP NetWeaver Portal

Web Dynpro ABAP applications can be run as standalone applications as well as iViews inside SAP NetWeaver Portal; SAP NetWeaver Portal provides a template for creating Web Dynpro ABAP-based iViews. A Web Dynpro ABAP application can also access SAP NetWeaver Portal functions by using the IF_WD_PORTAL_INTE-GRATION interface.

Web Dynpro ABAP applications can access the following functions from SAP NetWeaver Portal:

▶ Portal eventing

▶ Navigating with SAP NetWeaver Portal to other portal content by using the following:

  ▶ Object-based navigation

  ▶ Absolute navigation

  ▶ Relative navigation

The following steps are needed for integrating Web Dynpro applications using the Web Dynpro ABAP iView template:

1. Create a system for the SAP system in the portal system landscape.

2. Implement single sign-on (SSO) or user mapping between the portal and the ABAP system where the Web Dynpro ABAP application is running.

3. Create the Web Dynpro iView.

4. Assign the iView to a role that is assigned to the intended user group.

Figure 7.114 shows the overview of the portal integration for SAP Web Dynpro ABAP applications.

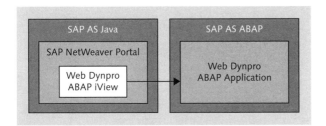

Figure 7.114 Web Dynpro ABAP—Portal Integration

When SAP Web Dynpro ABAP applications are integrated into SAP NetWeaver Portal as Web Dynpro ABAP iViews, they can make use of the portal eventing features. A Web Dynpro ABAP application can subscribe to events that other iViews on the same page as the Web Dynpro iView are firing. When subscribing to an event, the Web Dynpro ABAP application can also extract the event parameters passed by the application that fired the event. Also, a Web Dynpro ABAP application can fire events that other iViews on the same page can subscribe to. We will discuss the steps needed for these next.

Portal Eventing

Portal eventing is an eventing framework provided by SAP NetWeaver Portal, which the iViews running on the same page can use to interact with each other and pass data. The iViews on one SAP NetWeaver Portal page can be of various technologies, portal components, Web Dynpro Java, Web Dynpro ABAP, or Business Server Pages (BSP), but they all can make use of portal eventing to interact with one another. Portal eventing is a client-side framework that uses JavaScript to achieve the communication between various iViews.

A Web Dynpro application subscribes to a portal event. Whenever the portal event is triggered by another Web Dynpro or an iView that is not based on Web Dynpro, the event is passed to all of the iViews that have subscribed to the event. A Web Dynpro application can also raise a portal event.

Firing a Portal Event

Firing a portal event from a Web Dynpro ABAP application can be done by using the IF_WD_PORTAL_INTEGRATION interface. Listing 7.6 provides an example.

```
DATA LO_API_COMPONENT  TYPE REF TO IF_WD_COMPONENT.
DATA LO_PORTAL_MANAGER TYPE REF TO IF_WD_PORTAL_INTEGRATION.

LO_API_COMPONENT = WD_COMP_CONTROLLER->WD_GET_API( ).
LO_PORTAL_MANAGER = LO_API_COMPONENT->GET_PORTAL_MANAGER( ).

CALL METHOD lo_portal_manager->FIRE
  EXPORTING
    PORTAL_EVENT_NAMESPACE =
    PORTAL_EVENT_NAME      =
*     PORTAL_EVENT_PARAMETER =
*     PORTAL_EVENT_SCOPE     = IF_WD_PORTAL_INTEGRATION=>CO_EVENT_
SCOPE-CURRENT_WINDOW
      .
```

Listing 7.6 Firing a Portal Event

In Listing 7.6, note the following:

▶ PORTAL_EVENT_NAMESPACE
The namespace is used to uniquely distinguish each event.

▶ PORTAL_EVENT_NAME

This is the name of the portal event. The combination of the event namespace and the event name should be unique within the portal.

▶ PORTAL_EVENT_PARAMETER

This contains the data that will be exchanged between the views along with the event.

Subscribing to a Portal Event

Subscribing to a portal event by a Web Dynpro ABAP application can only be done by a view. Usually, the registration should be done in the WDDOINIT method of the view. Listing 7.7 shows the code for subscribing to a portal event.

```
DATA LO_API_COMPONENT  TYPE REF TO IF_WD_COMPONENT.
DATA LO_PORTAL_MANAGER TYPE REF TO IF_WD_PORTAL_INTEGRATION.

LO_API_COMPONENT = WD_COMP_CONTROLLER->WD_GET_API( ).
LO_PORTAL_MANAGER = LO_API_COMPONENT->GET_PORTAL_MANAGER( ).

DATA LO_API_CONTROLLER  TYPE REF TO IF_WD_VIEW_CONTROLLER.

LO_API_CONTROLLER ?= WD_THIS->WD_GET_API( ).

CALL METHOD lo_portal_manager->SUBSCRIBE_EVENT
  EXPORTING
    PORTAL_EVENT_NAMESPACE =
    PORTAL_EVENT_NAME      =
    VIEW                  = LO_API_CONTROLLER
    ACTION                = 'CHANGE_EVENT'
    .
```

Listing 7.7 Subscribing to a Portal Event

For registering to a portal event from a Web Dynpro ABAP view, you should already have an action that will be called when the event is triggered. The name of the action needs to be passed during registration.

The code for firing and registering to an event can be generated by using the Web Dynpro code wizard (Figure 7.115).

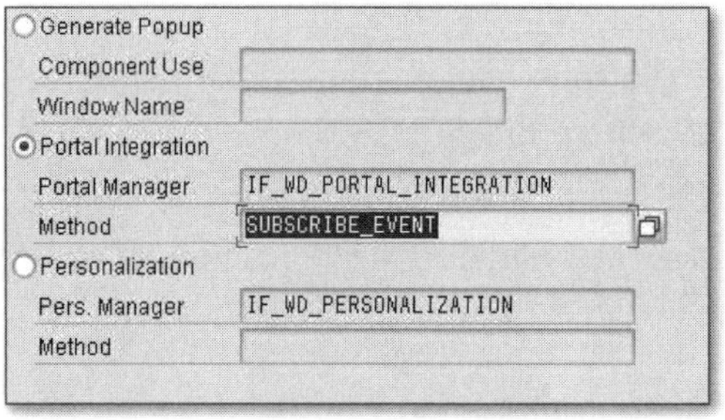

Figure 7.115 Web Dynpro Code Wizard

Extracting the Event Parameters

When you have subscribed to a portal event in a Web Dynpro ABAP application, you also need to extract the data that has been passed by the event. The information about the event can be extracted from the parameter WDEVENT passed to the event.

WDEVENT->PARAMETERS contains the name-value pairs as an internal table. The portal event parameter can be retrieved by using the key PORTAL_EVENT_PARAMETER from the internal table. Listing 7.8 shows a sample for this.

```
DATA: ls_parameters TYPE wdr_event_parameter.
FIELD_SYMBOLS: <ls_params> TYPE STRING.

READ TABLE wdevent->parameters INTO ls_parameters
    WITH KEY name = 'PORTAL_EVENT_PARAMETER'.
ASSIGN ls_parameters-value->* TO <ls_params> CASTING.
```

Listing 7.8 Extracting Portal Event Parameters

As shown in Listing 7.8, we retrieve all of the parameters from WDEVENT and then read the PORTAL_EVENT_PARAMETER key.

7.5 Summary

When you are implementing SAP NetWeaver Portal, you will normally integrate applications that are existing in your landscape. You will also very frequently be integrating business packages provided by SAP. Sometimes you will need to create new applications for providing content that does not exist anywhere in the landscape. In these scenarios, you will develop custom applications. Usually, when the application that needs to be developed does not frequently interact with an SAP backend, portal components technology is the preferred technology for developing custom applications; this is because portal components run directly on the SAP NetWeaver Portal and can take advantage of a lot of portal services.

When there is heavy interaction with SAP backends, Web Dynpro becomes the preferred technology, because it provides a graphical way of developing applications, thus reducing the development time. Web Dynpro comes in two flavors, Java and ABAP. Web Dynpro Java applications run directly on the portal server, whereas Web Dynpro ABAP applications run on the ABAP backend server and are integrated with the portal using Web Dynpro ABAP iViews. In this chapter, we have looked at these technologies and worked through some examples to get a basic idea of the development in various technologies. This chapter does not intend to provide a complete guideline for development; it rather aims to provide the basic concepts necessary to get started in development.

So far we have learned about implementing a standalone portal, meaning one portal acts as a single point of access for many applications running on the same or external system. In the next chapter, we will learn about implementing a federated portal network in which multiple SAP NetWeaver Portal systems or non-SAP NetWeaver portals interact together and provide content to the user.

This chapter explains the main concepts of and the available usage scenarios with a federated portal network. This chapter also covers the steps needed to implement such a network.

8 Federated Portal Network Implementation

The federated portal network (FPN) capabilities of SAP NetWeaver Portal allow it to share content between SAP and non-SAP portals distributed across an organization's landscape. With a federated portal network, you can reuse content and applications deployed throughout the organization, while still keeping the autonomy of individual units running independent portals. SAP NetWeaver Portal can form a FPN with other SAP NetWeaver Portals or other non-SAP portals, provided they are WSRP compliant. WSRP (Web Services for Remote Portlets) is an industry standard network protocol that defines standards for communication between portlets.

There are two main flavors of portal federation:

▶ **Content federation**
In this type of federation, there are two or more portal installations; however, all of the users log on to one portal, and all of the other portals are used for providing content. This type of federation has the advantage that the responsibilities for producing the content and rendering it to the users are separated.

▶ **Portal federation**
In this type of federation, there are two or more portal installations, and each portal can act as an independent portal serving content to its users. Also, each portal consumes content from other portals and also exposes content to other portals. The advantage of this type of federation is that it gives autonomy to each business unit to run its own portal for its users and at the same time expose content and consume content to and from other portals.

Each portal in a federation can be defined as a producer or consumer portal based on the role it plays in the federation. A *producer portal* is responsible for producing the content and exposing it to other portals. A *consumer portal* consumes the content provided by the provider portals and renders it to the users.

Before we look at the types of content sharing between the portals, let's look at some of the important FPN features:

▶ **Single user store**
In a portal federation, all of the portals can connect to a central user store. The portals, however, are also able to use the local users to serve the content.

▶ **Remote roles**
You can assign the users or groups of users to portal roles on a remote portal. The role is created and maintained on the remote producer portal and also executes on the remote portal.

▶ **RDLs**
Content administrators on a consumer portal can assign delta links to the portal content on remote producer portals.

▶ **Application sharing**
Content administrators can integrate WSRP-compliant portlets from non-SAP portals into SAP NetWeaver Portal. Also you can create WSRP-compliant iViews that can be consumed by non-SAP portals.

▶ **Caching**
A caching mechanism can be used to cache the portal objects on the consumer portals for reuse, thereby reducing the network traffic.

▶ **Personalization**
Users can personalize the remote iViews and pages in the same way they do the local iViews and pages.

In this introduction, we have discussed the basics of an FPN. In the coming sections, we will go into the details of each feature that we discussed, and we will also see how to implement these features in SAP NetWeaver Portal. Specifically, we will start by discussing the types of content sharing in an FPN. We will then see the steps needed to prepare the SAP NetWeaver Portal content sharing. Configurations for the content sharing involve creating FPN connections and WSRP connections, then exposing the content on producers, and consuming the content on consumers. In this chapter, we will discuss these topics in detail.

8.1   Types of Content Sharing

As introduced earlier, SAP NetWeaver Portal provides different ways of content sharing while implementing an FPN. Each content sharing type is suited for a different scenario. In this section, we will go into the detail of each sharing mode, discuss the advantages and disadvantages of these sharing types, and then see how these are implemented in SAP NetWeaver Portal.

8.1.1   Remote Role Assignment (RRA)

In remote role assignment (RRA), a user administrator on a consumer portal can assign users and user groups to roles on a remote producer portal. When the users log on to the consumer portal, they receive the content of the remote role from the remote producer portal. Figure 8.1 shows this use-case scenario.

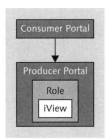

Figure 8.1   Remote Role Assignment

An important thing to note here is that the RRA feature is only available for SAP NetWeaver Portal, so you can't use a non-SAP portal as a producer for RRA.

RRA has the following advantages:

▶ Content creation can be federated because each producer portal will produce its own content. The consumer portal does not need to deal with content administration. The user administrators on the consumer portal just need to assign the users to a remote role.

▶ The producer portal does not need to manage the users and user assignments. Content administrators on the producer portal can just focus on content creation and the consumer portal takes care of users.

RRA has the following disadvantages:

▶ The consumer portal has no control over the actual content, and the administrators on the consumer portal cannot modify the content on the producer portal.

▶ Because administrators on a producer portal have minimum knowledge about the users and user groups accessing the content, they need to be careful about changing the content.

8.1.2　Remote Delta Links (RDL)

The remote delta links (RDL) feature allows the content administrator on the consumer portal to create delta links (discussed in Chapter 6) to portal content on a remote producer portal. These delta links can be configured and customized on the consumer portal as local content, so the content administrators on the consumer portal don't need to access the producer portal. The execution of the content applications still occurs on the producer portal, so when the RDLs are customized on the consumer portal, the original content on the producer portal remains unchanged. On the other hand, if the original content is changed on the producer portal, it reflects on the consumer portal too. Figure 8.2 shows the RDL use-case scenario.

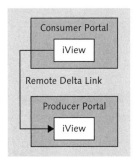

Figure 8.2　Remote Delta Link

RDL has the following advantages:

▶ Various object types, such as iViews, pages, worksets, and roles, are supported.

▶ The remote content on the consumer portal can be modified, even though the unmodified content still exists in the producer portal.

▶ The scenario of mixed content from consumer and producer portals running on the consumer is supported.

- Content can be personalized on the consumer.

RDL has the following disadvantages:

- After RDL has been created in the consumer portal, the original content in the producer portal cannot be deleted, cannot be moved, and cannot have its ID changed.
- A content administrator on the consumer portal is needed to maintain RDL.

8.1.3 WSRP Application Sharing

Web Services for Remote Portlets (WSRP) is an industry standard that defines the interfaces for integrating portlets running on portals from different vendors. SAP NetWeaver supports the WSRP 1.0 specifications. With the WSRP application sharing feature of SAP NetWeaver Portal, you can share content between SAP NetWeaver Portal and non-SAP portals. The non-SAP portal should also support WSRP specifications.

SAP NetWeaver Portal supports two modes of WSRP application sharing:

- SAP NetWeaver consumer and non-SAP producer
- Non-SAP consumer and SAP NetWeaver producer

Even though SAP NetWeaver Portal can serve as both a consumer and a producer, it is not recommended to use this integration to integrate content between two SAP NetWeaver Portal systems. When you are implementing a federation of SAP NetWeaver Portal systems, you should use RRA or RDL. In Figure 8.3, SAP NetWeaver Portal is acting as a consumer to a non-SAP producer portal, and in Figure 8.4, a non-SAP portal is acting as a consumer to an SAP NetWeaver Portal.

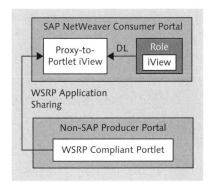

Figure 8.3 WSRP Application Sharing—SAP NetWeaver Consumer

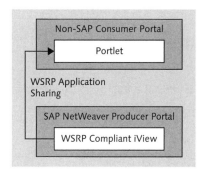

Figure 8.4 WSRP Application Sharing—Non-SAP Consumer

8.2 Preparing the Portals

Now that we are familiar with the basic concepts and types of FPNs, let's discuss the details of implementing a FPN. This section will discuss the various preparatory steps that need to be completed before content sharing can take place.

8.2.1 Setting Up Trust Between Portals

Setting up trust between the portals participating in a federation is the most important step in preparing portals for FPN. Unless the portals trust each other, no single sign-on (SSO) can be done for content sharing across portals. Trust between two portals is established by using logon tickets. The issuing server sends the logon tickets encrypted by the private key of the issuing server, and the receiving server reads the logon ticket after verifying with the issuer's public certificate.

Trust set up in SAP NetWeaver Portal can be done using the SSO wizard in SAP NetWeaver Administrator, and involves exchanging the server certificate files between the consumer and producer servers. Trust can be done either in one direction or in both the directions; the decision will depend on your scenarios and the type of content-sharing mechanism you are implementing.

When there is a connection made from the consumer portal to the producer portal, a logon ticket is issued by the consumer portal, and the producer system accepts the logon system if a trust has been established between the systems. This scenario is shown in Figure 8.5.

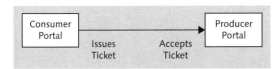

Figure 8.5 Logon Ticket—Consumer Portal Issues Ticket

To implement this scenario, you need to export the keystore certificate from the consumer portal, and it needs to be imported into the producer portal. This is needed in all of the content-sharing scenarios when implementing FPN.

In the second scenario, the producer portal issues the ticket, and the consumer portal accepts the ticket when trust has been established between the two portals (Figure 8.6).

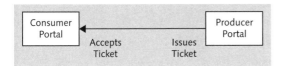

Figure 8.6 Logon Ticket—Producer Portal issues ticket

In this scenario, the keystore certificate is exported from the producer system and imported into the consumer system. This scenario is not normally needed; it is needed only in the scenario in RRA when you want the role assignment from the consumer portal to be automatically removed when a role has been deleted from the producer portal.

Now that you understand the basic concepts of setting up the trust, let's look at the steps for exporting and importing the certificates.

Exporting Certificate from the Ticket-Issuer Portal

To export the certificate from the ticket-issuer system, follow these steps:

1. Go to SAP NetWeaver Administrator on the ticket-issuer portal by going to *http://<host>:<port>/nwa*.

2. Go to CONFIGURATION • SECURITY • CERTIFICATES & KEYS • KEY STORAGE. You will get to the key storage page as shown in Figure 8.7.

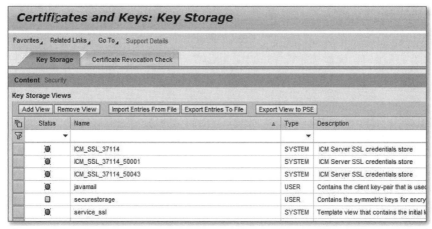

Figure 8.7 Key Storage

3. Choose TICKETKEYSTORE, and from the DETAILS OF VIEW "TICKETKEYSTORE" section, choose SAPLOGONTICKETKEYPAIR-CERT.

4. Click EXPORT ENTRY as shown in Figure 8.8.

Figure 8.8 Exporting Certificate

5. Choose BINARY X.509 CERTIFICATE FILE, and then click the DOWNLOAD link to download the certificate file (Figure 8.9).

6. Save the file on your local file system.

Next, let's look at the steps for importing the certificate file on the ticket-accepting system.

Figure 8.9 Saving the Certificate File

Importing a Certificate on the Ticket-Accepting Portal

To import a certificate, follow these steps:

1. Go to SAP NetWeaver Administrator on the ticket-issuer portal by going to *http://<host>:<port>/nwa*.

2. Go to CONFIGURATION • SECURITY • TRUSTED SYSTEMS • SINGLE SIGN-ON WITH SAP LOGON TICKETS.

3. In the TRUSTED SYSTEMS section, choose ADD TRUSTED SYSTEM • BY UPLOADING CERTIFICATE MANUALLY (Figure 8.10).

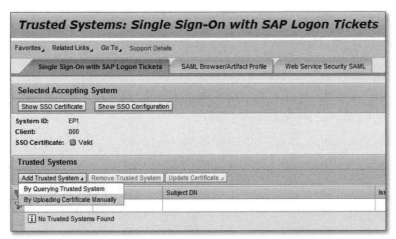

Figure 8.10 Add Trusted System

4. Enter the system ID of the ticket-issuing system and the client number. The client number for a Java system by default is 000. Also select the certificate file from your file system that you had exported from the ticket-issuing system as shown in Figure 8.11.

Figure 8.11 Trusted System Details

5. Click NEXT. The next screen shows the certificate details. Click FINISH to import the certificate. This will add the issues system as a trusted system in the ticket-accepting system. This can be seen from the trusted systems table where the newly added system appears (Figure 8.12).

Figure 8.12 Trusted System Added

With this step, the trust set up between a ticket-issuing system and a ticket-accepting system has been completed.

8.2.2 Setting Up a Registration Password

For security purposes, when setting up a producer portal, you can configure the portal so that any consumer portal wanting to register with this portal must enter a password. This password applies only to SAP NetWeaver Portal systems, not to non-SAP portals. Also, the same password applies to all of the SAP NetWeaver Portal consumers.

To set the registration password, follow these steps:

1. Log on to the producer portal on which you want to define the password, and go to SYSTEM ADMINISTRATION • FEDERATED PORTAL • SAP NETWEAVER – FPN CONNECTIONS • CONTROL PANEL.

2. Go to the CONNECTION OPTIONS tab.

3. Check REMOTE SYSTEMS MUST ENTER A PASSWORD TO CONNECT TO YOUR SYSTEM, and enter a password (Figure 8.13).

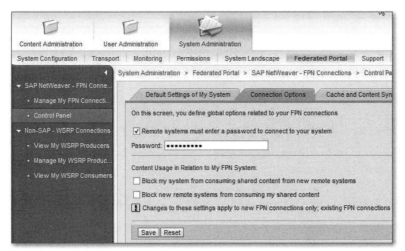

Figure 8.13   Setting Up Registration Password

4. Save your settings.

Now the consumer portal will need to enter this password when registering with this producer portal.

8.2.3   Setting the Root Browse Folder for Remote WSRP Usage

You can expose an SAP NetWeaver Portal producer to a non-SAP consumer portal. However, this may pose a security risk that could expose your whole portal content to the non-SAP portal. To avoid this risk, you can define a root portal content folder on the producer folder that should be visible to the non-SAP portal. All of the subfolders of this root folder are also visible to the non-SAP consumer folder.

To set up the root folder, follow these steps:

1. Log on to SAP NetWeaver Administrator, and go to CONFIGURATION • INFRA-STRUCTURE • APPLICATION MODULES.

2. In the module list, select the name COM.SAP.PORTAL.IVS.WSRPSERVICE, and then select AUTOGENPRODUCER1_0 (Figure 8.14).

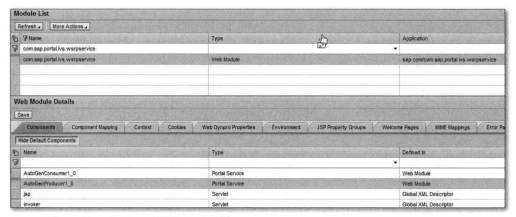

Figure 8.14 Setting a WSRP Root Folder

3. Go to the PORTAL SERVICE DETAILS section, and set the CONTENT_ROOT_FOLDER property to the appropriate folder on your portal. You can set this property value to a folder ID; for example, PCD:PORTAL_CONTENT/WSRP_CONTENT, as shown in Figure 8.15.

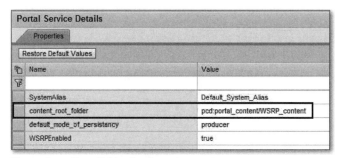

Figure 8.15 Root Folder Configuration

For non-SAP consumer portals to access content on SAP NetWeaver Portal producers, you need to create user IDs for the non-SAP consumer portal in the producer portal. The consumer portal needs to use this user ID and password to connect to the producer portal. The user ID on the producer portal can be created by going to the USER ADMINISTRATION tab.

8.2.4   Setting Default Connection Values

Default connection settings allow you to define the default connection parameters of a consumer portal for making connections to a producer portal. With this setting done, you will not need to enter the values every time you create an FPN connection (Figure 8.16). You can access the default connection settings wizard by going to SYSTEM ADMINISTRATION • FEDERATED PORTAL • SAP NETWEAVER – FPN CONNECTIONS • CONTROL PANEL, and choosing the DEFAULT SETTINGS OF MY SYSTEM tab.

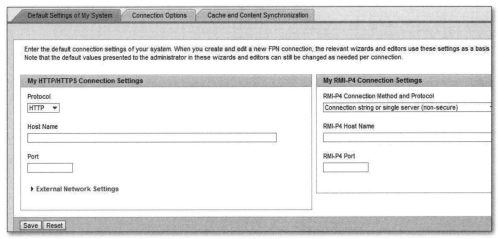

Figure 8.16   Setting Default Connection Values

When you create an FPN connection, the values will be filled in from your default settings; however, you can still override the settings for your FPN connection.

8.3   Managing FPN Connections

You need to create FPN connections to connect from one SAP NetWeaver Portal to another SAP NetWeaver Portal. Consumer portals can create the producer connections and then register with the producer portals. After registration, the consumer portal also shows up in the producer portal as the consumer portal.

To go to the FPN MANAGEMENT screen, navigate to SYSTEM ADMINISTRATION • FEDERATED PORTAL • SAP NETWEAVER – FPN CONNECTIONS • MANAGE MY FPN CONNECTIONS. Figure 8.17 shows the MY FPN CONNECTIONS tab.

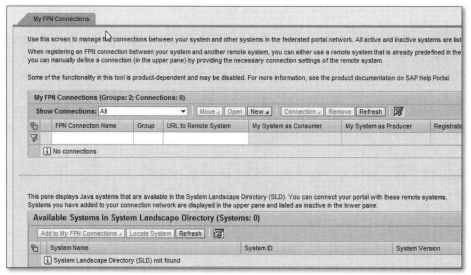

Figure 8.17 Manage FPN Connections

As you can see from Figure 8.17, apart from being able to create new FPN connections from scratch, you can also use systems from your System Landscape Directory (SLD) to create an FPN connection. For doing this, you can select a system from the SLD and click ADD TO MY FPN CONNECTIONS.

In the MY FPN CONNECTIONS section, you can see all of the consumers and producers for this portal. Figure 8.18 shows all of the types of entries you can see in the MY FPN CONNECTIONS table.

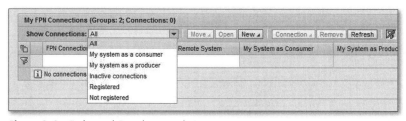

Figure 8.18 Federated Portal Network Connection Types

In this section, we will discuss the steps for creating an FPN connection. Also, for any sharing of content to take place between two portals, the consumer portal must be registered in the producer portal. We'll discuss registering and unregistering FPN connections in this section as well.

8.3.1 Creating an FPN Connection

To create an FPN connection, navigate to SYSTEM ADMINISTRATION • FEDERATED PORTAL • SAP NETWEAVER – FPN CONNECTIONS • MANAGE MY FPN CONNECTIONS, and click the NEW • FPN CONNECTION. Then you need to enter properties, as we'll discuss next.

General Properties

In the general properties screen, you need to enter the following properties:

▶ FPN CONNECTION NAME
The name of this connection appears on both the consumer and producer portals, so it is important to give a name that represents both portals.

▶ FPM CONNECTION ID
This is a unique ID to this connection. It is recommended to not leave this field blank.

▶ GROUP
You can create multiple groups to group various FPN connections. While creating the FPN connection, you can assign it to a group.

System Settings

The connection settings for the system are automatically picked up from the default settings that we defined earlier. You can still change these values for every FPN connection, but features exist to allow for a faster FPN connection creation. It is mandatory to provide the HTTP/HTTPS settings. The RMI-P4 section is only required if you plan to use content sharing by RDL.

As shown in Figure 8.19, if the connection is done through a message server, then you should select the LOAD-BALANCED VIA SAP MESSAGE SERVER entry. If your connection is made directly to the application server, then you should choose CONNECTION STRING OR A SINGLE SERVER. For both, you can choose either the secure or non-secure option. Please keep in mind that you can use the secure option only if the transport layer security has been implemented. RMI-P4 messages can be sent over both SSL and HTTPS secure protocols.

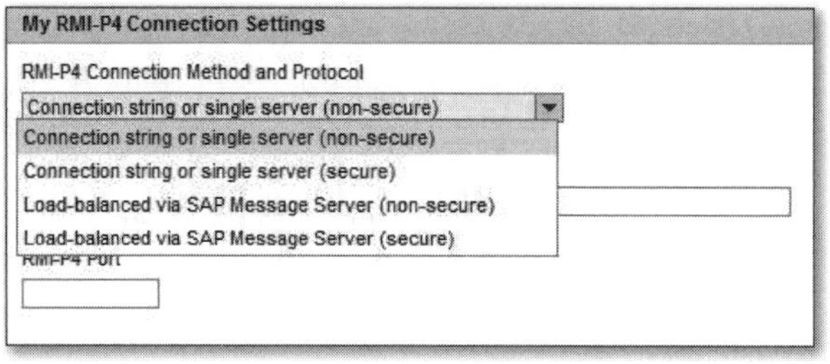

Figure 8.19   RMI-P4 Connection Settings

External network settings are required if there is a reverse proxy between your portal and the clients. You will need to enter the details of the reverse proxy server in the EXTERNAL NETWORK SETTINGS section (Figure 8.20).

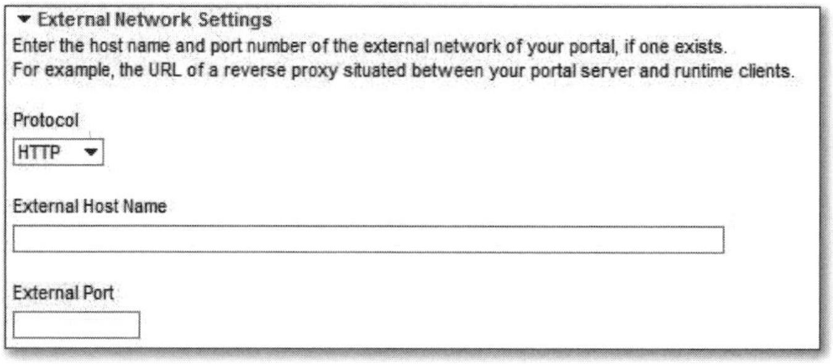

Figure 8.20   External Network Settings

Remote System Settings

For remote system settings, you need to enter the HTTP/HTTPS connection settings of the remote portal; the RMI-P4 connection settings only need to be entered if you want to use the RDL mechanism. Also, if there is a reverse proxy server between the remote portal and its clients, then you need to enter the external network settings for the remote portal.

Trust Configuration

You must make sure that trust has been established between the two portals as shown in Section 8.2.1. If trust has already been established, then you can skip the trust creation here. We have already seen how to establish trust using the SSO wizard of SAP NetWeaver Administrator; follow these steps to create trust between two portals using the FPN Trust Editor:

1. Navigate to System Administration • Federated Portal • SAP NetWeaver – FPN Connections • Manage My FPN Connections. The My FPN Connections tab appears.

2. Select an existing connection, and click Open.

3. In the editor, now choose Trust. The FPN Trust Editor appears.

4. In the Trust Configuration dropdown, choose the direction in which you want to establish trust.

5. Enter the logon credentials of a user on the remote system. The user must be assigned the Administrator role on the remote system.

6. Now click Create Trust to create trust between the two portals. Note that this is applicable only for two SAP NetWeaver Portal systems.

If you are unable to create the trust using the FPN Trust Editor (for example, if you are running the composition environment), you should use the SSO wizard.

8.3.2   Registering/Unregistering FPN Connections

For a consumer portal to consume content from a producer portal, it must be registered in the producer portal. When you register a portal, a two-way registration is already done if the portals are running on the same version; otherwise, only a one-way registration is done. Also, as we saw earlier, if the producer is configured such that a password is needed for every registration, then you will need to enter the required password as configured in the producer portal.

Follow these steps to perform the registration:

1. Navigate to System Administration • Federated Portal • SAP NetWeaver – FPN Connections • Manage My FPN Connections. The My FPN Connections tab appears.

2. Select an existing connection, and select Connection • Register.

3. Enter the registration password if needed.

This completes the registration process. The appropriate status appears in the Registration Status column. If you want to unregister a system, you need to follow similar steps as you just followed, except that in the second step, you will choose Connection • Unregister. The registration status changes appropriately.

8.4 Managing WSRP Connections

WSRP connections are needed if you want to use your SAP NetWeaver Portal as either a consumer or a producer with a non-SAP portal. With SAP NetWeaver Portal 7.3, you can do the following:

▶ Manage WSRP producers.

▶ View WSRP producers.

▶ View WSRP consumers.

We'll discuss each of these in the following sections.

8.4.1 Manage WSRP Producers

To create a WSRP producer for your SAP NetWeaver Portal, navigate to SYSTEM ADMINISTRATION • FEDERATED PORTAL • NON-SAP – WSRP CONNECTIONS • MANAGE MY WSRP PRODUCERS. Right-click WSRP CONTENT PRODUCERS, and select NEW • WSRP PRODUCER (Figure 8.21).

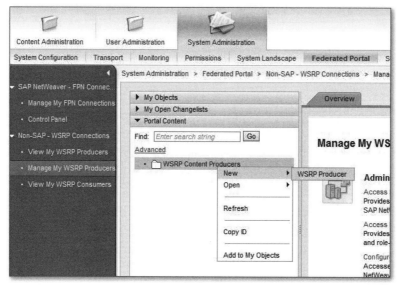

Figure 8.21 Creating a WSRP Producer

The following are the properties for creating the WSRP producer:

General Properties

▶ PRODUCER PORTAL NAME
This is the name that you want to define for the producer portal. This name should identify the producer portal.

▶ PRODUCER PORTAL ID
This is a unique ID given to the producer portal.

Figure 8.22 shows the GENERAL PROPERTIES screen for creating a producer portal.

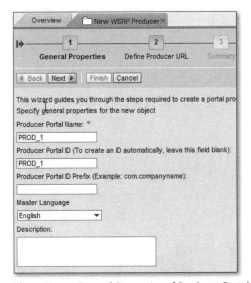

Figure 8.22 General Properties of Producer Portal

Define Producer URL

The WSRP connection to the non-SAP portal is made through Web Services running on the WSRP-compliant portal. You need to know the URL of the Web Services Definition File (WSDL) to connect to the non-SAP WSRP portal.

Figure 8.23 shows the screen for entering the WSDL URL for the WSRP producer.

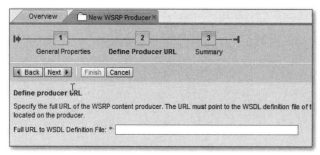

Figure 8.23 Define Producer URL

8.4.2 View WSRP Producers

After the creation of WSRP producers, you can view the producers you have created in two places. You can either go to System Administration • Federated Portal • Non-SAP – WSRP Connections • View My WSRP Producers, or you can go to System Administration • Federated Portal • Non-SAP – WSRP Connections • Manage My WSRP Producers, and expand the folder WSRP Content Producers. Figure 8.24 shows the View My Producers screen, and Figure 8.25 shows the Manage My Producers screen.

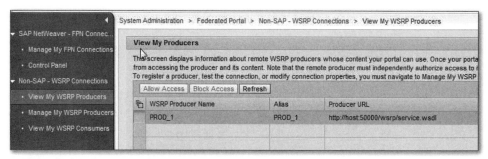

Figure 8.24 View My Producers

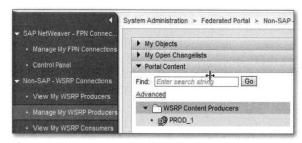

Figure 8.25 Manage My Producers

From the MANAGE MY PRODUCERS screen, you can select a producer, right-click, and perform the following actions:

1. Open properties.

2. Open the permissions.

3. Open the remote content producer URL.

4. Open the producer registration.

5. Open the connection tests.

6. Open system aliases.

For performing connection tests, you need to enter the user name and password for the remote content producer server.

In addition to managing and viewing producers, you can also manage and view consumers. To manage consumers, you need to navigate to SYSTEM ADMINISTRATION • FEDERATED PORTAL • NON-SAP – WSRP CONNECTIONS • MANAGE MY WSRP CONSUMERS; to view consumers, navigate to SYSTEM ADMINISTRATION • FEDERATED PORTAL • NON-SAP – WSRP CONNECTIONS • VIEW MY WSRP CONSUMERS.

8.4.3   View WSRP Consumers

To view the registered WSRP consumers for where SAP NetWeaver Portal is acting as a producer, navigate to SYSTEM ADMINISTRATION • FEDERATED PORTAL • NON-SAP – WSRP CONNECTIONS • VIEW MY WSRP CONSUMERS.

Figure 8.26 shows the screen with the list of connections.

Figure 8.26   View My WSRP Consumers

You can select a consumer and click the REMOVE button if you want to invalidate the registration of the consumer portal.

As you can see from Figure 8.26, you can allow or block access to a producer's content for each consumer from here. If you want to block the content access for any of its consumers, select the consumer for the list, and click BLOCK ACCESS. This will block that consumer from being able to access the producer's content. You can again allow access by selecting the consumer and clicking the ALLOW ACCESS button.

8.5   Exposing Content

At this point, we have discussed the initial steps needed for content sharing in FPN. We have seen how to prepare the portal for content sharing, and how to manage the FPN connections and WSRP connections. In this section, we will discuss how the content is exposed by the content producers so that it can be consumed by the consumers. Specifically, we will discuss the steps needed for exposing content in all three types of content sharing: RRA, RDL usage, and WSRP application sharing.

8.5.1   Remote Role Assignment Usage

For the content on a producer portal to be accessible on the consumer portals, appropriate permissions and actions must be set on the producer portal. Two types of authorizations are typically required: Administrators on the consumer portal should be able to search for roles on the producer portal, and users on the consumer portal should be able to run the content on the producer portal.

The following permissions and actions need to be assigned on the producer portal:

▶ **Role that is being exposed to the consumer**
The user administrator on the consumer portal should be assigned the role assigner level permissions on the producer portal. This will allow the user administrator to search for roles and assign remote roles to local users.

▶ **User pcd_service**
To any role that has the user PCD_SERVICE assigned to it, the following UME actions should be assigned:

  ▶ `Remote_Producer_Read_Access`

  ▶ `Remote_Producer_Write_Access`

▶ **End user permissions**
For the users that will be accessing the content from the producer portal, the portal content and systems should have the end user permissions enabled in the permissions editor. You can open the permissions editor by right-clicking on any portal content and selecting OPEN • PERMISSIONS.

8.5.2 Remote Delta Link Usage

For delta link usage, the content administrators on the consumer portal should be able to copy the content from the producer portal and create delta links. Also, the users accessing the content should have permissions to execute the content on the producer portal. The following permissions should therefore be applied on the producer portal:

▶ **Portal components**
Portal components will be accessed by the business users, so all of the portal components should have end user access enabled.

▶ **PCD content**
PCD content such as iViews, pages, worksets, and roles will be accessed by content administrators on the consumer portals, so they should be assigned read access on the producer portal. Also, the end user access should be enabled for all business users, because they will be executing the PCD content at runtime.

8.5.3 WSRP Application Sharing Usage

Exposing content for WSRP application sharing usage is recommended only for non-SAP consumers. For SAP NetWeaver consumers, RRA or RDL mechanisms should be used.

Non-SAP portals and WSRP do not support the portal permissions mechanism; you still need to set some permissions and iView properties to expose WSRP-compliant content to non-SAP consumers. The iViews that are being exposed must be WSRP compliant.

Two levels of permissions are needed:

▶ **Portal components**
The user on the producer portal that was created for the consumer portal should be given end user permissions.

▶ **iViews**

For the iViews that are being exposed, the consumer users should be given the end user permissions.

To set the iView properties for exposing the iView as a WSRP application, set the AUTHENTICATION SCHEME property of the iView being exposed to ANONYMOUS (Figure 8.27).

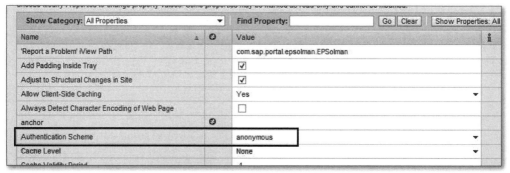

Figure 8.27 Authentication Scheme

Set the EXPOSE AS WSRP APPLICATION property of the iView as shown in Figure 8.28.

Figure 8.28 iView Expose as WSRP Application Property

8.6　Consuming Content

Content can be consumed by the consumer portals in one of the three ways discussed in Section 8.1. Now let's look at how the producer content is consumed by the consumer portals. This section assumes that the FPN connections have been established and tested, that the trust has already been established between the consumer and producer portals, and that all of the suitable permissions have been provided. In this section, we will see how the content from the producer portal is consumed by the consumer portal by using the three sharing types: RRA, RDL, and WSRP application sharing.

8.6.1　Remote Role Assignment Usage

Follow these steps for assigning remote roles to the local users or user groups:

1. Navigate to CONTENT ADMINISTRATION • IDENTITY MANAGEMENT.

2. Search for the role by selecting the data source as REMOTE DATA SOURCES.

3. Select the role, and assign users or user groups to it.

RRA usage is not described in detail here because role assignments have been discussed in detail in Chapter 6. Alternatively, you can also do the role assignment by searching for the users or user groups first and then assigning them the role.

8.6.2　Remote Delta Link Usage

You can create RDLs in two ways. Either you can directly add a remote object to a local object as a delta link, or you can first copy the remote content and paste it to the local portal content as a proxy, and then you can add this as a delta link to local objects.

To add a remote object to a local SAP NetWeaver Portal content object, follow these steps:

1. Open the page, workset, or role editor on the consumer portal.

2. In the portal catalog, select the producer portal in the REMOTE FPN PRODUCERS folder.

3. Browse the portal catalog of the producer, and select the object that you want to add.

4. Right-click the object, and select ADD IVIEW TO PAGE (if you are adding an iView to a page), or a similar message depending on the object types you are adding.

To add a remote object as a delta link on the consumer portal, follow these steps:

1. In the portal catalog, go to the folder REMOTE FPN PRODUCERS.

2. Browse the content of the producer portal, and select the object you want to copy. Right-click, and select COPY.

3. On the consumer portal, navigate to the folder where you want to create the delta link object. Right-click, and select PASTE.

After it is pasted successfully, this object will be available in the local portal catalog to be added to other portal objects.

8.6.3 WSRP Application Sharing Usage

Consumption of WSRP-compliant content on an SAP NetWeaver Portal is done by creating proxy-to-portlet iViews (for which SAP provides a template) on the consumer portal that represent the iView running on the producer portal. The proxy-to-portlet iViews can then be used on the local portal. Follow these steps to create a proxy-to-portlet iView:

1. In the content administration, navigate to the folder where you want to create the iView.

2. Right-click the folder, and select NEW • IVIEW • IVIEW FROM TEMPLATE.

3. From the available templates, select the PROXY-TO-PORTLET IVIEW (WSRP) (Figure 8.29).

4. Select the content producer, browse, and then select the iView/portlet.

5. Click NEXT, and then click FINISH. This should create the proxy-to-portlet iView in your local folder.

After the iView has been created, you work with this iView like other local iViews. You can assign it to pages, worksets, roles, and so on.

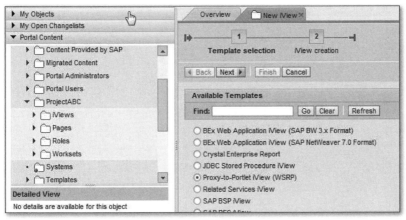

Figure 8.29 Proxy-to-Portlet iView

8.7 Summary

This chapter discussed the various types of content usage in FPN and how each scenario can be configured. We started with configuring the consumer and producer portals with the basic setup necessary for the network, such as creating the connections, establishing trust, and so on, and then went into detail about how content is shared by the producer portals and how content is then consumed by the consumer portals.

So far in this book, we have discussed implementing SAP NetWeaver Portal from the configurations and development point of view. Along with the implementation, it is very important to also have a disaster recovery plan to handle the unforeseen issues. In the next chapter, we will discuss the importance of disaster recovery and various strategies that can be used for disaster recovery in the context of SAP NetWeaver Portal.

Redundancy and regular backups of your system and data are important parts of the ongoing operations of any implementation. Because system failure and data loss can occur any time, it is important to build redundant systems and back up the data regularly to minimize losses.

9 Backup and Recovery

In the previous chapters, we've seen how to implement an SAP NetWeaver Portal project. After an implementation is complete, the most important job is to keep the portal up and running. A disaster—natural or due to human error— can occur any time. And a disruption in the operations of an SAP NetWeaver Portal can be disastrous for a business. *Disaster recovery* refers to the ability to recover the operation condition of your systems when a disaster strikes. Although some disasters are not within your control, some disasters can be avoidable with careful planning. Even if a disaster is not avoidable, however, with proper planning it may be possible to minimize the damage that the disaster causes. The following are some of the most common types of disasters:

▶ Natural calamity

▶ Hard drive crash

▶ Viruses destroying data

▶ Human error

▶ Stolen system

Backup refers to the act of copying files and data of a system to some other storage place with the intention of using this data in the event of a disaster, loss of data, or hardware failure. Restore refers to the act of retrieving the files or data that were backed up earlier, for using with the SAP NetWeaver Portal system. Backup and restore becomes an effective way to protect your system against a potential failure only if it is executed effectively as part of a backup and restore strategy. The backup and restore strategy should be carefully planned and tested properly before applying in a production environment.

A detailed discussion of the steps for implementing high availability is out of scope for this book because these steps depend on factors such as network, disk drive, database system, and so on, and the implementation steps would vary based on what type of infrastructure you have in your implementation. Instead, the purpose of this chapter is to give you a high-level overview of various concepts and components involved in planning and executing a backup and restore strategy. To begin, we discuss high availability, which is an important concept in disaster recovery that introduces the concept of redundancy. Then we will go on to discuss the backup and restore strategies that you should follow for SAP NetWeaver Portal. Because SAP NetWeaver Portal depends on the database for most of its operations, we will also discuss the backup and restore of an SAP NetWeaver Portal database instance.

Vendor Solutions

Many vendors provide custom backup and restore solutions with SAP systems; however, this chapter does not aim to discuss any vendor-specific solution for backup and restore.

9.1 Downtime and High Availability

As we have seen in earlier chapters, SAP NetWeaver Portal is usually the single point of access for users to access various enterprise applications, news feeds, internal corporate information, online training, and so on. If SAP NetWeaver Portal serves as the primary user interface (UI) to your organization's enterprise applications, services, and intranet, what happens if a disaster strikes, and it goes down? In many cases, the portal is your face to your customers, and every minute a portal is unavailable directly puts revenue at risk. If you lose that user who wanted to come in through the web, you've lost money. The portal is therefore an important piece to the revenue generation of many enterprises. With a properly architected solution, there would be no risk or less risk of losing that revenue. One of the most common methods to avoid downtime is to have redundant servers and route the users to the redundant servers when the primary server goes down. This concept is referred to as *high availability*.

The rule of thumb when it comes to proper architecture is to not put all your technology eggs in one basket. In other words, build your system with enough redundancy so that the whole cluster will not fail. When one server goes down, users may get thrown off for a moment, but when they reconnect, the message server sends them to another application server that is operational and has the capacity to carry the additional load. SAP is designed for redundancy so that if a server fails, another will take its place.

High availability for the SAP NetWeaver Portal should be part of a systemwide strategy. Therefore, apart from the SAP NetWeaver Portal system, be sure to also consider other components of the system, such as the database management system (DBMS), the network, and the hardware and operating system services.

From a high-availability viewpoint, there are three variants of SAP NetWeaver Portal:

▶ **Standard SAP NetWeaver Portal**
The standard SAP NetWeaver Portal already contains a range of possibilities to improve the availability of your system without purchasing additional software or hardware. You use a standard SAP NetWeaver Portal when you have no special additional requirements for high availability.

▶ **High-availability SAP NetWeaver Portal**
A high-availability SAP NetWeaver Portal system consists of additional hardware and software purchased from a third party. For example, you can use a cluster solution to protect the database or the enqueue service. You use a high-availability system when you need to ensure the fault-tolerant operation of your SAP system. A high-availability SAP system is robust without being fully disaster-proof.

▶ **Business continuity SAP NetWeaver Portal**
A business continuity SAP NetWeaver Portal system involves a standby SAP system, usually at a remote site. This enables you to recover from disasters such as the destruction of your primary SAP system. You use a business continuity SAP system for critical operations when it is essential that the system is always available. In the event of a disaster, such as a fire at the primary site, you can resume operations immediately or quickly from the standby site.

In this section, we discuss concepts involved in planning downtime, as well as the various SAP NetWeaver Portal services that are affected by unplanned downtime and the high-availability concept.

9.1.1 Planning Downtime for SAP NetWeaver Portal

When an SAP NetWeaver Portal is operational, you will need to plan a downtime of the portal from time to time for various reasons. You may have to do an upgrade of the SAP NetWeaver Portal because a new version of the portal has been released by SAP. Or, you may need to apply a specific support package to the portal to fix a certain bug that has been addressed by SAP. In all such cases, you will need to plan for a window when you can bring the portal down and perform these upgrades or patches. In this section, we will discuss the process and how a high-availability system can help.

Upgrade

An SAP NetWeaver Portal upgrade consists of different phases that may or may not require downtime. The different phases of an SAP NetWeaver Portal upgrade process are as follows:

▶ **Preparation: no downtime**
During the preparation phase, the upgrade analyzes the source system configuration and performs all preparations necessary for the upgrade, including compiling a list of all operations necessary for the system to reach the required target release.

To reduce the downtime by anticipating common problems, the upgrade executes some checks at the end of the preparation phase. These checks include file system space check, database version check, and instance ID check.

▶ **Shadow system installation: no downtime**
In this phase, SAPJup starts building the shadow system in the original database, under the same instance ID, but with different instance numbers for its instances and different database users and schemas.

After the setup is completed, the production system is ready to enter downtime. The upgrade prompts you to manually stop the dialog instances, the SAP Microsoft Management Console (SAP MMC), Software Deployment Manager (SDM) GUI, and in a high-availability scenario, the failover software as well as the central and SAP Central Services (SCS) instances along with their operating system services and daemons.

► **Switch to a new system with a new kernel: downtime**
When this phase has finished, the upgrade prompts you in a high-availability scenario to manually start the failover software, the remote SCS instance, the central instance, and the dialog instances.

Support Packages

Applying a support package to SAP NetWeaver Portal also consists of many stages that may or may not require downtime. Here we will look at the different stages of the support package upgrade of SAP NetWeaver Portal:

► **Update Java Support Package Manager (JSPM):** no downtime

► **Select updates:** no downtime

► **Check updates:** no downtime

► **Apply updates:** downtime

When applying support packages, only the applying updates step has a downtime when the kernel upgrade is actually made. All of the steps before that are preparatory and don't result in system downtime.

As with the upgrade process, during the last step, the support pack upgrade will prompt you to manually start the failover software, the remote SCS instance, the central instance, and the dialog instances.

9.1.2 SAP NetWeaver Portal Services and Unplanned Downtime

For high availability of SAP NetWeaver Portal, you can configure a software cluster of several SAP NetWeaver Portal instances. By installing additional software instances, you can build redundancy and thus reduce downtime. Clustering of SAP NetWeaver Portal instances and the switchover software together will provide high availability for SAP NetWeaver Portal. If one instance of the portal fails, the switchover software can send the client requests to a next available instance. Figure 9.1 shows a Java cluster architecture for with SAP NetWeaver Portal Java instances.

In this section, we will look at how some of the most important processes running inside SAP NetWeaver Portal are affected by downtime and the high-availability concept.

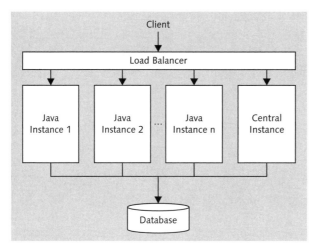

Figure 9.1 Java Cluster Architecture for High Availability

Web Container

SAP NetWeaver Portal includes a web container (highlighted in Figure 9.2) that enables the execution of Java servlets and Java Server Pages (JSPs).

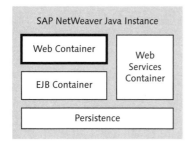

Figure 9.2 Web Container

Because JSPs are translated into servlets, they follow the same principles as servlets. Within a load-balanced Java cluster, all Java processes have the same Java components available. They are deployed in parallel, and the cluster elements use the database as a central information store. This means that all servers in the cluster share the same information.

Therefore, it does not matter which server in a cluster is accessed to provide HTTP services. However, you need to distinguish whether stateless or stateful servlets are accessed. Stateless servlets have no application state that is bound to the session. Therefore, every server in the cluster can run stateless servlets. In a high-availability environment, when a server fails, the next request for the servlet is directed to another server that handles the request without loss of session data. Stateful servlets have an application state that is bound to the session. For these servlets in a high-availability environment, you can implement HTTP session failover so that the session state is serialized and written to persistent storage (either the database or the file system). Therefore, if the server where the session was active fails, the session state can be retrieved on another server using the database.

EJB Container

The Enterprise JavaBeans (EJBs) run inside the EJB container of the SAP NetWeaver Java instance of the portal server (Figure 9.3). During application deployment, EJBs are deployed on all server processes in the cluster. For each call to an EJB, a system, which is external to the EJB container, dispatches the call to an EJB instance on a particular server process. This instance works locally; that is, it is not aware of the availability of other EJB instances in the cluster.

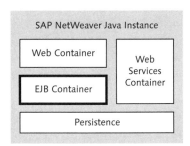

Figure 9.3 EJB Container

In a high-availability environment, if the server process where the instance resides fails, the call must be redirected to an available server process where a new EJB instance processes it. The redirection is transparent to the EJB.

Session EJBs in SAP NetWeaver Portal work locally and independently of each other. They are not clustered and do not communicate with other session EJBs on other server nodes in the cluster.

In a high-availability environment, failover for stateless session beans is provided by the RMI-P4 protocol, which redirects the call to an available server process. However, state preservation is available for stateful session beans through the session management system of SAP NetWeaver Portal.

Java Message Service (JMS)

Java Message Service (JMS) is the middleware API for sending and receiving asynchronous messages. JMS is a part of the Java Enterprise Edition (Java EE) standards. A *message-driven bean* (MDB) is an EJB that makes use of the JMS messages. In this section, we will discuss the failover mechanism for application using MDBs as well as for a client JMS application that does not use MDBs.

JMS Provider and Message-Driven Beans Failover

Failover in the context of JMS is the process of detecting a system failure (i.e., a server process crash) leading to unavailability of JMS resources (hosted on the failing server process) and migrating these resources to a backup server process.

Failover in the context of MDBs is the process of detecting a system failure (i.e., a server process crash) leading to unavailability of the JMS destination (hosted on the failing server process) to which the MDB is registered, and reconnecting the MDB after its destination has been migrated to a backup server process and made available again.

JMS Applications Failover

Applications using JMS only via MDBs do not need to implement their own failover logic because MDB failover is automatic and transparent to applications. Applications using JMS directly—that is, through the JMS API—have to implement their own failover logic because JMS failover is automatic but not transparent to applications. Some or all JMS resources (destinations and connection factories) become temporarily unavailable during the automatic JMS failover.

The JMS runtime objects—connections, sessions, producers, consumers, and so on—created before the failover are invalidated and have to be recreated. Applications can be notified of failover or other error conditions by registering an exception listener.

As discussed earlier, in a high-availability environment, the JMS applications need to implement their own logic to connect to the backup server instance if they are using the JMS API. However, if they are using the MDBs, they do not need to implement a custom logic for failover because the MDB failover is transparent to the applications.

Persistence Layer and Databases

SAP NetWeaver Portal stores all of its configurations and data on the system database. In this section, we see how the failover works in case of a database connection failure.

Persistent Cluster Configuration Database

SAP NetWeaver Portal uses the system databases to store all binaries and configuration information with the Configuration Manager. Therefore, this database is essential for the portal to function correctly.

OpenSQL is SAP's database abstraction layer that translates abstract SQL statements to native database SQL statements. It is recommended that you use OpenSQL as the standard when connecting to the database schema of SAP NetWeaver Portal. You can also use Native SQL if you do not want to use Open SQL.

Availability of the Database Access Layer

When the configuration database fails in a high-availability environment, SAP NetWeaver Portal tries to reconnect to the database. As soon as the database is accessible, the cluster becomes functional again: SAP NetWeaver Portal maintains a pool of database connections and handles broken connections as described in the "DB Reconnect" subsection later in this chapter.

An application that receives an `SQLException` should roll back its transaction and close the connection (handle) by calling `connection.close()`. After that, when the application requests a new connection, the connection pool returns a valid connection. If this is impossible—for example, due to database problems—an exception is thrown.

SAP Java Connector

SAP provides the SAP Java Connector (SAP JCo) to enable communication in the SAP NetWeaver AS between the ABAP and Java stacks. SAP JCo can be used for the internal communication of SAP NetWeaver AS, where the AS ABAP and SAP

335

NetWeaver Portal interact. The communication between SAP NetWeaver Java and the SAP backend system happens through a gateway, as shown in the Figure 9.4.

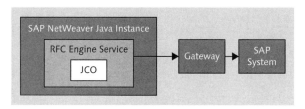

Figure 9.4 SAP Java Connector

With SAP NetWeaver Portal 7.3, instead of using the SAP JCo APIs, applications should move to Java Resource Adapter (JRA), which is the SAP JCo architecture. The SAP JCo remote function call (RFC) provider has been deprecated with release 7.10. You set up the SAP JCo by registering SAP NetWeaver Portal as an RFC server to an SAP gateway. This method, which is based on the RFC, works in both directions:

▶ **Inbound**
Java calls business application programming interfaces (BAPIs) and RFC-enabled function modules (RFM) on the ABAP side and acts as a client.

▶ **Outbound**
ABAP calls functions on the Java side that acts as a server.

Calls from the SAP system are processed by the SAP JCo RFC provider service of SAP NetWeaver Portal. It dispatches the call to a stateless session bean, which is registered in the Java Naming and Directory Interface (JNDI). Following the naming convention, the JNDI name used is identical to the name of the SAP function module. To parse the function calls from the SAP system correctly, the SAP JCo needs access to an SAP system repository.

In this section, we will discuss how the SAP JCo works and how it is related to the SAP system gateway. We will also discuss how the failure of a SAP NetWeaver Portal server in a cluster affects the SAP JCo.

Scenario for the SAP Java Connector
Let's first see how an SAP JCo RFC provider service works:

1. On startup of the SAP JCo RFC provider service (i.e., normally the startup of SAP NetWeaver Portal), the service does the following:

- ▸ Connects to the SAP system repository

- ▸ Registers itself at the gateway with a defined name

It is possible to register under different names and at different gateways. But note that there is only a 1:1 relation between a name and a particular gateway. This has implications for high availability that are discussed in this section.

2. An SAP system calls a function for the registered RFC destination. The function has to be defined in the repository.

3. The gateway forwards the call to the JCo RFC provider.

4. The JCo RFC provider looks in the JNDI for the EJB, which is registered under the same name as the function module in the SAP system.

5. The JCo RFC provider calls the method `processFunction(JCO.Function)` of the EJB.

6. The results of the call are passed to the gateway.

7. The gateway passes the results back to the SAP system.

Relationship of the Gateway to the Java Connector

The JCo RFC provider service can register under one name to one particular gateway. To register to the same gateway with a second server, another name has to be used. In the SAP system, you can configure an RFC connection under one name for one particular external program that has to be registered at the gateway. Optionally, you can specify a particular gateway for the connection.

Within a Java cluster, all Java servers configure the JCo RFC provider service identically. This means that a particular program registration is valid on all servers and points to the same gateway. The gateway balances requests between different servers that are registered under the same program name.

Java Servers in a High-Availability Cluster

If one Java server fails, the RFC connection still works with the other server in the cluster. However, if the gateway fails, the RFC connection no longer works because a particular program name can only be registered at one particular gateway.

You can set up the gateway in one of the following ways:

- ▸ Each SAP instance has its own gateway service, *sapgw<systemnumber>*, where external programs can be registered.

▶ With the standalone SAP gateway, you can install the gateway service separately from the SAP system, for example, on the same host as the Java server(s). In this case, the SAP system can access each external gateway under a different RFC connection.

Choose the gateway setup that best fits your application scenario. When you use an option with different RFC connections, the ABAP application has to be aware of this.

Naming Service

In a high-availability environment, the JNDI registry service provides failover by redirecting clients to a context instance on an available server process.

Remote clients use the JNDI registry service of one of the server processes in the cluster through a context instance. This instance is connected to the naming system of the server process, and all naming operations are performed there.

If the primary server fails, the JNDI registry service redirects naming operations to another server for processing. The redirection is transparent to clients.

P4 Service

Remote clients obtain a reference to the remote RMI-P4 objects on the server side by getting an `InitialContext` instance on a particular server process. Subsequent requests by this client are sent to the same server process.

In the event of server failure in a high-availability environment, the client request is dispatched to another server process where it gets a new `InitialContext` instance. There is also a mechanism that migrates the instance of the server-side remote object from the failed server process to another one. The same mechanism is the basis for the implementation of EJB failover.

Database Reconnect

In a high-availability environment, SAP NetWeaver Portal can automatically handle database errors, for example, when the database crashes or the network connection to the database fails. For Open SQL and Native SQL, the handling of database connection errors works as follows:

1. The Java Database Connectivity (JDBC) driver detects an error and throws an `SQLException` when database access fails.

2. SAP NetWeaver Portal classifies the error and propagates the exception to the caller. The connection is only closed in the event of a fatal connection error, in which case the following steps occur.

3. SAP NetWeaver Portal checks all connections currently in the connection pool:

   ▶ It immediately checks all idle connections and closes defective ones.

   ▶ It checks used connections only on release and closes defective ones.

4. SAP NetWeaver Portal alerts all other SAP NetWeaver Portal instances that a failure has occurred. Each SAP NetWeaver Portal instance checks its connections by performing the previous step.

5. In the event of subsequent connection requests, SAP NetWeaver Portal tries to create new connections and populates the connection pool again.

After error classification, all calls using the broken connection receive a well-defined `connection already closed` exception.

For a vendor SQL, the connection error handling is similar. The main difference is the deferred error classification that only takes place during the commit, rollback, and close of the connection. Before error classification, all calls using the broken connection receive database-specific exceptions. You should close SQL connections immediately when no longer required.

System Services

SAP NetWeaver Portal system is a set of software and hardware components that are hierarchically assembled into the fully functioning system. The interrelationship between the components of the SAP system is important for high availability. The individual components deliver services to one another. Therefore, if one component fails, the effect is felt by other parts of the system that rely on the delivery of services from the failed component to complete their tasks. This is especially true if a potential single point of failure (SPOF) is involved. If you do not provide a backup in the event of failure, unplanned system downtime can result.

How you protect your SAP NetWeaver Portal system services depends on your overall approach to high availability, for example, whether you are using a standard SAP system or a high-availability SAP system. In a standard configuration, certain services are unprotected (e.g., enqueue, message, and database), whereas in a high-availability configuration, you can protect vulnerable services.

In a high-availability SAP NetWeaver Portal system, you can replicate vulnerable services, such as the enqueue, message, and database services by using, for example, cluster solutions or switchover solutions

Switchover Software

You can protect servers through redundancy, resulting in a significantly shorter switchover time. When the primary SAP NetWeaver Portal system fails, the operations can switch to a secondary system quickly.

SAP NetWeaver Portal has its own enqueue and message service. SAP NetWeaver Portal depends on a database that stores configuration and business data. In a switchover environment, these are both protected by redundancy—that is, by running another application server instance on the second host or on computers outside the protected system. If the software becomes unavailable, a switchover is initiated by first shutting down the SCS instances and then restarting them on the second host.

To optimize the efficiency of this system, the second host is often used to run the database. The first host acts as failover for the database. This means that under normal operation, one host runs SAP NetWeaver Portal, and the other runs the database, which optimizes the use of the available computing resources. In a failover, both systems share one host, which leads to a reduction in performance during failover.

In a high-availability environment, you can use switchover software for the database host and the application host on which the enqueue and message services are running. Automatic failure detection and automatic restart (on a standby host) are thereby ensured.

SAP Central Services

For high availability of SCS, you can follow the methods described next.

Message Service

The *message service* is the system communications hub, acting as a name server to return the required service on request. It distributes the cluster events and enables service-to-service communication. It also provides information for load balancing over the SAP Web Dispatcher.

If the message service fails, this disturbs the communication between the cluster nodes. The only way to protect the message service from failure is to use switchover software. After the switchover software restarts the message service, cluster communication continues.

Enqueue Service

The *enqueue service* provides a central lock table for logical locks on database objects to protect these objects from unsynchronized writes by the SAP NetWeaver Portal programs.

When the enqueue service fails, all open transactions have to be rolled back to prevent inconsistencies. If the enqueue service fails, the applications with requested locks get an exception that has to be handled by the application.

You can solve this problem in the following ways:

▶ **Basic solution: switchover software for failover protection**
You need to at least protect the enqueue service with switchover software. This makes sure that the enqueue service can be restarted and is available again. However, even with switchover software, transactions open at the time of failure have to be rolled back.

▶ **Advanced solution: standalone enqueue replication service for protection of the internal system state**
You can also use the standalone enqueue replication service, which maintains a replica of the lock table. This replica can be used in the event of failover to restore the lock table without the need to roll back transactions.

> **Note**
>
> There might be restrictions for the product availability of the standalone enqueue replication service.

For full protection of your enqueue service, we recommend you use *both* of these solutions.

9.2 Backup and Restore Strategy

SAP NetWeaver Portal backup and restore strategy planning is difficult because it's very different from the SAP backend backup and restore. SAP NetWeaver Portal backup can be done either at the component level or the whole system level. It is usually better to go for the system backup option because the whole SAP NetWeaver Portal system can be brought back up in case of system failure. Also SAP NetWeaver Portal components and their configurations are usually interdependent, and they need to be backed up together.

As part of an SAP NetWeaver Portal strategy, it is important to identify what needs to be backed up. For components that use database-like storage, it is enough to back up the database. Applications running on SAP NetWeaver Portal usually use the same database schema that SAP NetWeaver Portal uses. Also, SAP NetWeaver Portal and SAP AS Java share the same database. So in the majority of the cases, backing up the database shared by SAP NetWeaver Portal and SAP AS Java is sufficient to restore the portal. The strategy for backup and restore should include a reliable test of the backup system to make sure that restore can be done from the backup.

SAP NetWeaver Portal stores the configuration data in the database, so restoring the database will effectively bring the SAP NetWeaver Portal back. Many applications also use the SAP NetWeaver Portal database. These applications can be safe with the database backup. Some applications store their configuration data in files on the file system. Restoring these can be difficult if the file system is not backed up. Databases usually have built-in functionality for recovery based on a certain point in time. These features can be used to make the database backups.

The main other challenge associated with SAP NetWeaver Portal backup is being able to restore the data on other systems with which SAP NetWeaver Portal integrates. In the event of a SAP NetWeaver Portal crash, if the database is restored to a point of time, the other related systems should also be restored close to that point of time. If the data that is stored on these systems is dynamic, then an effective backup and restore strategy for that system will also be needed.

After you have successfully implemented a recovery from a backup, it is important to ensure that the restore has been done successfully by performing the following checks:

▸ Check whether the component can be started properly either by checking the log files on the system or by using the operating system's built in process monitoring tools.

▸ Check whether the restored component is working properly by running functionality related to the component that has been restored.

9.3 Backup of SAP NetWeaver Portal

Because SAP NetWeaver Portal runs on AS Java, in most cases, it is sufficient to back up and restore AS Java. In this and subsequent sections, we will see how to back up and restore SAP NetWeaver Portal as well as AS Java. Backing up SAP NetWeaver Portal with AS Java and the related database provides the safety needed to restore a system in the event of data loss.

The various scenarios in which an SAP NetWeaver Portal backup can be used are listed here:

▸ The SAP system upgrade fails.

▸ The operating system fails, or there is a problem with the file system.

▸ The database crashes.

Backup can usually be done online or offline. Offline backup can only be done when the system is offline. The disadvantage of offline backup is that it needs system downtime, so it cannot be done on a daily basis. However, the advantage of an offline backup is that a complete backup of the system can be done. This backup can be used to restore the full system to an earlier state reliably.

Offline backup should necessarily be done at the following stages of an SAP NetWeaver Portal system:

▸ After initial installation

▸ Before an upgrade

▸ After an upgrade

Whenever an offline backup of the SAP NetWeaver Portal system is done, the Java development kit (JDK) installation directory should also be backed up. This will ensure that you have the correct version of the JDK while you are restoring the system. After the initial offline backup, you should be doing regular offline backups every week.

Online backup, as the name suggests, can be done while the system is running. It does not require the system downtime and hence can be used for daily or more regular backups. Online backup is normally done for incremental backups. Online backup does not guarantee a complete and reliable backup of all components of the system.

After you have completed a full offline backup, you should do regular online backups of the following components:

▶ **Database**
Backup of data as well as logs should be done. Also if the applications on the SAP NetWeaver Portal use multiple data sources, then those databases should also be backed up.

▶ **File system**
You should create a backup of the SAP system installation directory */usr/sap/<SID>*.

You should usually have a planned schedule of regular online and offline backups to help restore from a sudden data loss. We discuss this later in the chapter; however, keep in mind that any suggestion about the schedule should only serve as a suggestion, and you should plan your backup and restore strategy with your implementation requirements in mind.

9.4   Restore of SAP NetWeaver Portal

In the previous section, you learned about backing up SAP NetWeaver Portal and SAP AS Java. In the event of a data loss, you need to restore the SAP NetWeaver Portal system to its original state from a backup by following these steps:

1. Shut down the SAP NetWeaver Portal system.

2. Install a new SAP NetWeaver Portal using SAPInst, or restore the file system from the offline backups that you created.

3. Import the database backup using the tools provided by the database vendor.

4. Overwrite the SAP system directory */usr/sap/<SID>*.

5. Start the system.

The SAP NetWeaver Portal is now restored with the last backup. Figure 9.5 shows the steps in the restoration of SAP NetWeaver Portal.

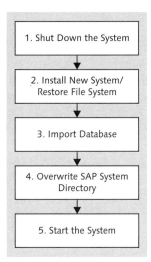

Figure 9.5 Restoring SAP NetWeaver Portal

9.5   SAP NetWeaver Portal Database Backup

Because SAP NetWeaver Portal stores all of the configurations in the database, a consistent database is key to running SAP NetWeaver Portal properly. You should back up the data and log entries so that in the case of a failure, the database instance can be brought back to a consistent state by restoring the data and the log entries.

In this section, we will see the various ways of backing up the database for SAP NetWeaver Portal. In Section 9.5.3, we'll also see how to activate and deactivate automatic log backup for the database.

9.5.1   Backup Templates and Data Carriers

For doing any data or log backup, the first thing that you have to do is define a backup template. In the backup template, you define the type of backup and the type of data carrier that will be used, for example, a tape device or a file system. The backup templates are stored in the file *dbm.mmm.*

A backup template has the following properties:

▶ **Name of the template**
You can specify any name for the template. The names of backups do not depend on the name of the backup template.

▶ **Backup type**
The backup type can be one of the following:

- ▶ Full data backup

- ▶ Incremental data backup

- ▶ Log backup

- ▶ Automatic log backup

Table 9.1 shows which types of backup are possible with various data carriers (discussed next).

Data Carrier	Backup Types	Comments
File (FILE)	▶ Data backup ▶ Log backup ▶ Automatic log backup	
Tape (TAPE)	▶ Data backup	You can use an autoloader.
Pipe (PIPE)	▶ Data backup ▶ Log backup	Automatic log backups to pipes are not possible.

Table 9.1 Data Carrier Types

▶ **Data carrier**
You must define whether the data carrier is a tape device or the file system. You need to enter the name of the tape device in the operating system, the path and file name of the file in the file system, or the path and name of the pipe.

The system adds a sequence number to the name of each new backup file for log backups to files. The system assigns the numbers sequentially as long as the history of the log backups is not interrupted. If the log backup history is interrupted (e.g., if the database instance is initialized), the system begins numbering at 001 again.

The system also uses sequential numbers if you carry out multiple log backups for one database instance onto different data carriers and thereby to files with different file names.

The following is an example of the file names for backups.

▶ *LogUri.001*

▶ *LogKai.002*

▶ *LogOleg.003*

▶ *LogUri.004*

▶ *LogUri.005*

Also, if automatic log backup is switched on, the system stores all backup files under the same file name and adds the sequential number:

▶ *autoLog.001*

▶ *autoLog.002*

▶ *autoLog.003*

▶ *autoLog.004*

▶ *autoLog.005*

Figure 9.6 shows a screenshot of the backup template wizard for a MaxDB database. In MaxDB, the template is called a backup medium.

Figure 9.6 Backup Template

Figure 9.7 shows the various properties of a backup template.

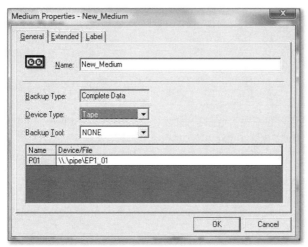

Figure 9.7 Backup Template Properties

▶ **Size of data carrier**

You can select the size of the data carrier for the data backup. The size of log backups in files is the size of the log segment plus the space required for system information. Figure 9.8 shows the size-related properties of the backup template.

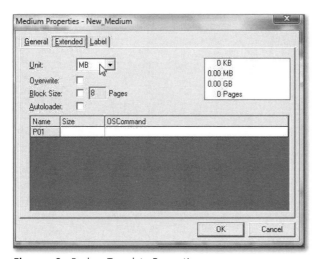

Figure 9.8 Backup Template Properties

▶ **Overwritable**

If the OVERWRITE property is set to true, the same backup file can be used more than once, and the data carrier is overwritten.

▶ **Block size**

The BLOCK SIZE property defines the block size that the system uses to write backups into the data carrier.

When defining a backup template, you can choose the type of backup template you want to use. The radio buttons in Figure 9.9 show the types of backup that you can choose from. The screenshots shown here are from a MaxDB database; you can, however, use the specific tool from your database vendor.

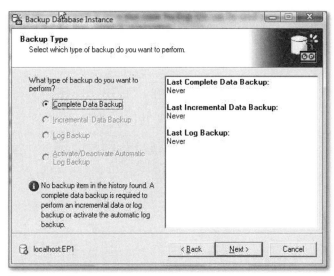

Figure 9.9 Backup Type

9.5.2 Backing Up Data

Data can be lost due to a variety of reasons, including disk failure or a damaged data area. Because of this reason, you need to back up your data regularly. A prerequisite to starting a backup is to have a backup template. Now that you know how to create a backup template, let's use this backup template while doing the actual backup.

There are two types of data backup:

▶ **Complete data backup**
In this backup, the entire data area is backed up.

▶ **Incremental data backup**
In this backup, only the delta changes to the data are backed up.

When you are doing a backup for the first time, you need to do a complete backup. Thereafter, you can do incremental backups. You can perform a backup either using the backup wizard or using the command-line tools. In this section, we will cover both options for backing up the database.

Backup Using the Backup Wizard

Let's look at using the backup wizard for backing up the data. For the purpose of this chapter, we will make use of the backup wizard provided by MaxDB database because it is the default database provided by SAP. If your database is different, you should look at the tools provided by your database vendor.

For MaxDB, follow these steps for backing up your data:

1. Start the Database Manager GUI and go to INSTANCE_NAME • BACKUP • BACKUP WIZARD as shown in Figure 9.10.

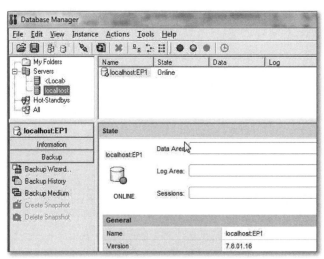

Figure 9.10 Backup Wizard

2. You will be asked to log in to the database instance. Enter your credentials as shown in Figure 9.11.

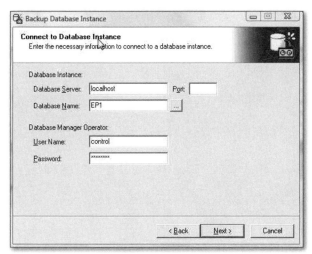

Figure 9.11 Log In to the Database Instance

3. After entering the credentials, you will be connected to the database instance. You can now choose the type of backup you want to do: complete backup, incremental backup, or log backup.

4. Select the template/medium that you want to use for this backup. You saw how to create a backup template earlier in Section 9.5.1.

5. You will now see a review page, where you can review the details you have entered and the click the START button to start the backup (Figure 9.12).

Backup Using a Command-Line Utility

Along with the backup wizard, you can also start the backup using a command-line utility instead of using a wizard-based interface. The command-line utility for MaxDB is `backup_start`. Using `backup_start`, you can back up the data area or the log area of the database. You can also use the following commands during the backup session:

▶ `backup_state`
This command gives the status of the ongoing backup. The backup can take a long time to complete, so you will need to use this command to get the status.

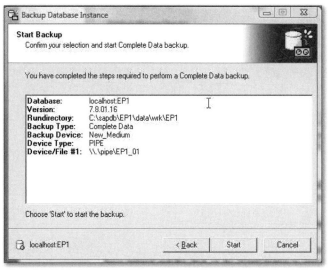

Figure 9.12 Backup Start

▶ `backup_cancel`
This command is used to terminate a database backup operation while it is running.

▶ `backup_replace`
When the backup operation is interrupted because the data carrier is full, you will need to use this command to replace the carrier to continue the backup.

▶ `backup_ignore`
When you are performing a backup to a group of data carriers and one of the data carriers is full, you can use this command to ignore the warning message and continue the backup operation with the remaining data carriers.

The syntax of the backup_start command-line utility is given here:

```
>backup_start <medium> [<backup_type>] [AUTOIGNORE]
```

`<medium>` is the name of the backup template you want to use for this backup.

`<backup_type>` is the type of backup that you want to perform. Possible values for this are listed here:

▶ `DATA`: Complete data backup

▶ `PAGES`: Incremental data backup

▶ `LOG`: Log backup

AUTOIGNORE is used to set the AUTOIGNORE flag for continuing the backup while ignoring the data carrier full warning.

9.5.3 Backing Up Log Entries

Along with data backups, log backups are also required to recover the database after some system failures. The log entries are where all changes to the database are logged. If the log area is damaged, then the database can only repeat the most recent data changes, which it was not able to write to the data area. The system can repeat the data changes using redo log entries of the log area if the database has a breakdown but the log area was not damaged. Regular log backups are important because the database system can only overwrite saved log segments of the log area with new redo log entries. If the database system cannot write any more redo log entries into the log area (log area is full), the database stops.

To do a log backup, you need to fulfill the following prerequisites:

▸ You must have created at least one complete data backup.

▸ You must have created a backup template.

▸ The database instance must be in either ONLINE or ADMIN operational states.

As we saw in Section 9.5.2, redo log entry backup can also be done in a similar way by using the backup wizard or command-line tool `backup_start`. You have seen this process in detail earlier, and you just need to make sure you provide the appropriate parameter for the backup type and the data carrier.

You should switch on the automatic log backup so that the system backs up all of the redo log entries automatically. When you configure the database parameter `LOG_SEGMENT_SIZE`, the system will trigger a backup as soon as a log segment reaches that size.

In systems where you expect a large number of redo log entries to be generated continuously, you should set the automatic log backup to ON because your log segment size will get filled up quickly. You can use the Database Manager GUI to activate and deactivate the automatic log backup.

To activate automatic log backup, you need to fulfill the following prerequisites:

▸ You should have performed one complete data backup.

▸ The database instance must be running in the ONLINE operational state.

In this section we will discuss the steps for activating and deactivating automatic log backups using the backup wizard as well as the MaxDB Database Manager GUI.

Activating and Deactivating Using the Backup Wizard

You can activate and deactivate automatic log backups with the backup wizard by following these steps:

1. Launch the backup wizard.

2. Make sure you have created a backup template.

3. Choose the backup template that you created for log backup, and change the parameter for activating or deactivating automatic log backup.

Activating and Deactivating Using the Database Manager GUI

You can activate or deactivate automatic log backup with the Database Manager GUI also. To do so, make sure that your database instance is running in ONLINE mode and the backup templates are available. Follow these steps to activate or deactivate:

1. Launch the Database Manager GUI, and choose your database instance (Figure 9.13).

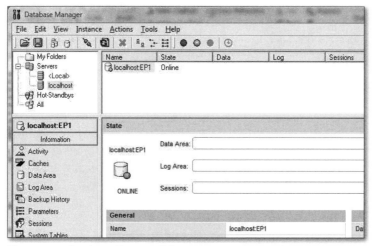

Figure 9.13 Database Manager GUI

2. Right-click the database instance, and choose SET AUTO LOG ON/OFF as shown in Figure 9.14.

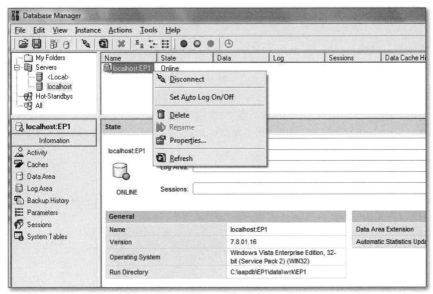

Figure 9.14   Auto Log On/Off

As we said earlier, you must have performed one complete backup of data for this to work; otherwise, you will get an error message as shown in Figure 9.15.

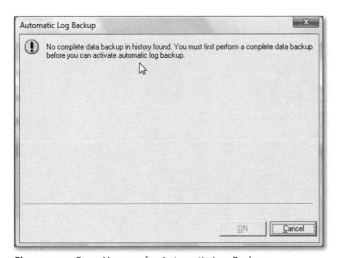

Figure 9.15   Error Message for Automatic Log Backup

9.6 SAP NetWeaver Portal Database Restore

In the previous section, we saw how the database and log entries for SAP NetWeaver Portal can be backed up using various methods. In this section, we will discuss how the database can be restored from a backup performed earlier. As we said earlier, we will look at the restore for MaxDB database because MaxDB is the default database provided by SAP. If your database is different, the steps for your database vendor may be different and you should refer to the documentation provided by them.

MaxDB provides a recovery wizard that can be used for performing the restore. Let's look at the steps involved in database restore using the MaxDB recovery wizard.

1. Make sure that the database instance is running in the operational state ADMIN.

2. Launch the MaxDB Database Manager GUI from the server. (The Database Manager GUI is part of the MaxDB installation.)

3. In the Database Manager GUI, launch the recovery wizard by going to <INSTANCE> • RECOVERY • RECOVERY.

4. Enter the connection details and your credentials.

5. Choose the type of restore you want to perform as shown in Figure 9.16.

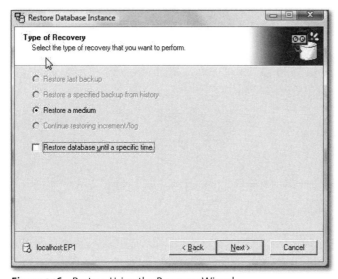

Figure 9.16 Restore Using the Recovery Wizard

You have the following options:

- ▶ Restore last back up
- ▶ Restore a specified backup from history
- ▶ Restore a medium
- ▶ Continue restoring increment/log
- ▶ Restore database until a specific time (provide a time until which you want to restore the database)

Choose the appropriate option, and then click Next.

6. If you have selected Restore a medium, you will be prompted to select the medium; otherwise, you will be prompted to insert the required data container and then the recovery can start.

9.7 Summary

Disaster recovery and backup and restore strategy planning for SAP NetWeaver Portal is an important strategy that should be developed for your implementation as early as possible. As part of this process, you should consider the whole system: network infrastructure, operating system, disk drives, and especially databases. Because all of the SAP NetWeaver Portal configurations are stored in the database, we spent a considerable amount of time on discussing database backup and restore in this chapter.

In the next chapter we will explain the process of monitoring an SAP NetWeaver Portal system to make sure the system is running efficiently and to detect symptoms of any upcoming failures. We will learn about logging and tracing and see how to configure the system for monitoring.

Monitoring SAP NetWeaver Portal is necessary to identify problems before a failure occurs. This involves using various monitoring tools provided by SAP.

10   Monitoring Technology and Logging

The monitoring of any system is necessary to make sure that problems can be detected early and action can be taken to prevent failure or system downtime. SAP NetWeaver Portal and AS Java provide a number of tools that help monitor the running system, the most important of which is SAP NetWeaver Administrator. This chapter will explain the functions provided by SAP NetWeaver Administrator and the steps to use them for monitoring.

SAP NetWeaver Portal also provides tools for reporting user activities, which can be used for monitoring SAP NetWeaver Portal. In this chapter, we will see how to use and configure the portal activity reports and the activity data collector service.

Apart from the monitoring tools, logging and tracing are the most common methods used to make sure a system is running properly and to detect problems at an early stage. *Logging* provides useful information at the system level, whereas *tracing* provides information regarding the applications running on the system. In this chapter, we will see how logging and tracing can be configured so that you can get the right information from logs when needed. We will specifically discuss the change recording of Portal Content Directory (PCD) objects, which is new to SAP NetWeaver 7.3. Using this functionality, you can configure logging for PCD object changes.

Finally, we will discuss some of the SAP tools that can help troubleshoot issues with SAP NetWeaver Portal.

10.1   Using SAP NetWeaver Administrator for Monitoring

SAP NetWeaver Administrator is a web-based tool for monitoring and configuring SAP NetWeaver Portal and AS Java. As we have seen in previous chapters, you can launch the SAP NetWeaver Administrator by going to *http://<host>:<port/nwa*.

In SAP NetWeaver Administrator, you can access various monitors provided by SAP, and you can configure the monitors that you want to see. SAP NetWeaver Administrator also provides a SYSTEM OVERVIEW page where you can see the overall status of all of the critical components of the system. In this section, we'll first look at the SYSTEM OVERVIEW page and then discuss how various important monitors can be viewed and configured.

10.1.1   System Overview

SAP NetWeaver Administrator provides a wide variety of tools to monitor SAP NetWeaver Portal and SAP AS Java. In this section, we will take a close look at the tools available for use. Many of these tools are available in the AVAILABILITY AND PERFORMANCE tab of SAP NetWeaver Administrator. The SYSTEM OVERVIEW tab inside this gives a snapshot of the overall status of the system (Figure 10.1).

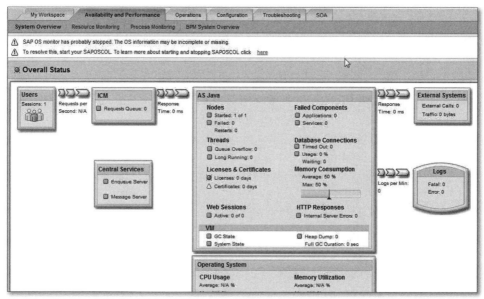

Figure 10.1   Overall Status of System

The overall status screen gives a snapshot of the user sessions, Internet Communication Manager (ICM), central services, AS Java, operating system, database, and so on. Also, if you look at this screen carefully, you will realize that more than just giving an overall status, it shows the various components as they are accessed in a user interaction with SAP NetWeaver Portal.

On the left side, with the screen lists the user sessions. When users connect to SAP NetWeaver Portal, the connections are routed to the AS Java through an ICM. The AS Java in turn connects to external systems, connects to the database, and runs on the operating system. The overall status screen shows the green, yellow, and red color icons to indicate the health of a particular component.

From the individual component here, you can go to a particular component to manage and configure it. For example, when you click the status area for AS JAVA NODES, you get the option to MANAGE JAVA SERVER NODES, as shown in Figure 10.2.

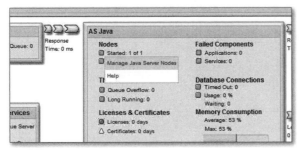

Figure 10.2 Manage from the Overall Status Dashboard

When you click the MANAGE JAVA SERVER NODES, you will be taken to the page where you can manage the Java server nodes as shown in Figure 10.3.

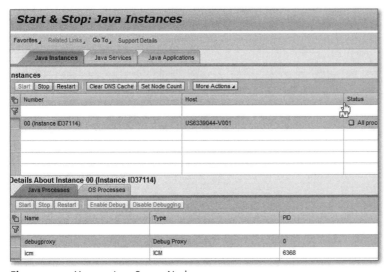

Figure 10.3 Manage Java Server Nodes

Similarly, you can select the CENTRAL SERVICES section, click ENQUEUE SERVER, and look at all of the locks in the enqueue server.

10.1.2 Resource Monitoring

The RESOURCE MONITORING tab inside the AVAILABILITY AND PERFORMANCE tab of SAP NetWeaver Administrator helps monitor various resources of SAP AS Java and SAP NetWeaver Portal. From here, you can perform the following monitoring activities:

▶ JCO MONITORING
Helps monitor the Java Connector (JCo) connections, displaying various cached metadata, and setting trace levels. The metadata cache is part of JCo monitoring, and helps in viewing the metadata of backend remote function calls (RFCs) that have been cached on the portal.

▶ DISTRIBUTED TRANSACTIONS
Provides monitoring and configuration of Java Transaction API (JTA) transactions. You can monitor pending and completed transactions and view details about them.

▶ SESSION MANAGEMENT
Helps manage and monitor various sessions in the application server.

▶ LOCKS
Helps monitor all of the locks created in the Java system.

▶ SYSTEM PERFORMANCE STATISTICS
Gives various performance statistics of the Java system. If you are familiar with Transaction STAD in an ABAP system, this gives similar statistics, such as response times, CPU usage, memory consumption, and so on.

▶ HISTORY REPORTS
Provides historical reports of the server regarding various metrics such as resource consumption, error statistics, and so on. You can choose the time period for showing the historical reports, and you can also view the reports in graphical or tabular formats.

Figure 10.4 shows the various tools available within the RESOURCE MONITORING tab.

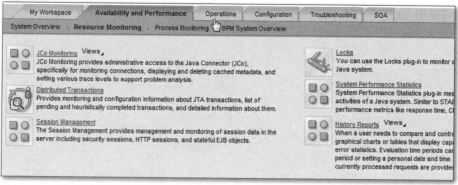

Figure 10.4 Resource Monitoring

In the following subsections, we will see how to use and configure various resources used by SAP NetWeaver Portal and AS Java.

JCo Monitors

JCo Monitoring provides the following three tools:

▶ Connection monitor

▶ Metadata cache

▶ Traces

Connection Monitor

The *connection monitor* helps you in monitoring all of the JCos in the system. You can select a Java instance and a cluster node to view the connections specific to that system (Figure 10.5).

Connection Monitor	Metadata Cache	Traces					
Connections							
Instance: EP1 00 ▾ Cluster Node: 3711450 ▾							
Cluster Node	Partner Host	Connection Type	Function	Group	Thread Name	Thre

Figure 10.5 Connection Monitor

From the connection monitor, you can select a connection to see the details of that connection. The CONNECTION DETAILS section comes below the connection monitor. Figure 10.6 shows the various connection detail attributes that can be seen on the connection monitor.

Connection Details		
Application Attributes		**Communication Attributes**
Partner Host:		Connection Type:
ABAP Client:		Conversation ID:
ABAP User:		DSR Passport:
Function:		Last Time Stamp:
Group:		State:
Thread Name:		Unique ID:
Thread ID:		Server Instance:
Session ID:		Cluster Node ID:

Figure 10.6 Connection Details

Metadata Cache

The *metadata cache* is the information about a backend RFC that is stored on the SAP NetWeaver Portal side in the cache. When a Web Dynpro Java application accesses an ABAP backend using an RFC, the application server retrieves and stores the metadata of the RFC in the server cache. This helps improve the performance of the RFCs. The metadata cache tool gives you a way to view the cached metadata on your server. You can choose an ABAP server, and then you can see the metadata stored for that particular server.

When an RFC interface changes, the metadata related to that RFC also changes. If you still have the older metadata loaded when the RFC has changed, you will get a runtime exception when you execute the application. To avoid this, the metadata cache tool provides you with an option to clear the cache.

Figure 10.7 shows the screen for the metadata cache. As shown here, you can select the ABAP APPLICATION SERVER ID and click the CLEAR button to clear the cache for that ABAP server.

You can also see the metadata cache in terms of function modules, classes, and structures; for example, you can select one particular object and click CLEAR to clear the cache for that particular object. After the cache has been cleared, the metadata information is re-downloaded the next time the application is accessed, and the metadata is stored in the cache. One important thing to note here is that the cache is lost when the server is restarted; when the applications are accessed by the user after a restart, the metadata is downloaded and cached again.

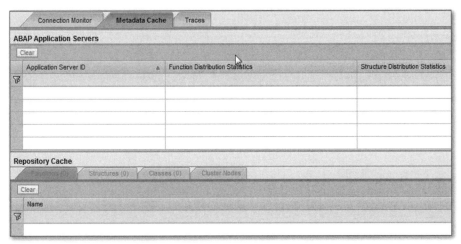

Figure 10.7 Metadata Cache

Traces

Traces allow you to configure various parameters related to the JCo traces (Figure 10.8). You can activate or deactivate tracing for JCo connections, set the trace levels, configure the path for the trace files, and so on. You can do these configurations for each node within an instance.

Connection Monitor	Metadata Cache	Traces		

Traces

Modify | Save | Cancel | Mass Operation...

Instance	Cluster Node ID	Path to Trace Files	RFC Trace	JCo Trace Level

Figure 10.8 JCo Traces

365

Distributed Transactions

The distributed transactions tool provides monitoring and configuring information about JTA transactions. You can get a list of pending and completed transactions and details about all transactions. The distributed transactions tool has two tabs: one that gives an overview of the overall status of transactions in the Java system (TRANSACTION SERVICES) and one that gives detailed monitors for the transactions (ADVANCED MONITORS).

Figure 10.9 shows the DISTRIBUTED TRANSACTIONS: MONITORING AND TROUBLE-SHOOTING overview page. As you can see, it provides an overview of pending transactions, unrecoverable transactions, commit ratios, and so on.

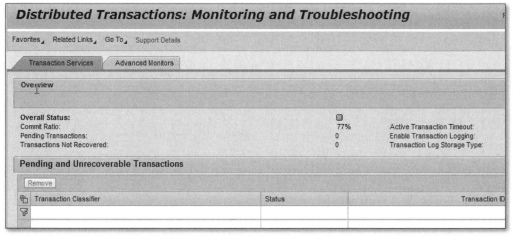

Figure 10.9 Distributed Transactions

From the list of PENDING AND UNRECOVERABLE TRANSACTIONS, you can select a transaction and remove it from the list.

Advanced monitors available inside the distributed transactions monitor give a more detailed analysis of the transactions going on in the system. Here you can get the number of active, completed, committed, and rolled back transactions. For the rolled back transactions, you can also get the counts of the various reasons the transactions rolled back; for example, rollback triggered by application, rollback triggered by timeouts, and so on.

Figure 10.10 shows the ADVANCED MONITORS tab with various details of the transactions in the system. Figure 10.11 and Figure 10.12 show the MONITORS PER RESOURCE MANAGER and MONITORS PER TRANSACTION CLASSIFIER, respectively.

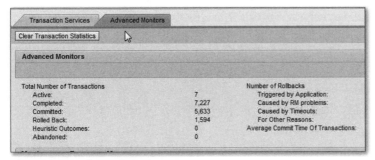

Figure 10.10 Advanced Monitor

Monitors per Resource Manager		
Resource Manager Name	Total Completed Transactions	Commit Ratio
Local RM com.sap.engine.services.dbpool.spi.CommonManagedConnectionImpl	6,912	77%
!SAP_JMS_RA!$@#javax.jms.MessageListener	108	100%

Figure 10.11 Monitors per Resource Manager

Monitors per Transaction Classifier			
Transaction Classifier	Total Completed Transactions	Commit Ratio	Application Rolled Back
[DC Name: sap.com/com.sap.portal.pcd.pcm.roles.rolecontainer, BC-PIN-PCD]	4	100%	0
[DC Name: sap.com/com.sap.netweaver.bc.uwl, EP-BC-UWL]	5	100%	0
[DC Name: com.adobe/DocumentServicesLicenseManager, BC-SRV-FP]	2	100%	0
[DC Name: sap.com/tc~je~threaddump~app, BC-JAS-ADM-MON]	1,034	100%	0
[DC Name: sap.com/com.sap.xi.mdt.soa, BC-XI-IS-WKB]	84	100%	0

Figure 10.12 Monitors per Transaction Classifier

Session Management

The session management tool allows you to monitor the various use sessions that are active in the system. This includes all of the connections to the server, whether the user is accessing SAP NetWeaver Portal, SAP NetWeaver Administrator, or other features of SAP AS Java. For each user connection to the system, it provides the following data (Figure 10.13):

▶ TOTAL NUMBER OF REQUESTS

▶ TOTAL ACTIVE REQUESTS

▶ LONGEST ACTIVE REQUEST (MS)

▶ LONGEST RESPONSE TIME (MS)

▶ OVERALL CPU USAGE (MS)

▶ OVERALL DB TIME (MS)

▶ ALLOCATED MEMORY

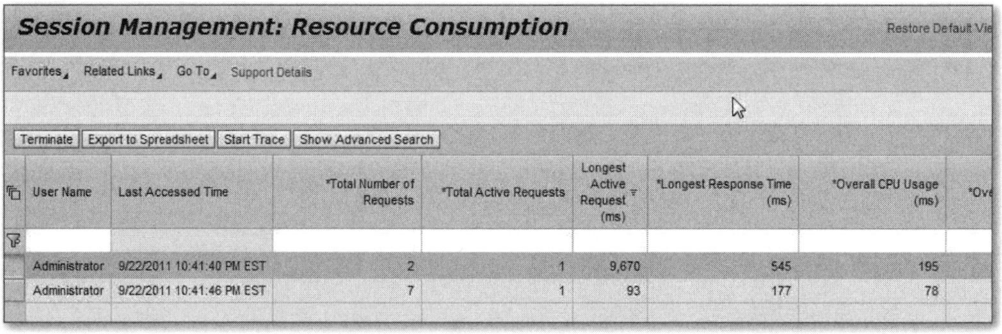

Figure 10.13 Session Management

The combination of the data provided here gives a very good base to be able to analyze the performance of the system. Also, you can easily identify from here what component is going to be bottlenecked in the future. The whole idea of monitoring is to be able to detect problems at an early stage so that appropriate steps can be taken, and a system failure or downtime can be avoided.

In Figure 10.13, you can select any user session, and the details of that session can be seen in the section below on the same screen. The session detail tells you what components of the system are being accessed by that particular user session (Figure 10.14).

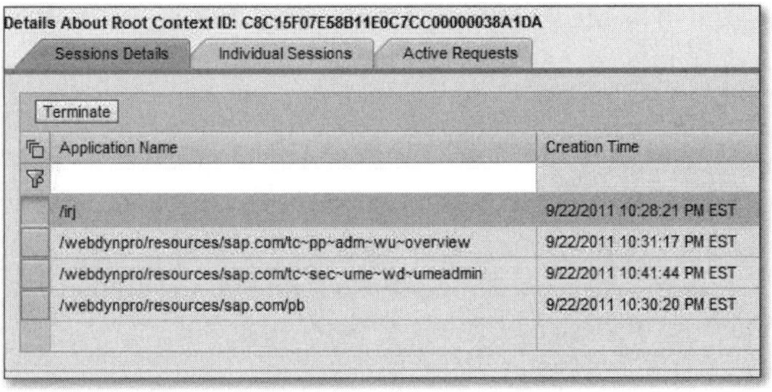

Details About Root Context ID: C8C15F07E58B11E0C7CC00000038A1DA

| Sessions Details | Individual Sessions | Active Requests |

Terminate

Application Name	Creation Time
/irj	9/22/2011 10:28:21 PM EST
/webdynpro/resources/sap.com/tc~pp~adm~wu~overview	9/22/2011 10:31:17 PM EST
/webdynpro/resources/sap.com/tc~sec~ume~wd~umeadmin	9/22/2011 10:41:44 PM EST
/webdynpro/resources/sap.com/pb	9/22/2011 10:30:20 PM EST

Figure 10.14 Session Details

Locks

The enqueue server manages the system locks in AS Java. The enqueue server does not communicate with the persistent storage like a database; instead, it records the current locks in the system in its internal memory. When an application needs to modify shared data, the application requests a lock to be set by the enqueue server. If the enqueue server does not already have a lock that collides with this request, it sets the lock; otherwise, it rejects the lock.

The locks tool of SAP NetWeaver Administrator allows you to see current locks in the system, create locks, and delete locks. You can select an existing lock and view the details of the lock; for example, user name, lock mode, lock arguments, and so on. Figure 10.15 shows the SYSTEM LOCKS table of AS Java.

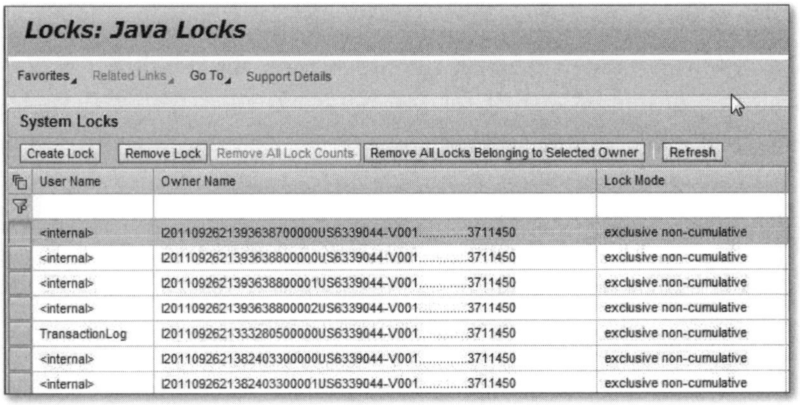

Locks: Java Locks

Favorites   Related Links   Go To   Support Details

System Locks

| Create Lock | Remove Lock | Remove All Lock Counts | Remove All Locks Belonging to Selected Owner | Refresh |

User Name	Owner Name	Lock Mode
<internal>	I20110926213936387000000US6339044-V001............3711450	exclusive non-cumulative
<internal>	I20110926213936388000000US6339044-V001............3711450	exclusive non-cumulative
<internal>	I20110926213936388000001US6339044-V001............3711450	exclusive non-cumulative
<internal>	I20110926213936388000002US6339044-V001............3711450	exclusive non-cumulative
TransactionLog	I20110926213332805000000US6339044-V001............3711450	exclusive non-cumulative
<internal>	I20110926213824033000000US6339044-V001............3711450	exclusive non-cumulative
<internal>	I20110926213824033000001US6339044-V001............3711450	exclusive non-cumulative

Figure 10.15 Java Locks

When you select a row from the table that displays the locks, the details are shown below the locks table.

System Performance Statistics

The system performance statistics section of SAP NetWeaver Administrator gives the statistics for the various requests that have come to SAP NetWeaver Portal or AS Java. If you have worked on the ABAP stack, this may remind you of Transaction STAD, which provides performance statistics for each user request.

This tool lists all of the incoming and outgoing calls to and from the server and maintains the statistics for all of these calls. You can filter the call list based on incoming and outgoing calls to monitor the two types of calls individually. It maintains the following statistics:

▶ Server node

▶ Memory usage

▶ Response time

▶ DB calls

▶ DB time

▶ CPU time

▶ Action

This is an excellent tool that gives you details about each request and can help in analyzing which request is performing badly. You have various filter criteria available to filter the call list. As shown in Figure 10.16, you have a filter for incoming or outgoing calls at the top-left side. Then you have various search criteria for advanced searching of the calls. The CALL LIST table lists all of the calls per the search criteria. When you select a call, the CALL DETAILS section (Figure 10.17) is updated with the details of that call.

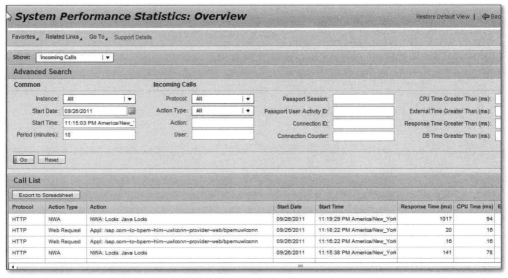

Figure 10.16 System Performance Statistics—Call List

Figure 10.17 System Performance Statistics—Call Details

History Reports

History reports show the historical reports of the system, and you can customize what you want to see in the reports. You can evaluate various statistics such as resource consumption, error statistics, and so on, which can be shown in either graphical or tabular form. The history reports tool has the following sections:

- HISTORY REPORTS
  - DISPLAY tab
  - CONFIGURE tab
- MONITOR BROWSER

The CONFIGURE tab allows you to create or edit reports. You can create or change the following attributes of any report:

▶ REPORT NAME

▶ DEFAULT REPORT TYPE

  ▶ SINGLE CHART

  ▶ CHART PER NODE

  ▶ CHART PER INSTANCE

▶ DEFAULT REPORT TIME UNITS

  ▶ MINUTES

  ▶ FIVE MINUTES

  ▶ QUARTERS

  ▶ HOURS

▶ MONITORS

  ▶ Many monitors are available by default with the application server. You can add or remove monitors from the report.

Figure 10.18 shows the screenshot for creating a history report. You can select values for the DEFAULT REPORT TIME UNIT and the DEFAULT REPORT TYPE fields from the dropdown lists.

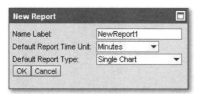

Figure 10.18 Creating a History Report

After a report has been created with basic values, you need to assign monitors to the report. The monitors that you assign will correspond to the type of reports you want to see. As shown in Figure 10.19, SAP delivers many different kinds of monitors that you can add to your report.

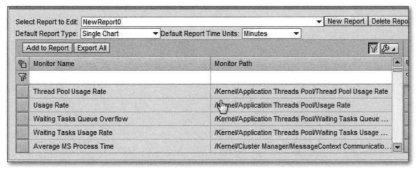

Figure 10.19 Adding Monitors to a History Report

If you select a monitor and click ADD TO REPORT, this will add the monitor to the report. The selected monitors are listed to the right, as shown in Figure 10.20. This table means that the monitors that are part of this table will be shown in the report.

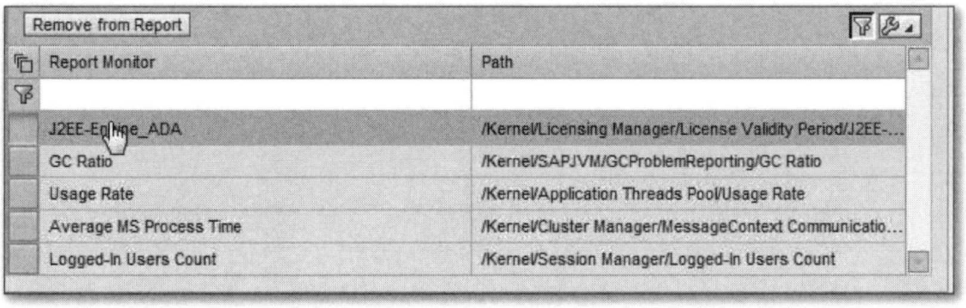

Figure 10.20 Monitors Added to a Report

From this table, you can select a monitor and click REMOVE FROM REPORT to remove the monitor from the report.

We have seen how to create and configure history reports. Now let's see how the history report looks after these configurations. The DISPLAY tab of the HISTORY REPORTS section shows the graphical report. Figure 10.21 shows the history report of the AS Java in graphical mode. The colored lines represent the various monitors that were chosen for this report. The graph also has a legend that shows which color represents which monitor.

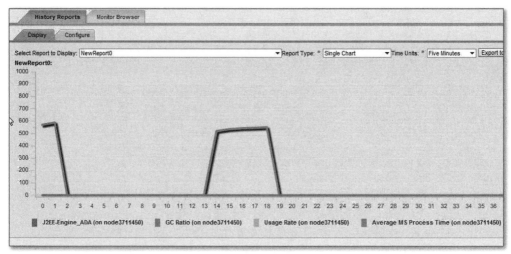

Figure 10.21 History Report

If you place the cursor on any point in the chart, you can see the current values for various monitors at that time. Figure 10.22 shows one such scenario.

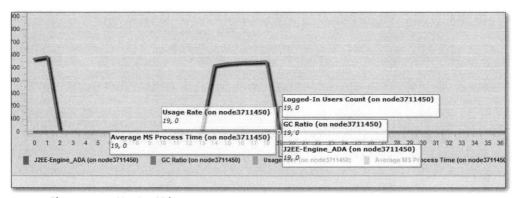

Figure 10.22 Monitor Values

The History Reports section also provides a Monitor Browser section from where you can view and configure all of the monitors available in the system. For each type of monitor, you can see the following in the Monitor Browser section:

▶ List of monitors
▶ Status of monitors

▶ Details of monitors

▶ Configurations of monitors

Figure 10.23 shows a list of all of the monitors available in the system. You can search for and go to any monitor to see the details about that monitor. The list also shows the status of the monitor; that is, whether the monitor is active or inactive.

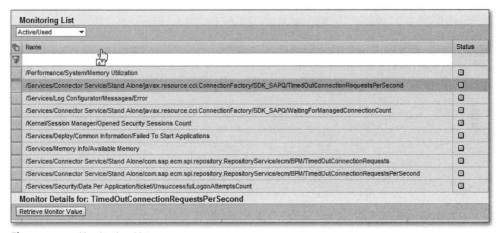

Figure 10.23 Monitoring List

When you click a monitor in this list, the details of the monitor are shown in the details view (Figure 10.24) just below the MONITORING LIST. Here you get the following details about the monitor:

▶ SERVER NODE ID

▶ CURRENT VALUE

▶ LAST REPORTING TIME

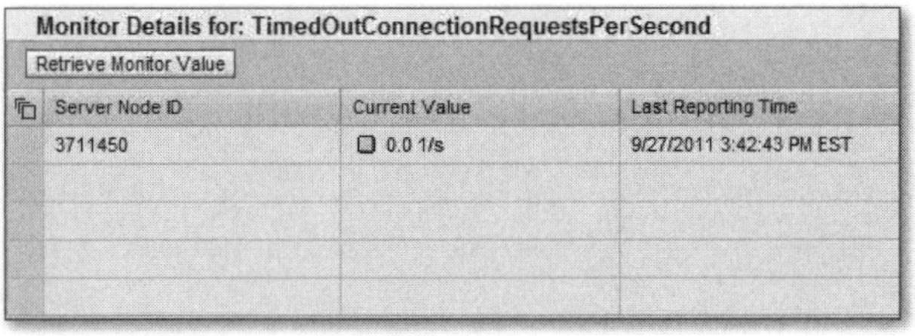

Figure 10.24 Monitor Details

Also, along with the details view, a monitor configuration view (Figure 10.25) appears just below the monitor details view on the same screen. In this screen, you can configure various parameters related to the monitor. You can do the following activities from the monitor configuration view:

▶ Deactivate a monitor

▶ Restore the monitor configuration to default values

▶ Change the following configurations and save:

    ▶ DESCRIPTION

    ▶ COLOR CHANGING THRESHOLDS

    ▶ DATA COLLECTION METHOD

    ▶ PERIOD

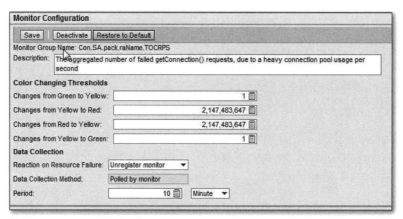

Figure 10.25   Monitor Configuration

10.2   Activity Reporting

SAP NetWeaver Portal provides two types of reporting functionality for the portal usage:

▶ Portal activity report

▶ Activity data collector

The *portal activity report* provides the number of users who logged in to the SAP NetWeaver Portal during a specified period of time. It also gives a report of what iViews/pages were requested by the users.

The *activity data collector* tool provides more detailed reports about the portal usage. The additional data provided can be the response time, details of the logged-in user, browser type of the user, and so on.

In this section, we will learn how these tools are enabled and used in SAP NetWeaver Portal.

10.2.1 Portal Activity Report

The portal activity report is a tool for administrators to evaluate the usage of the SAP NetWeaver Portal on a regular basis. Administrators can get the following information from the portal activity report:

▶ Number of users logged in during a specific period

▶ Details of the users who logged in

▶ Number of users who visited each page and iView

The portal activity report feature of SAP NetWeaver Portal depends on the following three components provided by SAP:

▶ **Data collection service**
The data collection service runs inside SAP NetWeaver Portal as a service and collects raw data from the Portal Runtime (PRT) about the users who are logged in and the iViews and pages they are accessing. The data collection service is part of SAP NetWeaver Portal and is activated by default. There is one data collection service per node of SAP NetWeaver Portal. The data collection service uses the SAP NetWeaver Portal database to store the raw data collected from the PRT.

▶ **Aggregator application**
Because there is one data collection service per node of SAP NetWeaver Portal, you need another application to combine the data regarding portal usage from all of the nodes and store it centrally. The aggregator application does this aggregation and stores the data in the portal database. The aggregator application deletes the raw data generated by the data collection service after generating the aggregated data.

▶ **iView template**
SAP NetWeaver Portal provides an iView template for the portal activity report. The portal iView reads data from the aggregated data created by the aggregator application. You can use this iView template to create your iViews; you can also configure the iView to show different types of data and different time periods.

Figure 10.26 shows the workflow of how portal activity reporting works.

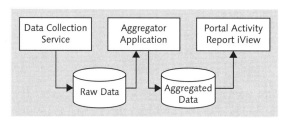

Figure 10.26 Portal Activity Report Workflow

For portal activity reporting to work, you need to configure the data collections service. We'll explore how to configure the data collection service in the following subsections. We will also explain how you can create iViews for the portal activity report. If you don't want to use the SAP iView templates and instead want to create your own application to use the data provided by the aggregator application, you can do this by directly accessing the database tables where the aggregator application stores the data. The aggregator application doesn't require any configuration, but we will discuss the tables that can be used for this information.

Configuring the Data Collection Service

To activate the data collection service and to configure the data collection, you need to configure the activity report service. You can do this from the SAP NetWeaver Administrator.

Follow these steps to configure the data collection service:

1. Log on to SAP NetWeaver Administrator by going to *http://<host>:<port>/nwa*.

2. Navigate to CONFIGURATION • INFRASTRUCTURE • APPLICATION MODULES (Figure 10.27).

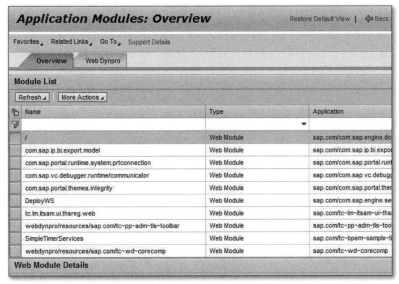

Figure 10.27 Application Modules

3. Select the service COM.SAP.PORTAL.ACTIVITYREPORT.CORE, and set the property ACTIVATE PORTAL ACTIVITY REPORT to TRUE. This will activate the data collection service. The data collection service is deactivated by default.

4. The data collection service can be configured with the following properties as needed:

   ▶ FIRST DAY OF THE WEEK: Sets the first day for weekly reports.

   ▶ GATHER IVIEW STATISTICS: Enables or disables the gathering of iView statistics.

   ▶ GATHER PAGE STATISTICS: Enables or disables the gathering of page statistics.

   ▶ NUMBER OF DAYS FOR DAILY DATA RETENTION

   ▶ NUMBER OF DAYS FOR HOURLY DATA RETENTION

   ▶ NUMBER OF DAYS FOR MONTHLY DATA RETENTION

   ▶ NUMBER OF DAYS FOR QUARTERLY DATA RETENTION

   ▶ NUMBER OF DAYS FOR WEEKLY DATA RETENTION

   ▶ SAVE INTERVAL (MINUTES)

5. Save the settings after configuration changes are done.

Creating Portal Activity Report iViews

A portal activity report iView enables you to create and display various types of reports of the number of users logged in, number of times an iView is visited, and so on. SAP provides an iView template for creating portal activity reports.

To create a portal activity report iView, follow these steps:

1. Log on to SAP NetWeaver Portal, and navigate to CONTENT ADMINISTRATION.

2. Right-click the folder where you want to create the iView, select NEW • IVIEW FROM TEMPLATE, and then select the PORTAL ACTIVITY REPORT IVIEW template (Figure 10.28).

Figure 10.28 Portal Activity Report Template

3. Enter the iView properties to create the iView. After the iView has been created, open the iView for editing.

4. Define the type of report and the reporting period. Figure 10.29 shows the options for the type of report, and Figure 10.30 shows the options for the reporting period. You can create the following types of reports:

   ▶ NUMBER OF USERS WHO LOGGED ON

   ▶ DETAILS ABOUT THE USERS WHO LOGGED ON

   ▶ PAGE/IVIEW ACTIVITY

You can also select the following reporting periods:

- CURRENT DAY'S ACTIVITY
- MOST RECENT ACTIVITY
- FIXED PERIOD

Based on these parameters, the iView is created and saved.

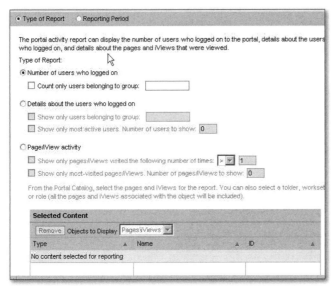

Figure 10.29 Type of Report

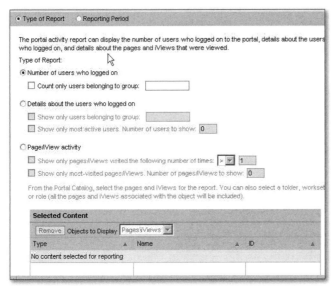

Figure 10.30 Reporting Period

Directly Accessing Database Tables

SAP provides the iView template that can be readily used for creating the usage reports for SAP NetWeaver Portal. However, in some scenarios, you might want to develop your own custom application to provide the usage data to the users in a custom way. For this purpose, you can access the aggregated database directly. The following are the tables that hold the aggregated data in the database:

▶ **WCR_USERSTAT**
Holds information about the number of users who logged on to the portal.

▶ **WCR_WEBCONTENTSTAT**
Holds information about the content that was viewed.

▶ **WCR_USERFIRSTLOGON**
Holds information about the first logon of each user and how many pages and iViews the user viewed.

▶ **WCR_USERPAGEUSAGE**
Holds information about which users viewed which pages.

▶ **WCR_AGGINFO**
Holds information about all aggregations.

10.2.2 Activity Data Collector

The activity data collector is a tool provided by SAP that helps monitor user and content activity. It records each request to SAP NetWeaver Portal and writes the details of the request to the collector files. You can activate and configure the activity data collector to change the way it collects data; in order to do this, you need to configure the portal service *com.sap.portal.*activitydatacollector.

The data collected by the activity data collector can be used by analytics tools to create reports. SAP NetWeaver Portal does not include a tool to provide reporting out of this data.

To activate and configure the activity data collector, follow these steps:

1. Navigate to SYSTEM ADMINISTRATION • CONTENT STATISTICS • DATA COLLECTION CONFIGURATION, and select the CONFIGURATION tab.

2. The ACTIVATE DATA COLLECTION checkbox can be used to activate or deactivate the data collection.

3. If you are activating the data collection, the following important parameters need to be entered and saved:

   ▶ BASE FILE NAME
   File name that will be used for generating the files.

   ▶ DIRECTORY NAME
   Directory where the files will be saved.

   ▶ FILE ENCODING
   Encoding for the data file.

   ▶ MAX FILE SIZE
   Maximum size of each file. After the maximum size is reached, a new file is opened.

   ▶ MAX STORAGE ALLOCATION
   Maximum storage allocated for the data collection files. If no value is entered, then there is no limit for the storage size, but if a size is mentioned, then the new file starts overwriting the oldest files after the maximum storage space has been used.

   ▶ MAIN FILE FORMAT
   Stores the format of the main file. We will discuss the file formats in this section.

   ▶ ADDITIONAL FILE FORMAT
   Stores the format of the additional files.

You can define the format in which the activity data collection file should be saved. The file format determines what data is saved to the data files and in what format.

The file format is a string with the grammar listed in Table 10.1. The important components of the file format are opCode, parameter, and the special character code. In the following subsection, we will discuss these components and see how the format can be defined. We also discuss how the time pattern can be used in the file format.

Element	Definition
File format	`<ELEMENT> *`
ELEMENT	`<OPCODE> | <LITERAL> | <SPECIAL_CHAR>`
OPCODE	`%O<OpCode>[(<Parameter>)]%` (See the next section for a list of valid opCodes and their parameters.)
LITERAL	`, | : | ;`
SPECIAL_CHAR	`%S<Special character code>%` (See the "Special Character Codes" section later for a list of valid special character codes.)

Table 10.1 File Format Grammar

OpCodes and Parameters

OpCodes return information about the portal request, or the iView/page and portal component that were run in response to the request. Some opCodes require one or more parameters, which are specified in parentheses immediately following the opCode, without quotation marks. Multiple parameters are separated by a comma. The opCodes listed in Table 10.2 return information derived directly from the request.

OpCode	Description
`rfo.rh()<header name>`	Value of the request header specified in the `<header name>` parameter. For example, the opCode `rfo.rh(Content-Type)` returns a string similar to `application/x-www-form-urlencoded`.
`rfo.hrh()<header name>`	Hashed value of the request header specified in the `<header name>` parameter.
`rfo.an`	Portal application of the portal component triggered by the request.

Table 10.2 opCodes Retrieved Directly for Request

OpCode	Description
rfo.cn	Portal component triggered by the request.
rfo.in	Name of iView triggered by the request.
rfo.pu	PCD URL of the iView triggered by the request.
rfo.hpu	Hashed value of the PCD URL of the iView triggered by the request.
rfo.ct	Indicates whether a page or iView was triggered by the request. Returns either page or iView.
rfo.up(<namespace>, <property name>)	Value of the user property as specified by the namespace and property name attributes, where the namespace attribute is optional. If no namespace is added, the default UME namespace is used.
rfo.un	Name of the logged-in user.
rfo.hun	Hashed value of the name of the logged-in user.
rfo.ut	Type of user: either authenticated (n) or anonymous (a).
rfo.sid	HTTP session ID.
rfo.qs	Query string of the URL that triggered the request.
rfo.hqs	Hashed value of the query string of the URL that triggered the request.
rfo.bt	Browser type.
rfo.uid	A unique ID for the portal request, which can be used to correlate the current request record with a record for the same request in a different data collector file.
rfo.st	Indicates whether the iView/page is embedded in a page (child) or not embedded in a page (root).

Table 10.2 opCodes Retrieved Directly for Request (Cont.)

The opCodes listed in Table 10.3 return information not derived from the request.

385

OpCode	Description
rfo.np	Navigation path of the iView/page. The path is the navigation node name of the iView/page.
rfo.sh	Server host name.
rfo.sp	Server port.
rfo.nid	Node ID.
rfo.t(<time pattern>)<time zone>	Current time when request was made, in the specified format and time zone. See the "Time Pattern" and "Time Zone" sections later in this chapter.
adc.pt	Time to process the request, in milliseconds.

Table 10.3 opCodes Not Derived from Request

Special Character Codes

Table 10.4 lists the special character codes.

Character Code	Description
nl	New line
dq	Double quote
sq	Single quote
bs	Backspace
tab	Tab

Table 10.4 Special Character Codes

Time Pattern

The time pattern is a string that is similar to the pattern used for the java.text. SimpleDateFormat class and is made up of the characters as shown in Table 10.5.

Symbol	Description
y	Year
M	Month in year
w	Week in year
W	Week in month
D	Day in year
d	Day in month
F	Day of week in month
E	Day in week
a	AM/PM
H	Hour in day (0–23)
k	Hour in day (1–24)
K	Hour in am/pm (0–11)
h	Hour in am/pm (1–12)
m	Minute in hour
s	Second in minute
S	Millisecond
z	Time zone

Table 10.5 Characters in a Time Pattern

A time pattern may contain any separator character except the following:

`% ( ) , { }.`

Time Zone

The time zone is a string with the syntax shown in Table 10.6.

387

Element	Definition
TIME ZONE	GMT\<SIGN>\<HOURS>:\<MINUTES>
SIGN	+ | -
HOURS	\<DIGIT> | \<DIGIT>\<DIGIT>
MINUTES	\<DIGIT>\<DIGIT>
DIGIT	[0-9]

Table 10.6 Time Zone Elements

For example, GMT+2:00 is a valid time zone, and the following is a valid file format:

```
%Orfo.t(d-MMM-yyyy  kk:mm:ss,z)%%Stab%%Orfo.un%%Stab%  %Orfo.rh(Content-
Type)%%Snl%
```

The format writes the following for each portal request:

- The time of the request, in the given format
- A tab character
- The user who was authenticated for the request
- A tab character
- The value for the content-type request header
- A new line character

10.3 Logging and Tracing

SAP NetWeaver Portal creates logs based on the central logging system of SAP NetWeaver AS Java. You can view the logs and traces from the Log Viewer tool provided by SAP NetWeaver Administrator. To make sure that your system is functioning properly, you should be looking at the system logs regularly. They give important clues to what is happening inside the system.

In the context of logging and tracing, it is important to understand the difference between logs and traces. *Log files* are generally for the system messages and are monitored by system administrators to gauge the functioning of the system and for error analysis. Logs are always switched on in the system, and they are necessary for troubleshooting in case of issues. SAP NetWeaver Administrator gives you the ability to configure your log settings based on which messages you want to see and which messages should go to which categories. *Trace files* are usually used by developers to analyze the functioning of the applications at runtime. Traces are usually deactivated because they involve a performance hit on the server, and they are switched on if needed to analyze any issue related to the applications. Even though there is a conceptual difference between logs and traces, all of the configurations related to logs and traces are together referred to as log configuration. In this chapter, all of the configurations we discuss for logging also apply to traces.

To analyze the information from the logs in the desired manner, you need to configure logging in SAP NetWeaver Portal. You can do this using the SAP NetWeaver Administrator and the Offline Configuration Tool (Config Tool). The Config Tool provides more advanced log configuration options than SAP NetWeaver Administrator. In this section, we will see how log configuration is done with these tools.

10.3.1 Log Configuration with SAP NetWeaver Administrator

Log configuration with SAP NetWeaver Administrator provides options for configuring the severities of log controllers. Log controllers in AS Java are objects to manage the writing of logs and traces. Two types of log controllers are provided by SAP:

▶ **Category**
A category refers to messages from a specific problem area. It is used to store log messages. Examples of problem areas include the database, networking, and so on.

▶ **Location**
Locations refer to messages originating from various source code areas. They are used by developers and are organized along code packages.

For the log configuration in SAP NetWeaver Administrator, follow these steps:

1. Log in to SAP NetWeaver Administrator, and navigate to TROUBLESHOOTING • LOGS AND TRACES • LOG CONFIGURATION. You can also go to the configuration page by going directly to *http://<host>:<port>/nwa/log-config*. You will be taken to the LOG CONFIGURATION: JAVA page as shown in Figure 10.31.

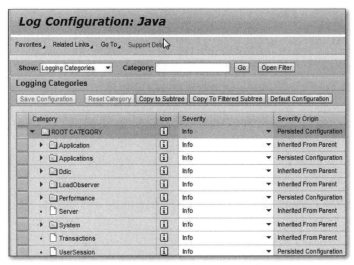

Figure 10.31 Logging Category in SAP NetWeaver Administrator

On the top-left side of Figure 10.31, you will notice a dropdown. The dropdown has the values LOGGING CATEGORIES and TRACING LOCATIONS. The selection in this dropdown determines what is shown on the screen. Figure 10.31 only shows the logging categories as selected in the dropdown. When you select TRACING LOCATIONS, you will see the locations listed, as in Figure 10.32.

2. From the list, you can select a category and location to change the configuration.

3. To change the severity of the category or location, go to the SEVERITY column, and select the appropriate severity. This will set the severity of the selected category or location. The severity can have the following values:

   ▸ ALL
   The lowest severity. Log controllers with such a severity log all of the messages regardless of their severity.

   ▸ DEBUG
   For debugging purposes, with extensive and low-level information.

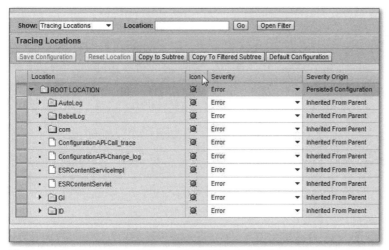

Figure 10.32 Tracing Locations in SAP NetWeaver Administrator

▶ PATH
For tracing the execution flow; for example, entering and leaving a method, looping and branching operations, and so on.

▶ INFO
Informational text, mostly for announcing what has already been performed.

▶ WARNING
Announces that the application can recover from an anomaly and fulfill the required task but needs attention from a developer/operator.

▶ ERROR
Announces that the application can recover from an error, but it cannot fulfill the required task due to the error.

▶ FATAL
Announces that the application cannot recover from an error, and the situation causes fatal termination.

▶ NONE
The highest severity. Log controllers with such a severity suppress all of the messages logged into them, except for the messages with the same severity.

After changing the SEVERITY setting, you can save the configuration. There are two buttons on the screen COPY TO SUBTREE and COPY TO FILTERED SUBTREE. If you select the COPY TO SUBTREE button, the new configuration will be copied to the entire subtree of the selected node. If you have used a filter to filter the list of categories or locations (Figure 10.33) on the screen, the COPY TO FILTERED SUBTREE button will apply the configuration to the subtree in the filtered list.

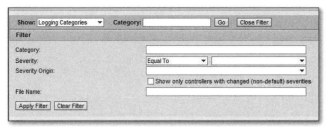

Figure 10.33 Filter for Categories and Locations

4. The preceding process will apply the log configuration change to the entire system. Sometimes, however, you may want to do log configuration on one specific instance and not on the entire system. To do this, click the PER INSTANCE CONFIGURATION tab (Figure 10.34) tab below the CATEGORY or LOCATION lists.

Figure 10.34 Per Instance Configuration

The tab will show the list of instances in the system. You can select the specific instances and change the severity level from the SEVERITY column. This will change the severity level only for that instance.

10.3.2 Log Configuration with the Config Tool

Using the Config tool, you can do more advanced configurations related to logging and tracing. Also, as discussed earlier, you can use the Offline Config tool even when the system in not online.

With the Offline Config tool, you can perform the following configurations related to logging:

▶ Log controllers configuration

▶ Log formatters configuration

▶ Log destinations configuration

▶ Log archiving configuration

Log Controllers Configuration

Log controllers are Java objects that manage the writing of logs and traces. There are two types of controllers, as we have seen earlier: location controller and category controller. Using the Config tool, you can add, edit, or remove the location and category controllers. To add a log controller, follow these steps:

1. Start the Config tool, and navigate to CLUSTER • <TEMPLATE_NAME> • INSTANCE • LOG CONFIGURATION (Figure 10.35).

Figure 10.35 Log Configuration in the Config Tool

2. Navigate to the desired node within either the CATEGORIES node or the LOCATIONS node where you want to create a new category or location.

3. Click the NEW button. You'll be asked to enter a name for the new category or location. Enter the desired name, and click OK.

The category or location will be created. Categories are named according to their location in the hierarchical structure. The root category is labeled with the forward slash (/). and all of the other nodes are in reference to this root category. Each level in the hierarchy is again separated by the / character (Figure 10.36). For example, to create a test category under the root, you enter the name as "/Test"; and to create a category sys under the Test node, you enter the name as "/Test/sys".

Figure 10.36 New Log Controller Name

Locations are separated by a period (.) in the hierarchy, and the hierarchical structure is similar to the Java package naming convention. For example, for creating a test location named under a folder named "com," you enter "com.Test" as the name of the location.

To edit a log controller, select the log controller from the hierarchy, categories, or locations. On the right side you can change the severity from the SEVERITY dropdown (Figure 10.37).

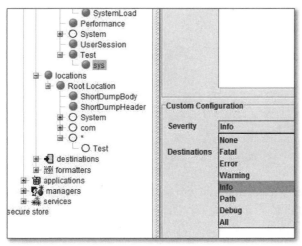

Figure 10.37 Editing the Log Controller

To add a log destination to the controller, click ADD. You will get a list of destinations. You can select a destination and click OK to add the destination to the controller.

394

Log Formatters Configuration

Logs can print the log message in different formats. These formats are ListFormatter, TraceFormatter, and XMLFormatter. To create a new formatter, follow these steps:

1. Start the Config tool, and navigate to CLUSTER • <TEMPLATE_NAME> • INSTANCE • LOG CONFIGURATION (refer to Figure 10.35).

2. Select any formatter from the list. For the details screen, click NEW. You will be asked to enter the name of the formatter.

3. Enter a name, and click OK to create the formatter.

4. From the TYPE dropdown, you can select the type of the formatter (Figure 10.38).

   The following types of formatters are available:

   ▶ LISTFORMATTER
   Formats the logs in a list format that can be consumed by other applications.

   ▶ TRACEFORMATTER
   Formats the logs in human-readable format. You can specify a pattern that can be used for this.

   ▶ XMLFORMATTER
   Formats the logs in XML format.

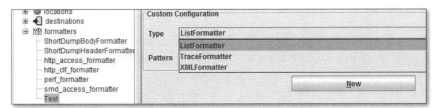

Figure 10.38 Creating a Log Formatter

If you have chosen the TRACEFORMATTER as the formatter type, then you can define a pattern for the TraceFormatter. The pattern allows you to specify the message data fields, with place holders of the form `"%[[-]<width>[-]]<type>"`, interspersed with arbitrary text that you want to have included in formatted messages. If you put a dash in front of the `<width>` of the field to be printed, the field is aligned on the right; if you use a trailing dash, it is aligned on the left. If you flank the value of `<width>` with dashes on both sides, you will get a centered field. If you omit the alignment, the field is left-aligned. The `<type>` that specifies the field can be one of the following:

▶ `i`: Message identification.

▶ `p`: Time stamp in milliseconds since January 1, 1970 00:00:00 GMT.

▶ `d`: Time stamp in readable form.

▶ `c`: Log controller through which the message was issued.

▶ `a`: Application on behalf of which the message was issued.

▶ `l`: Location of origin.

▶ `u`: User on behalf of which the message was issued.

▶ `S`: Session on behalf of which the message was issued.

▶ `T`: Transaction on behalf of which the message was issued.

▶ `o`: DSR (Distributed Statistics Record) component on behalf of which the message was issued.

▶ `e`: DSR user on behalf of which the message was issued.

▶ `r`: DSR transaction on behalf of which the message was issued.

▶ `t`: Thread that emitted the message.

▶ `g`: Group indentation.

▶ `s`: Message severity.

▶ `m`: Formatted message text.

To print a single % sign, insert a %%. With group indentation, width is interpreted as the indentation for each level with a standard value of 1, and alignment is ignored. As an example, the standard pattern `"%24d %-40l [%t] %s: %m"` lets the trace formatter print the date and time of the message in a 24-character column aligned to the left, followed by the right-aligned location truncated from the left to 40 characters, the thread name in brackets, and finally the severity name and the formatted message text separated with a colon. A typical message would then look like this:

May 11, 2001 11:17:42 AM ...g.TraceFormatterTest.testStdPattern() [main] Info: test standard pattern

Log Destinations Configuration

A log destination defines where you want your log message to be written and is an object to which you assign a formatter. To create or edit a destination, follow these steps:

1. Start the Config tool, and navigate to CLUSTER • <TEMPLATE_NAME> • INSTANCE • LOG CONFIGURATION (refer to Figure 10.35).

2. Choose any destination, and on the details screen, choose NEW.

3. Enter a new name, and click OK. The new destination will appear in the tree structure.

4. You can choose the severity of messages from the SEVERITY drop down (Figure 10.39).

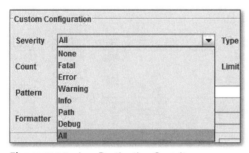

Figure 10.39   Log Destination Severity

5. You can choose the destination type from the TYPE dropdown. The allowed values are FILELOG and CONSOLELOG. If you select FILELOG, the logs are written to files; if you select CONSOLELOG, then the logs are written to the console (Figure 10.40).

Figure 10.40   Log Destination Type

If you have selected FILELOG as the destination type, then you need to enter the COUNT field. This field specifies how many files will be generated before the oldest file starts getting overwritten by the new file. The LIMIT field specifies the maximum size of each file before a new file gets created.

The PATTERN field defines the actual file where the log will be written. Also, the FORMATTER field allows you to select a formatter from the formatters defined.

Log Archiving Configuration

By default, SAP generates five log files with a maximum size of 10MB each. When the five files have been filled, the system starts overwriting the oldest file. This makes you lose older log files that you may need later to troubleshoot problems. For this reason, you might want to activate log archiving. If log archiving is enabled, the older set of five files are archived instead of being overwritten. This configuration is done in the log manager. Follow these steps to configure archiving:

1. Start the Config tool, and navigate to CLUSTER • <TEMPLATE_NAME> • MANAGERS • LOGMANAGER (Figure 10.41).

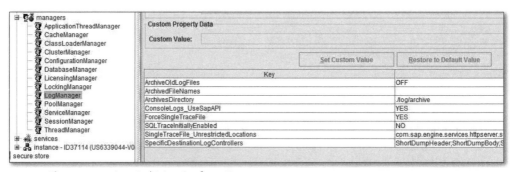

Figure 10.41 Log Archiving Configuration

2. Set the property ARCHIVEOLDLOGFILES to ON. By default, it is set to OFF.

In the ARHIVESDIRECTORY property, you can define the path on the file system where the log files will be stored.

10.4 Viewing Logs

SAP NetWeaver Portal logs can be viewed using the following tools:

- ► SAP NetWeaver Administrator
- ► Command line
- ► SAP Management Console (SAP MC)

In this section, we will discuss how to use these tools to view logs and traces from the SAP NetWeaver Portal server.

10.4.1 SAP NetWeaver Administrator

The Log Viewer in SAP NetWeaver Administrator allows you to view all of the logs and traces generated in the AS Java system. These logs are useful for monitoring the system as well as troubleshooting issues.

You can access the Log Viewer by logging in to the SAP NetWeaver Administrator and navigating to the TROUBLESHOOTING tab, choosing LOGS AND TRACES, and then clicking the LOG VIEWER link as shown in Figure 10.42.

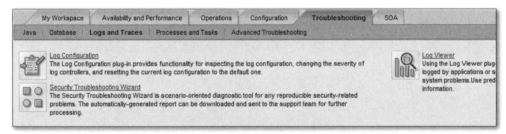

Figure 10.42 Log Viewer in SAP NetWeaver Administrator

Figure 10.43 shows the LOG VIEWER: OVERVIEW screen. The LOG VIEWER screen provides a list of all of the messages that have been generated. Here you can filter the messages based on severity, category, location, application, and so on. To see the details of a particular message, click the + icon in the DETAILS column. This will show that particular message in detail.

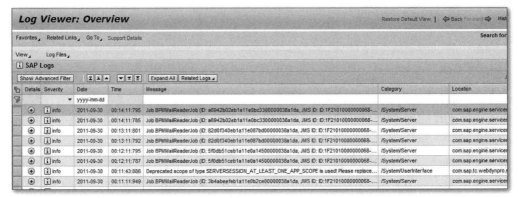

Figure 10.43 Log Viewer Overview

Figure 10.44 shows the details of a message. You can also click the SHOW ADVANCED FILTER button to make some advanced filter choices.

Figure 10.44 Message Details

You can download the content from the log viewer by selecting LOG FILES • DOWN-LOAD CONTENT from the menu in the screen.

10.4.2 Command Line

You can use the command line to view the list of formatted logs and trace files. SAP has provided a tool, lv.bat (for Windows), that can be used for viewing the logs and traces on the command line. The `lv` tool is provided in the same directory as the Config tool. To view the log files on the command line, navigate to the Config tool directory, and execute this command:

```
>lv.bat <file_name>
```

This will output the file on the screen. Figure 10.45 shows the output of the console log viewer. To get a list of all of the available options with the console log viewer, execute this command:

```
>lv -h
```

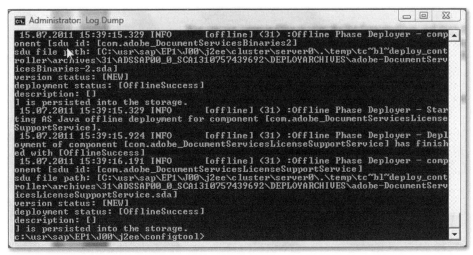

Figure 10.45   Console Log Viewer

10.4.3   Management Console

The SAP Management Console (MC) gives you tools to view logs and traces at the instance level as well as at the individual node level. At the instance level, you can select the trace file that you want to open and then view the file.

As shown in Figure 10.46, you can select the instance, right-click, and navigate to ALL TASKS • VIEW TRACE FILE or ALL TASKS • VIEW DEVELOPER TRACES. If you select VIEW TRACE FILE, the console gives you the instance-level system log.

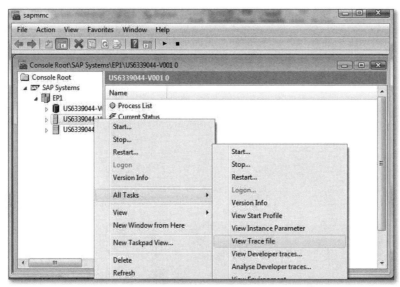

Figure 10.46 Instance Level Trace from the Management Console

If you select the VIEW DEVELOPER TRACES option, you will be given a list of all of the trace files and log files available in the instance (Figure 10.47). When you select a file and click OK, the selected file will be loaded (Figure 10.48).

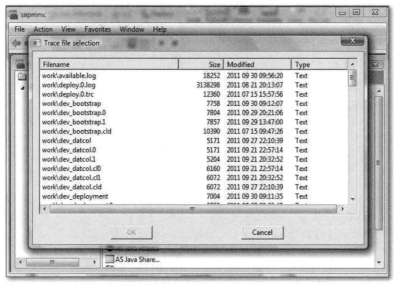

Figure 10.47 Trace File Selection

Figure 10.48 Viewing the Trace File

You can also navigate to the individual process in the MC, right-click, and select Developer Trace to load the trace for that process. You can see the same traces from the web-based management console also.

10.5 Logging for SAP NetWeaver Portal PCD Objects

Changes to PCD objects can be made by content administrators, transport mechanisms, or the generic creator service that is used in content creation via XMLs. The changes made to the PCD objects can also be logged and used for troubleshooting when needed. SAP NetWeaver Portal provides an admin traceability service that is responsible for logging all of these changes. Configuration of the admin traceability service can be done using the Config Tool and SAP NetWeaver Administrator.

The admin traceability service can log the following types of changes related to PCD objects:

▸ Creating an object
▸ Deleting an object

- ▸ Renaming an object
- ▸ Sorting the child list of an object
- ▸ Redefining the target of a delta link
- ▸ Importing a unit object
- ▸ Changing permissions of an object
- ▸ Deploying to Generic Portal Application Layer (GPAL) applications that are already used by objects in the portal

The admin traceability service can also log changes to some portal configurations such as changes to service configurations, changes to portal display rules, and so on. In this section, we will first see how to configure PCD objects, and then we will discuss how the admin traceability service is configured.

10.5.1 Configuring Portal Content Directory Objects Logging

By default, the PCD changes are written to the following folder (in Windows):

C:\ usr\sap\<System ID>\J<instance ID>\j2ee\cluster\change\log

The file name of the log file by default is *changes#.log* (Figure 10.49). If you want to specify another location, you can do that using the Config Tool.

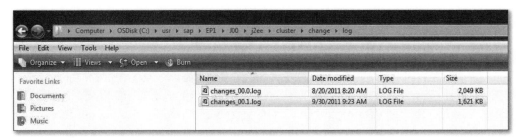

Figure 10.49 PCD Changes Log File Location

To configure the log file location, login to the Config Tool, navigate to <Template> • Log Configuration • Destinations, and create a new destination. (We discussed creating destinations in Section 10.3.) After you have created the destination, go to Categories • System • Changes, add the destination, and save your changes. The category Changes should now look like Figure 10.50.

Figure 10.50 Custom Destination for PCD Logging

After this change, you will need to restart the cluster for your changes to take effect.

10.5.2 Configuring Admin Traceability Service

The admin traceability service is activated by default in SAP NetWeaver Portal. To deactivate or activate the admin traceability service, log in to SAP NetWeaver Administrator, and navigate to CONFIGURATION • INFRASTRUCTURE • JAVA SYSTEM PROPERTIES.

In the SERVICES tab, search for the service PCD GENERIC LAYER (Figure 10.51), select it, and click the ADVANCED PROPERTIES button.

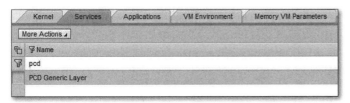

Figure 10.51 Portal Content Directory Generic Layer Service

All of the properties related to the PCD GENERIC LAYER service will be listed in the EXTENDED DETAILS section. In the EXTENDED DETAILS section, search for and select the property PCD.GL.ADMINTRACEABILITY.ACTIVE. You will see that by default the property is set to TRUE (Figure 10.52), which means it is activated by default. If you want to deactivate the service, you can click the MODIFY button and set the value to FALSE.

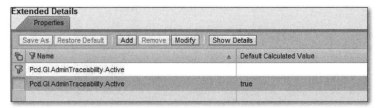

Figure 10.52 Activating/Deactivating Admin Traceability

After making sure that admin traceability is activated, you need to specify the objects that you need to be logged. Search for and select the property Pcd. Gl.AdminTraceability.IncludedObjectClasses. In Figure 10.53, notice that by default all classes (*) are logged; however, you can use this property to restrict the logging if needed.

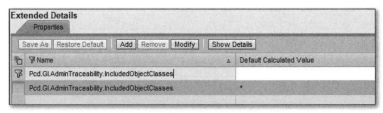

Figure 10.53 Restricting Objects for Logging

For example, to log all classes that start with "com.test", you need to enter "com. test.*". To enter multiple entries, separate them with a semicolon (;). You can include the portal content objects by giving their path in the PCD. For example, you can add all objects in a folder named "Test" inside the portal content by adding "portal_content/Test/*".

You can also assign the objects' paths to each severity level by changing the following properties related to each severity level:

▸ Pcd.Gl.AdminTraceability.IncludedPaths.Debug

▸ Pcd.Gl.AdminTraceability.IncludedPaths.Path

▸ Pcd.Gl.AdminTraceability.IncludedPaths.Info

▸ Pcd.Gl.AdminTraceability.IncludedPaths.Warning

▸ Pcd.Gl.AdminTraceability.IncludedPaths.Error

10.6   Troubleshooting

SAP NetWeaver Portal provides many tools within the portal for troubleshooting purposes (Figure 10.54). These tools are inside the SYSTEM ADMINISTRATION • SUPPORT section. In this section, we will look at how some of these tools can be used for troubleshooting purposes.

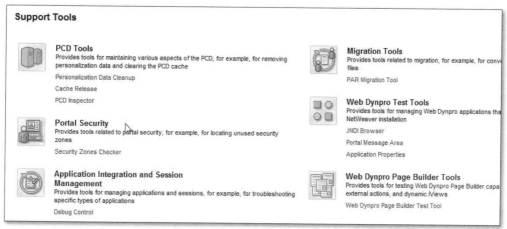

Figure 10.54 Troubleshooting Tools

10.6.1   Personalization Data Cleanup

The personalization data cleanup tool is within the PCD TOOLS category shown in Figure 10.54, and can be used for removing the PCD personalization done for specific users of objects. Sometimes you will see inconsistency in the data or screens seen by various users, as some users have personalized their screens knowingly or unknowingly. You can perform the following actions with this tool:

▶ Remove personalization for objects for a specific user

▶ Remove personalization for objects for all users

▶ Remove personalization for all users

You can access the personalization data cleanup tool by navigating to SYSTEM ADMINISTRATION • SUPPORT. Figure 10.55 shows that in the personalization data cleanup tool, you can search either for the user or for the object to remove the personalization data.

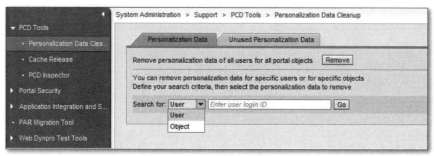

Figure 10.55 Personalization Data Cleanup

After selecting the specific user or object, you can click the REMOVE button to remove the personalization data.

The tool also provides an option to remove all unused personalization data. Cleaning up unused personalization data on a regular basis will improve the user performance of SAP NetWeaver Portal. To do the cleanup, you need to go to the UNUSED PERSONALIZATION DATA tab of the personalization data cleanup tool. Figure 10.56 shows the screen for removing the unused personalization data.

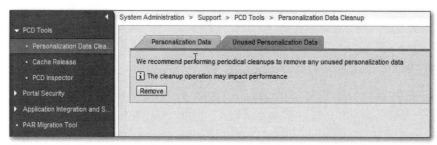

Figure 10.56 Unused Personalization Data

10.6.2 PCD Cache Release

The PCD cache is found in the PCD TOOLS category in Figure 10.54, and stores the PCD objects being used. Some objects in the cache may be shared by many users, whereas some objects are only used by a single user; for example, any personalization data that is specific to a user.

The PCD cache release tool includes an option to release all of the objects from the cache. You can access the cache release tool by navigating to SYSTEM ADMINISTRA-

TION • SUPPORT in SAP NetWeaver Portal. As shown in Figure 10.57, clicking the RELEASE CACHE button results in the releasing of all PCD cache objects.

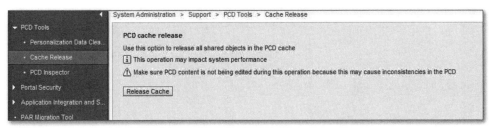

Figure 10.57 PCD Cache Release

10.6.3 Security Zones Checker

The purpose of a security zone is to make sure that SAP NetWeaver Portal users access only the applications and services that are appropriate to their roles in the organization. Changes in the organization may cause changes to the security zone hierarchy, which may leave zones in the PCD that are no longer required. The security zones checker tool is located in the PORTAL SECURITY category in Figure 10.54, and scans portal content and displays unused security zones. To use the security zone checker, navigate to SYSTEM ADMINISTRATOR • SUPPORT • PORTAL SECURITY • SECURITY ZONES CHECKER.

Figure 10.58 shows the security zones checker tool inside SAP NetWeaver Portal.

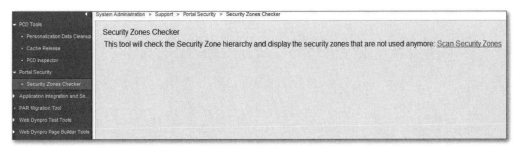

Figure 10.58 Security Zones Checker

10.6.4 Support Role

SAP NetWeaver Portal provides a built-in role for support purposes. The role is called SUPPORT and is provided in the path PORTAL CONTENT • CONTENT PROVIDED BY SAP • ADMIN CONTENT • SUPPORT. The path is shown in Figure 10.59.

Figure 10.59 Support Role

Whenever you need support from outside, for example, from SAP, you can assign this SUPPORT role to a user and provide that user ID to the support people. The SUPPORT role provides read-only access to the following:

- JNDI
- PCD
- Portal registry
- Security zone
- Client framework environment configurations

Figure 10.60 shows the structure and content of the SUPPORT role.

Name	Entry Point	Visible	Sort Priority	Merge
▼ Support	✓	✓	100.0	Yes*
▼ Browse	☐	✓	100.0	Yes*
• JNDI	☐	✓	100.0	Yes*
• PCD	☐	✓	100.0	Yes*
• Portal Registry	☐	✓	100.0	Yes*
• Security Zones	☐	✓	100.0	Yes*
▼ Check	☐	✓	100.0	Yes*
• Cluster Theme Integrity	☐	✓	100.0	Yes*
▼ OBN Tools	☐	✓	100.0	Yes*
• OBN Report	☐	✓	100.0	Yes*
• OBN Source	☐	✓	100.0	Yes*
• OBN Target	☐	✓	100.0	Yes*
• Navigation Options Checker	☐	✓	100.0	Yes*
▼ Information Configuration	☐	✓	100.0	Yes*
• EPCF	☐	✓	100.0	Yes*

Role Content — New ▲ Open, Remove, Cut, Copy, Paste, Edit Connection, Move Up, Move Down, Reset Object, Refresh Object

Figure 10.60 Support Role Structure

10.7   Summary

Monitoring a system is an important part of keeping a system healthy and running. It is important to be able to identify any problems early, so that corrective actions can be taken and any failure can be avoided. SAP NetWeaver Administrator groups together a collection of tools that can be used for monitoring portals; for example, portal activity reports and the activity data collector tool can be used for monitoring usage of the portal, details of logged-in users, and details of iViews/pages the users have accessed. This information allows you to analyze which various user groups access the portal most often, and which content is accessed most often.

Logs and traces give important clues about the system and applications running on the portal. While logs give the system messages, traces provide the application-specific messages reported by the applications themselves. SAP NetWeaver Portal provides many tools to configure logging and tracing to suit your needs, and we discussed the various configuration options available.

Finally, we also discussed some of the troubleshooting tools that SAP NetWeaver Portal provides as part of its system administration. After reading this chapter, you should understand the configuration and usage of various monitoring and logging tools available with SAP NetWeaver Portal.

This completes the last chapter of the book. In the appendices following this chapter, we provide a blueprinting questionnaire sample, a list of useful resources and products related to SAP NetWeaver Portal, information about upgrading to 7.3, and some useful SAP Notes.

Appendices

A   Blueprinting Questionnaire Sample

In Chapter 5, we discussed the steps for blueprinting for an SAP NetWeaver Portal implementation. We also discussed what questions an SAP NetWeaver Portal consultant should ask the client for preparing a blueprint of the implementation. The purpose of this appendix is to provide a sample questionnaire that consultants can use as the starting point and adapt for their implementation-specific needs.

Introduction	
Client	
Location(s)	
Key business	
Clients	
Suppliers	
Competitors	
Project leader	
Existing SAP client	

Project Overview	
General	
Planned start	
Planned end	
Total number of users	
Planned project phases	
Phased approach	

First go-live date	
Goals of the project (business drivers)	
Describe the main objective of the client's portal project.	
Describe the main vision of the client's portal project.	

Resources

Project manager	
Portal role administrator	
Web security administrator	
Web developer	
Content specialist	
Graphics specialist	
Business process experts	
Backend system experts	
Workflow developer	

Identify any other internal or external partners, and describe their role on the portal project.

Sizing and Scalability	
Is the portal expected to be available constantly?	
What is the peak number of concurrent users the client expects the portal to handle, and how many web requests does the client expect every day?	
How many different roles does the client expect to issue?	
Does the client plan on making the portal available to more users in future phases?	
To how many locations will the client make the portal available now and in future phases?	
How many unifiers will the client's company use along with HRNP (drag and relate)?	
How many documents will be stored in the portal?	
Will indexing be needed in the portal?	

Security	
Describe the authentication method that the client plans for authentication of the portal user.	
Digital certificate	
Windows NT/2000 authentication	
Netegrity SiteMinder authentication	
Other. Please specify.	

If the client will use user ID and password authentication, check and describe the following.	
HTTP basic authentication (Before the portal user enters the portal, the browser prompts the user for a user ID and password.)	
Form-based logon (The portal displays an initial start page to the user. The page contains entry fields where the user can enter a user ID and password.)	

If using digital certificates, what certification authority (CA) will issue certificates? Indicate below.	
SAP Trust Center Service	
Other. Please specify.	

Will SSL be used for encryption?	
Would the client like to provide anonymous access to the enterprise portal?	

For which backend systems would the client like to provide single sign-on (SSO)? Indicate below.	
SAP systems. Please specify versions.	
Unifier projects. Please specify.	
Internet/extranet web servers. Please specify.	
Other. Please specify.	

Describe any custom development needed.	

User Management and Roles	
Does the client plan to import roles from R/3 systems into the PCD?	
Has the client deployed a corporate LDAP to store users? Please describe.	
If the client is already using a corporate LDAP to store users, then answer the following questions.	
Which schema is used for the directory?	
Other. Please specify.	
Describe the directory architecture.	
Is one server used for the entire organization?	
Are multiple servers (a forest with referrals between servers) being used? Please specify.	
Describe how the directory stores users.	
Is a user stored directly under the group?	
Are users stored in one branch and groups in another? Please specify.	
Describe how roles are defined in the corporate directory.	
What LDAP server product does the client use or plan to use? iPlanet Directory Server, Novell NDS eDirectory, or Microsoft Active Directory Service?	
Other. Please specify.	
If the client's user management is not currently based on LDAP services, then answer the following questions.	
Which schema is to be used for the directory?	

Please specify which extensions.	
Other. Please specify.	
Describe the directory architecture.	
Is one server to be used for the entire organization (a tree)?	
Are multiple servers (a forest with referrals between servers) to be used? Please specify.	
Describe how the directory will store users.	
Is a user to be stored directly under the group?	
Are users to be stored in one branch and groups in another? Please specify.	
Describe how roles are to be defined in the corporate directory.	
Will the client integrate user management with SAP systems?	
Does the client currently use SAP Central User Administration (CUA)?	
Is a self-registration function for users needed? Please describe.	
Will users be able to decide whether (and when) they want to become registered portal users with personalized content?	

Branding and Personalization	
Describe visuals and examples of the branding for the portal (such as screenshots).	

Does a website (intranet or extranet) exist for a template or guide for branding the portal? If yes, ask for screenshots.

Describe the requirements for look and feel.

Will the look and feel be consistent across users?

Does the client require a different look and feel depending on the user, project phase, and so on?

Will the client require one consistent header or multiple headers?

What determines multiple headers?

Will the client require a change to the double-row navigation that is standard with SAP NetWeaver Portal?

Content Integration

Will the client develop custom iViews? If yes, what type(s) (URL-based, Java, etc.)?

Will the content be accessed from disparate systems? If yes, what systems?

Will the client develop custom drag and relate scenarios? If yes, how many, and what components will be involved?

Knowledge Management

List/describe the present document management system(s).

List the present content management systems(s).	
Does the client use a search engine?	
Indicate what KM components the client will use and in which phase.	
Content Management (CM)	
Document Classification and Retrieval (TREX)	
Collaboration	
Application Sharing	

Does the client have to support collaborative authoring scenarios? If yes, please describe.

Does the client have existing document management guidelines (naming conventions, documentation duties, etc.)? If yes, please attach guidelines.

What kind of approval workflow does the client need when publishing information? Please describe.

Does the client plan to replicate metadata or content from external repositories to its web content management system? If yes, please specify the type of repository and expected amount of data.

List any other services and features that will be used from KM (retrieval, classification, web authoring, version control, workflow, and etc.).

Mobile

If the client has mobile requirements, answer the questions below.

List and describe the requirements.

Which mobile devices?	

Components

Indicate which components the client wants to integrate (please specify applications with exact version, where applicable).

SAP ERP	
SAP R/3	
Oracle	
PeopleSoft	
Other	
Platform(s): UNIX, NT, and so on	
Web-enabled?	
Collaboration	
eRoom	
Covia	
WebEx	
Microsoft Outlook	
Lotus Notes	
Other	
Platform(s): UNIX, NT, and so on	
Web-enabled?	

Information	
Yahoo! Content	
External News	
Other	
Platform(s): UNIX, NT, and so on	
Web-enabled?	
Business Warehouse	
SAP NetWeaver BW	
Other	
Platform(s): UNIX, NT, and so on	
Web-enabled?	
Does the client intend to integrate IACs (Internet Application Components) or WAS (Web Applications)? If yes, please specify.	
Does the client intend to integrate an existing Microsoft Exchange infrastructure?	
Legacy Systems	
Specify systems and versions	
Platform(s): UNIX, NT, and so on	
Web-enabled?	
Databases	
Specify database systems and versions	
Platform(s): UNIX, NT, and so on	
Web-enabled?	

Other Components (please also identify if these applications are web-enabled)

Are all of these portal applications using TCP/IP? If no, please specify.

Are all of the client's portal applications accessible via HTML? If no, please specify.

How many of the client's existing applications are not web-enabled?

Business Package for MSS

How many employees will have access to MSS?	
What MSS services is the client interested in?	
Describe the client's current use of reporting tools, including SAP NetWeaver BW.	

Business Package for ESS

Define the SAP HR modules implemented.	
Are there existing modifications to the SAP source code that could lead to complications with ESS?	
How many employees will have access to ESS?	

Are all users of ESS internal users?	
List all ESS services that the client requires.	
Is workflow a requirement (training and events)?	
If the ESS service address is maintained, what are the other area implications?	
Will the client implement ESS web reporting? If so, from what source (R/3, SAP NetWeaver BW, etc.)?	
Will the client want to hide or remove buttons, change header or text, alter programming functions, or create or modify ESS services and transactions?	

Internationalization and Languages	
What languages would the client like the portal to support?	
What languages do the client's browsers support?	
In what languages does the client prefer the administration of the portal?	
Does the client have portal users in different time zones?	
Please indicate the different time zones the client's portal users are in.	

Alerts and Notifications	
What alerts and notifications does the client expect the portal to provide, if any?	

Reporting

What reports need to be included in the portal?

Answer the following questions about the portal analytics.

Does the client intend to measure user activity? If yes, please specify the type of indicator the client would like to obtain.	
What analytical reports does the client need (e.g., user activity, number of document views and downloads, etc.)?	
Does the client expect indicators regarding response times, number of hits, and average system load?	
Does the client want to track the number of downloads per document?	
Does the client want to track the number of views/subscriptions per document?	

B   Useful Resources and Products

In this appendix, we will discuss the following tools that are handy when working with SAP NetWeaver Portal UI-based applications:

- HTTPWatch (*www.httpwatch.com*)
- IE Developer Toolbar (*www.microsoft.com/download/en/details.aspx?id=18359*)

These tools are very useful during the development and troubleshooting of web-based applications.

B.1   HTTPWatch

HTTPWatch is an HTTP sniffer tool that integrates to your web browser and can give you a lot of insight into the performance of your web-based applications. You can analyze the HTTP requests that are going from the web browser to the SAP NetWeaver Portal server. For downloading the tool and for details about the browser compatibility, go to *www.httpwatch.com*.

After you have installed the HTTPWatch tool, you should be able to launch it by going to VIEW • EXPLORER BAR • HTTPWATCH in Internet Explorer. There are various versions of the HTTPWatch tool with varying features. Figure B.1 shows a screenshot from the basic version of HTTPWatch.

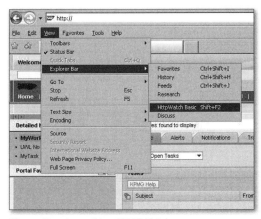

Figure B.1   Launching HTTPWatch

Figure B.2 shows the console that comes up when you launch HTTPWatch.

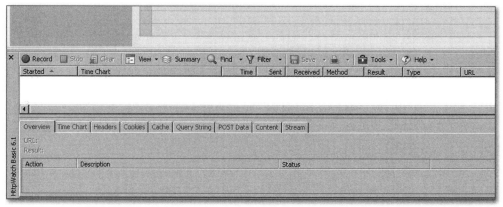

Figure B.2 HTTPWatch Console

When you are ready to capture a browser request, you need to start the recording by clicking the RECORD button. When you click RECORD, HTTPWatch is ready to record all of the HTTP requests going from the browser. Now go ahead and perform the browser activities that you want to analyze, and click the STOP button in HTTPWatch console when you are done.

Figure B.3 shows the recording done for all of the HTTP requests sent from your browser during the recording.

Started ▲	Time Chart	Time	Sent	Received	Method	Result	Type	URL
+ 7.293		0.051	1401	265	GET	200	image/gif	http://golitsapd30.go-d01.local:50100/ir
+ 7.296		0.058	1401	267	GET	200	image/gif	http://golitsapd30.go-d01.local:50100/ir
+ 7.301		0.052	1394	256	GET	200	image/gif	http://golitsapd30.go-d01.local:50100/ir
+ 7.313		0.075	1388	262	GET	200	image/gif	http://golitsapd30.go-d01.local:50100/ir
+ 7.332		0.033	1434	126	GET	304	image/gif	http://golitsapd30.go-d01.local:50100/ir
+ 7.414		0.263	1652	126	GET	304	text/html	http://golitsapd30.go-d01.local:50100/ir
+ 7.449		0.006	1347	126	GET	304	application/x-jav...	http://golitsapd30.go-d01.local:50100/w
		7.678	45339	37334	48 requests			

Figure B.3 HTTPWatch Recording

As shown in Figure B.4, you can export the result to a Microsoft Excel or CSV file, or you can save it in the HTTPWatch format that saves it as a file with an .hwl extension.

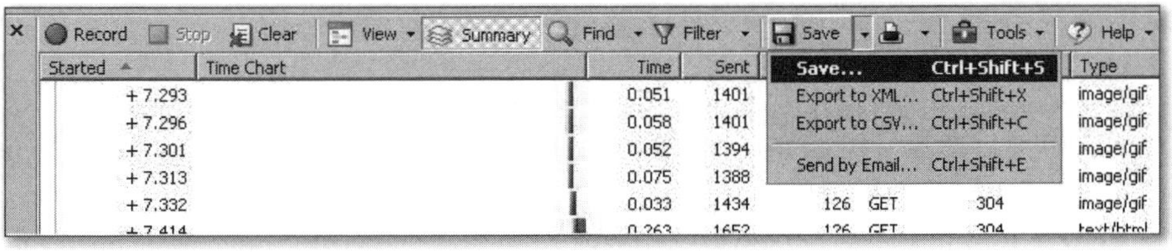

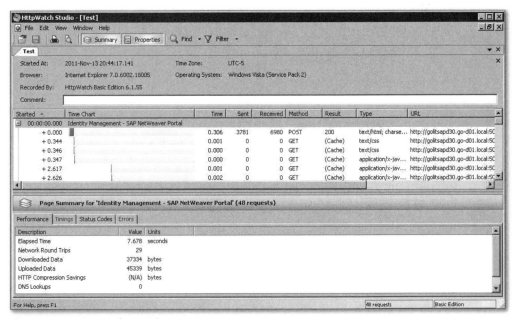

Figure B.4 Saving the HTTPWatch Result

As shown in Figure B.5, you can then use the saved log file to do analysis of your HTTP requests. It can give some really useful insights into improving the performance of your applications. You can see each HTTP request that was part of the request and how much time was taken in that request.

Figure B.5 HTTPWatch Log File

From here, you can analyze which requests are taking more time to load, and then you can focus on those items to improve the performance. Also it tells you which resources are being loaded from the server and which resources are being loaded from the cache. This can give you important clues about which additional resources can be cached to improve performance.

B.2   Internet Explorer Developer Toolbar

IE Developer Toolbar is an add-on to the Internet Explorer browser provided by Microsoft that can be used to understand and troubleshoot web pages. This tool can be used extensively with SAP NetWeaver Portal to understand and troubleshoot your portal web pages. With the IE Developer Toolbar, you can perform the following activities:

- Understand and modify the Document Object Model (DOM) of any web page.
- Locate and select specific elements on a web page.
- View HTML object class names, IDs, and details.
- Outline tables, table cells, images, or selected tags.
- Validate HTML, CSS, WAI, and RSS web feed links.
- Display image dimensions, file sizes, path information, and alternate (ALT) text.
- Resize the browser window to a new resolution.
- Selectively clear the browser cache and saved cookies from the browser. You can also choose from all objects or those associated with a given domain.
- Display a fully featured design ruler to help accurately align and measure HTML objects on web pages.
- Find the style rules used to set specific styles on any element.
- View the formatted and syntax-colored source of HTML and CSS.

You can download and install the IE Developer Toolbar add-on from the following URL:

www.microsoft.com/download/en/details.aspx?id=18359

You can launch the IE Developer Toolbar by going to VIEW • EXPLORER BAR • IE DEVELOPER TOOLBAR in the Internet Explorer as shown in Figure B.6.

The IE Developer Toolbar opens at the bottom of Internet Explorer as shown in Figure B.7.

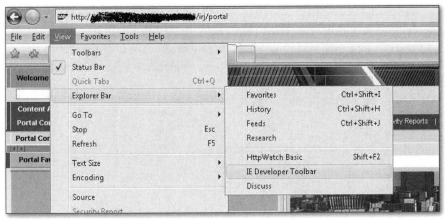

Figure B.6 Launching the IE Developer Toolbar

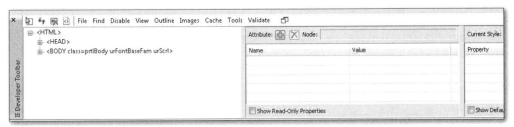

Figure B.7 IE Developer Toolbar

As shown in Figure B.8, you can traverse through the HTML DOM and go to a particular element to see the various attributes and styles of that element.

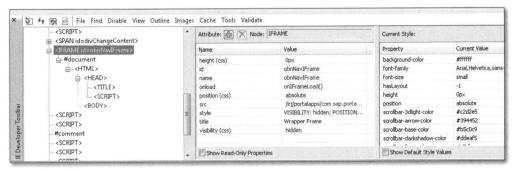

Figure B.8 Traversing the HTML DOM

You can also click an element on the page, and the IE Developer Toolbar will navigate to that element in the HTML DOM. To enable this feature, you need to click the SELECT ELEMENT BY CLICK button located on the top-left corner of the IE Developer Toolbar and represented by an arrow as shown in Figure B.9.

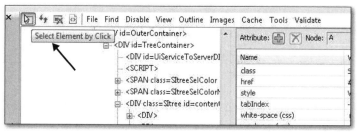

Figure B.9 Select Element by Click

The IE Developer Toolbar also provides many other features that you should explore to help you when troubleshooting your pages.

C Upgrading Applications for SAP NetWeaver Portal 7.3

Since SAP NetWeaver Portal 7.3 is pretty new at the moment, many customers might be upgrading their existing SAP NetWeaver 7.0-based portals to the 7.3 versions. For information on the preparation and steps for upgrading your portal to SAP NetWeaver 7.3, go to *http://service.sap.com/instguides*. You will need an S-user ID and password to login.

The standard upgrade process should be able to upgrade your PRT to SAP NetWeaver Portal 7.3 without requiring any manual migration steps. However, if you have done some custom development on your portal, then you will need to consider your options for migrating to the 7.3 version. Specifically, you are most likely to encounter these types of applications to migrate:

▸ Web Dynpro Java applications

▸ Portal applications

C.1 Web Dynpro Java Applications

Web Dynpro Java applications written for SAP NetWeaver Portal 7.0 are source compatible with SAP NetWeaver Portal 7.3 but not binary compatible. This means that you don't need to change the source code of your Web Dynpro applications, but you will need to import them into SAP NetWeaver Developer Studio (NWDS) 7.3, compile, and then deploy on SAP NetWeaver 7.3. Applications developed for SAP NetWeaver CE versions 7.1 and higher are, however, binary compatible with SAP NetWeaver Portal 7.3 and can be deployed directly.

NWDS 7.3 provides an Application Projects Migration Wizard that can help you migrate the Web Dynpro Java applications. When you important the older applications into NWDS 7.3, NWDS automatically detects that applications need to be migrated and guides you through the migration process. You can then compile the applications and deploy them on SAP NetWeaver Portal 7.3.

C.2   Portal Applications

Portal applications that were developed for up to SAP NetWeaver Portal 7.3 versions were deployed in a portal archive (PAR) format. However, all of the portal applications for 7.3 versions need to be deployed in enterprise archive (EAR) format. For the purpose of migration, SAP NetWeaver Portal 7.3 provides a PAR Migration Tool that can convert your existing PAR applications into EAR applications, which can then be deployed onto the SAP NetWeaver Portal 7.3.

You can run the PAR Migration Tool by navigating to SYSTEM ADMINISTRATION • SUPPORT • PAR MIGRATION TOOL.

Figure C.1 shows a screenshot of the PAR Migration Tool.

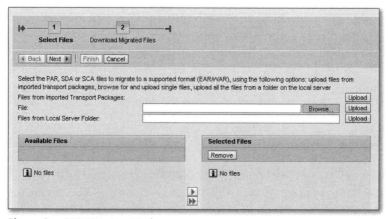

Figure C.1   PAR Migration Tool

As shown in Figure C.2, you can choose your PAR files and upload them into the PAR Migration tool. Then you can select the PAR files that you want to migrated and add them to the SELECTED FILES section by clicking on the ADD SELECTED FILES button with the right arrow icon. Click NEXT to migrate the selected PAR files(s).

As shown in Figure C.3, the PAR Migrate Tool migrates the PAR file to the EAR file format and gives you the option to download it. You can download it and deploy it on SAP NetWeaver Portal 7.3.

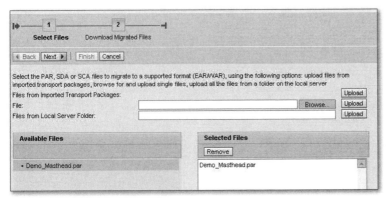

Figure C.2   Migration of PAR Files

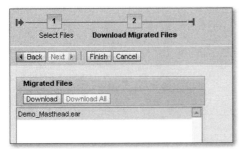

Figure C.3   Download the Migrated EAR File

D   Useful SAP Notes

In this appendix, we will list some of the most useful SAP Notes that you may need while working with SAP NetWeaver Portal 7.3. The primary component for looking up SAP Notes for SAP NetWeaver Portal is EP-PIN, and the URL is *http:// service.sap.com/notes*.

You will need an S-user ID and password to access the following SAP notes:

▶ **Note 1531306: Central Note for SAP NetWeaver 7.30 EP/EPC**
This is the central note for SAP NetWeaver Portal 7.3 and serves as the entry point for all notes related to issues with SAP NetWeaver Portal 7.3.

▶ **Note 1624827: SAP NetWeaver Portal 7.3 Content Packaging Guidelines**
With SAP NetWeaver Portal 7.3, SAP has made changes in the way you can package your applications. Now you don't have to package your portal content, portal applications, Web Dynpro Java applications, and J2EE applications separately. All of these can now be packaged together into one software component. This packaged software component can be deployed on a customer's SAP NetWeaver Portal.

▶ **Note 1633173: Navigation Steps to Change Portal Theme Settings**
With SAP NetWeaver Portal 7.3, the navigation for theme settings has changed. This note will explain the steps that were needed for SAP NetWeaver Portal versions 7.0–7.2 and the new steps needed for SAP NetWeaver Portal 7.3.

▶ **Note 1407472: Release Restrictions for SAP NetWeaver Portal 7.3**
This note gives the information on the restrictions or features not working at the time of the release of SAP NetWeaver Portal 7.3. This note keeps getting updated as the restrictions are removed.

▶ **Note 1627935: Known Issues for SAP NetWeaver Portal 7.30 SP04**
This note is for the known issues with SAP NetWeaver Portal 7.3 SP04 at the time of the release. There is a similar note (1611646) for SAP NetWeaver Portal 7.3 SP03 version.

▶ **Note 1564996: Change Recording—Changing the ID of a Portal Root Folder**
Change recording of portal content is a new feature that was introduced with SAP NetWeaver Portal 7.3. This note gives information on the issues related to change recording of folders that are configured as the root of the change recording location.

▶ **Note 1530174: Upgrade to SAP NetWeaver EP/EPC 7.30**
This is the central note for all issues related to the upgrade of SAP NetWeaver Portal from earlier versions to the 7.3 version.

▶ **Note 1504296: SAP NetWeaver Portal 7.30 — Removed APIs**
Some of the APIs that were part of earlier versions of SAP NetWeaver Portal have been removed from the 7.3 version. This note lists all of the APIs that have been removed.

▶ **Note 1498875: AJAX Framework Page — Issues Detected in SAP NetWeaver 7.30**
This note contains the list of all notes for issues related to the AJAX framework page of SAP NetWeaver Portal 7.3.

▶ **Note 1166135: Central Note for AJAX Framework Page with SAP NetWeaver**
This note serves as the central note for all of the limitations related to the AJAX framework page. This note also explains now to enable the new SAP Signature Design theme for SAP NetWeaver Portal. The SAP Signature Design theme offers a harmonized UI for SAP's diverse products as well as an advanced interaction theme. It is based on a new portal theme (font type and size, color scheme, etc.) and can be integrated into the Ajax-based framework page (layout, header, navigation iViews, content area). The Ajax framework page and the new SAP Signature Design for SAP NetWeaver Portal are globally available for SAP NetWeaver Portal starting with EhP 2 for SAP NetWeaver 7.0 and SAP NetWeaver 7.30.

▶ **Note 1257108: Collective Note — Analyzing Issues with Single Sign-On (SSO)**
This is the central note for all SSO issues with SAP NetWeaver Portal. There are various scenarios for SSO implementation, and this note discusses the issues associated with these scenarios.

▶ **Note 1398273: Federated Portal Network (FPN) — Specific Component Note**
This is the central note that provides information about the most common problems related to the federated portal network (FPN) implementation. This note also tells you the information SAP Support will need in case you need help from SAP.

▶ **Note 880482: Central Note — Federated Portal Network (SAP NetWeaver 7.0)**
This is the central note that covers all information not included in the official "Implementing a Federated Portal Network" scenario documentation provided on the SAP Help Portal at the following URL:

*http://help.sap.com/saphelp_nw04s/helpdata/en/5b/9f2d4293825333e10000000a15
5106/frameset.htm*

The information in this note includes known integration issues, workarounds, updated information, and restrictions in SAP NetWeaver Portal. Refer to the contents of this central note and to other related notes that may be linked to this note. For a list of general known limitations of the portal in SAP NetWeaver Portal, see SAP Note 853509. Also the limitation note (853509) should be looked at before reviewing this note. Even though this note is related to SAP NetWeaver Portal 7.0, this should be referenced for SAP NetWeaver Portal 7.3 also, until a separate note for this version becomes available.

▶ **Note 1295662: Interoperability Between Two Portals in FPN Environment**
This note is for checking whether a combination of portals is supported in a federated portal implementation. Also, this note discusses the Upgrade Dependency Analyzer tool to check the dependencies to other portals if you want to upgrade a portal to a newer release.

▶ **Note 1604912: Errors in PAR-WAR Migration**
Until the SAP NetWeaver Portal 7.0 version, the portal development components used to be deployed in the form of a PAR (portal archive) file. However, starting from the SAP NetWeaver Portal 7.3 version, the PAR format has become obsolete, and it only accepts the WAR (Web Archive) format for portal component applications. The WAR format is a Java EE standard, and SAP NetWeaver Portal 7.3 complies with the Java EE standards. SAP NetWeaver Portal 7.3, however, provides a PAR Migration Tool, which you can use to migrate your existing PAR file to the WAR format. This note discusses issues with the PAR Migration Tool.

▶ **Note 1538600: Defining Portal URL Aliases for SAP NetWeaver Portal 7.30**
This note talks about defining the portal URL alias as defined in the documentation at the following URL:

*http://help.sap.com/saphelp_nw73/helpdata/en/48/1d5d0171364269e10000000a42
1937/frameset.htm*

Sometimes the changes that you make to the *web.xml* file do not take effect because the process of changing the *web.xml* file was changed from SAP NetWeaver 7.0X and 7.30 due to the change in the J2EE engine.

E   The Author

Manish Chaitanya is an SAP NetWeaver Portal and web technology expert with experience in handling multiple SAP NetWeaver Portal implementations for global customers. Manish works as the SAP NetWeaver Portal practice lead for MOURI Tech LLC (*www.mouritech.com*), which is a USA-based premier consulting company for global SAP solutions. Manish has worked with many customers in defining their portal implementation strategy and has managed their portal implementation from the blueprinting through go-live and post go-live stages. Manish lives in New Jersey, USA with his wife Uttora, and their two kids Pranjal and Prakriti. He can be reached via email at *manishc@mouritech.com*.

Index

X

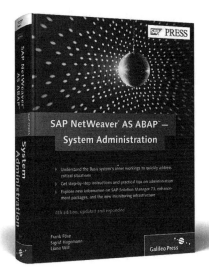

Understand the Basis system's inner workings to quickly address critical situations

Get step-by-step instructions and practical tips on administration

Explore new information on SAP Solution Manager 7.1, enhancement packages, and the new monitoring infrastructure

Frank Föse, Sigrid Hagemann, Liane Will

SAP NetWeaver AS ABAP— System Administration

As a system administrator, you know that SAP NetWeaver AS ABAP is the core of an SAP system. This book provides essential information on the main concepts and tools of SAP NetWeaver AS ABAP, as well as new information about SAP Solution Manager 7.1 and the new monitoring infrastructure. This all-inclusive resource teaches you a holistic approach to administration, and can also be used to prepare for the Certified Technical Consultant exam.

747 pp., 4. edition 2012, 79,95 Euro / US$ 79.95
ISBN 978-1-59229-411-4

>> www.sap-press.com

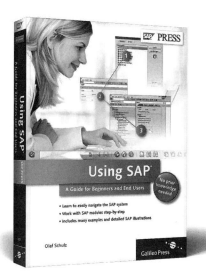

Learn to easily navigate the SAP system

Work with SAP modules step-by-step

Includes many examples and detailed SAP illustrations

Olaf Schulz

Using SAP:
A Guide for Beginners and End Users

This book helps end users and beginners get started in SAP ERP and provides readers with the basic knowledge they need for their daily work. Readers will get to know the essentials of working with the SAP system, learn about the SAP systems' structures and functions, and discover how SAP connects to critical business processes. Whether this book is used as an exercise book or as a reference book, readers will find what they need to help them become more comfortable with SAP ERP.

388 pp., 39,95 Euro / US$ 39.95
ISBN 978-1-59229-408-4

>> www.sap-press.com

Interested in reading more?

Please visit our website for all
new book releases from SAP PRESS.

www.sap-press.com